CSET 110-111 Foundation-Level Mathematics
Teacher Certification Exam

By: Sharon Wynne, M.S.
Southern Connecticut State University

"And, while there's no reason yet to panic, I think it's only prudent that we make preparations to panic."

XAMonline, INC.
Boston

Copyright © 2008 XAMonline, Inc.
All rights reserved. No part of the material protected by this copyright notice may be reproduced or utilized in any form or by any means, electronic or mechanical, including photocopying, recording or by any information storage and retrievable system, without written permission from the copyright holder.

To obtain permission(s) to use the material from this work for any purpose including workshops or seminars, please submit a written request to:

XAMonline, Inc.
21 Orient Ave.
Melrose, MA 02176
Toll Free 1-800-509-4128
Email: info@xamonline.com
Web www.xamonline.com
Fax: 1-781-662-9268

Library of Congress Cataloging-in-Publication Data

Wynne, Sharon A.
    Foundation Level Mathematics 110, 111: Teacher Certification / Sharon A. Wynne. -2nd ed.
    ISBN 978-1-58197-608-3
    1. Foundation Level Mathematics 110, 111   2. Study Guides.   3. CSET.
    4. Teachers' Certification & Licensure.   5. Careers

Disclaimer:

The opinions expressed in this publication are the sole works of XAMonline and were created independently from the National Education Association, Educational Testing Service, or any State Department of Education, National Evaluation Systems or other testing affiliates.

Between the time of publication and printing, state specific standards as well as testing formats and website information may change that is not included in part or in whole within this product. Sample test questions are developed by XAMonline and reflect similar content as on real tests; however, they are not former tests. XAMonline assembles content that aligns with state standards but makes no claims nor guarantees teacher candidates a passing score. Numerical scores are determined by testing companies such as NES or ETS and then are compared with individual state standards. A passing score varies from state to state.

Printed in the United States of America œ-1

CSET: Foundation Level Mathematics 110, 111
ISBN: 978-1-58197-608-3

TEACHER CERTIFICATION STUDY GUIDE

About the Subject Assessments

CSET™: Subject Assessment in the Mathematics examination

Purpose: The assessments are designed to test the knowledge and competencies of prospective secondary level teachers. The question bank from which the assessment is drawn is undergoing constant revision. As a result, your test may include questions that will not count towards your score.

Test Version: There are three versions of subject assessment for Mathematics tests in California. The Mathematics Subtest I (110) emphasizes comprehension in Algebra and Number Theory; Mathematics Subtest II (111) in Geometry Probability and Statistics; Mathematics Subtest III (112) for Calculus and the History of Mathematics. The first two subtests taken together represent the Single Subject Teaching Credential in Foundational-Level Mathematics authorizing the teaching of general mathematics, algebra, geometry, probability and statistics, and consumer mathematics. The Mathematics examination guide is based on a typical knowledge level of persons who have completed a _bachelor's degree program_ in Mathematics.

Time Allowance and Format: You will have 5 hours to finish the test. Part of the test will consist of multiple-choice questions; part of the test will consist of focused and extended constructed-response questions. There are 60 multiple-choice questions and 8 focused constructed-response questions in the three subtests. If you fail one part of the exam, but not the other, you only need to re-take the part you have failed.

Weighting: There are 24 multiple-choice questions and 3 focused constructed-response questions in Subtest I for Algebra; 6 multiple-choice questions and 1 focused constructed-response questions for Number Theory. There are 22 multiple-choice questions and 3 focused constructed-response questions in Subtest II for Geometry; 8 multiple-choice questions and 1 focused constructed-response questions for Probability and Statistics.

Additional Information about the CSET Assessments: The CSET™ series subject assessments are developed _National Evaluation Systems._ They provide additional information on the CSET series assessments, including registration, preparation and testing procedures, study materials such as three topical guides, one for each subtest, that are all together about 107 pages of information including approximately 57 additional sample questions.

FOUNDATION LEV. MATH.

TEACHER CERTIFICATION STUDY GUIDE

TABLE OF CONTENTS

Page Numbers

ALGEBRA (SMR Domain 1) 1

0001 Algebraic Structures (SMR 1.1) 1

Skill a. Apply basic properties of real and complex numbers in constructing mathematical arguments (e.g., if a < b and c < 0, then ac > bc) 1

Skill b. Know that the rational numbers and real numbers can be ...ordered and that the complex numbers cannot be ordered, but that any polynomial equation with real coefficients can be solved in the complex field 9

Skill c. Know why the real and complex numbers are each a field, and that particular rings are not fields (e.g., integers, polynomial rings, matrix rings) 14

0002 Polynomial Equations and Inequalities (SMR 1.2) 16

Skill a. Know why graphs of linear inequalities are half planes and be able to apply this fact (e.g. linear programming) 16

Skill b. Prove and use the following: The Rational Root Theorem for polynomials with integer coefficients, The Factor Theorem, The Conjugate Roots Theorem for polynomial equations with real coefficients, The Quadratic Formula for real and complex quadratic polynomials The Binomial Theorem 25

Skill a. Analyze and solve polynomial equations with real coefficients using the Fundamental Theorem of Algebra 45

0003 Functions (SMR 1.3) 59

Skill a. Analyze and prove general properties of functions (i.e., domain and range, one-to-one, onto inverses, composition, and differences between relations and functions) 59

Skill b. Analyze properties of polynomial, rational, radical, and absolute value functions in a variety of ways (e.g., graphing, solving problems) 64

Skill c.	Analyze properties of exponential and logarithmic functions in a variety of ways (e.g. graphing, solving problems)	89

0004 Linear Algebra (SMR 1.4) 92

Skill a.	Understand and apply the geometric interpretation and basic operations of vectors in two and three dimensions, including their scalar multiples and scalar (dot) and cross products	92
Skill b.	Prove the basic properties of vectors (e.g., perpendicular vectors have zero dot product)	99
Skill c.	Understand and apply the basic properties and operations of matrices and determinants (e.g., to determine the solvability of linear systems of equations)	101

GEOMETRY (SMR Domain 2) 104

0001 Parallelism (SMR 2.1) 104

Skill a.	Know the Parallel Postulate and its implications, and justify its equivalents (e.g., the Alternate Interior Angle Theorem, the angle sum of every triangle is 180 degrees)	104
Skill b.	Know that variants of the Parallel Postulate produce non- Euclidean geometries (e.g. spherical, hyperbolic)	109

0002 Plane Euclidean Geometry (SMR 2.2) 110

Skill a.	Prove theorems and solve problems involving similarity and congruence	110
Skill b.	Understand, apply, and justify properties of triangles (e.g., the Exterior Angle Theorem, concurrence theorems, trigonometric ratios, Triangle Inequality, Law of Sines, Law of Cosines, the Pythagorean Theorem and its converse)	118
Skill c.	Understand, apply, and justify properties of polygons and circles from an advanced standpoint (e.g., derive the area formulas for regular polygons and circles from the area of a triangle)	124

TEACHER CERTIFICATION STUDY GUIDE

Skill d. Justify and perform the classical constructions (e.g., angle bisector, perpendicular bisector, replicating shapes, regular n-gons for n equal to 3, 4, 5, 6, and 8) 143

Skill e. Use techniques in coordinate geometry to prove geometric theorems 146

0003 Three-Dimensional Geometry (SMR 2.3) 149

Skill a. Demonstrate an understanding of parallelism and ..perpendicularity of lines and planes in three dimensions 149

Skill b. Understand, apply, and justify properties of three-dimensional objects from an advanced standpoint (e.g., derive the volume .. and surface area formulas for prisms, pyramids, cones, cylinders, and spheres) 152

0004 Transformational Geometry (SMR 2.4) 158

Skill a. Demonstrate an understanding of the basic properties of isometries in two- and three dimensional space (e.g., rotation, translation, reflection) 158

Skill b. Understand and prove the basic properties of dilations (e.g., similarity transformations or change of scale) 162

NUMBER THEORY (SMR Domain 3) 167

0005 Natural Numbers (SMR 3.1) 167

Skill a. Apply the Fundamental Theorem of Arithmetic (e.g., find the greatest common factor and the least common multiple, show that every fraction is equivalent to a unique fraction where the numerator and denominator are relatively prime, prove that the square root of any number, not a perfect square number, is irrational) 167

Skill b. Use the Principle of Mathematical Induction to prove results in number theory 169

Skill c. Prove and use basic properties of natural numbers (e.g., properties of divisibility) 171

Skill d. Know and apply the Euclidean Algorithm 174

TEACHER CERTIFICATION STUDY GUIDE

PROBABILITY AND STATISTICS (SMR Domain 4) 176

0005 Probability (SMR 4.1) 176

Skill a. Prove and apply basic principles of permutations and combinations 176

Skill b. Illustrate finite probability using a variety of examples and ... models (e.g., the fundamental counting principles) 177

Skill c. Use and explain the concept of conditional probability 180

Skill d. Interpret the probability of an outcome 181

Skill e. Use normal, binomial, and exponential distributions to solve ..... and interpret probability problems 182

0006 Statistics (SMR 4.2) 185

Skill a. Compute and interpret the mean, median, and mode of both discrete and continuous distributions 185

Skill b. Compute and interpret quartiles, range, variance, and standard deviation of both discrete and continuous distributions 186

Skill c. Select and evaluate sampling methods appropriate to a task (e.g., random, systematic, cluster, convenience sampling) and display the results 190

Skill d. Know the method of least squares and apply it to linear regression and correlation 191

Skill e. Know and apply the chi-square test 193

FOUNDATION LEV. MATH.

CONSTRUCTED-RESPONSE EXAMPLES 195

ANSWER KEY TO PRACTICE PROBLEMS 201

ESSENTIAL TIPS FOR EVERY MATH TEACHER 205

WEB LINKS 213

SAMPLE TEST 217

ANSWER KEY 249

RIGOR TABLE 250

RATIONALES FOR SAMPLE QUESTIONS 251

TEACHER CERTIFICATION STUDY GUIDE

Great Study and Testing Tips!

What to study in order to prepare for the subject assessments is the focus of this study guide but equally important is *how* you study.

You can increase your chances of truly mastering the information by taking some simple, but effective steps.

Study Tips:

1. Some foods aid the learning process. Foods such as milk, nuts, seeds, rice, and oats help your study efforts by releasing natural memory enhancers called CCKs (*cholecystokinin*) composed of *tryptophan*, *choline*, and *phenylalanine*. All of these chemicals enhance the neurotransmitters associated with memory. Before studying, try a light, protein-rich meal of eggs, turkey, and fish. All of these foods release the memory enhancing chemicals. The better the connections, the more you comprehend.

Likewise, before you take a test, stick to a light snack of energy boosting and relaxing foods. A glass of milk, a piece of fruit, or some peanuts all release various memory-boosting chemicals and help you to relax and focus on the subject at hand.

2. Learn to take great notes. A by-product of our modern culture is that we have grown accustomed to getting our information in short doses (i.e. TV news sound bites or USA Today style newspaper articles.)

Consequently, we've subconsciously trained ourselves to assimilate information better in neat little packages. If your notes are scrawled all over the paper, it fragments the flow of the information. Strive for clarity. Newspapers use a standard format to achieve clarity. Your notes can be much clearer through use of proper formatting. A very effective format is called the *"Cornell Method."*

> Take a sheet of loose-leaf lined notebook paper and draw a line all the way down the paper about 1-2" from the left-hand edge.
>
> Draw another line across the width of the paper about 1-2" up from the bottom. Repeat this process on the reverse side of the page.

Look at the highly effective result. You have ample room for notes, a left hand margin for special emphasis items or inserting supplementary data from the textbook, a large area at the bottom for a brief summary, and a little rectangular space for just about anything you want.

3. **Get the concept then the details**. Too often, we focus on the details and don't gather an understanding of the concept. However, if you simply memorize only dates, places, or names, you may well miss the whole point of the subject.

A key way to understand things is to put them in your own words. If you are working from a textbook, automatically summarize each paragraph in your mind. If you are outlining text, don't simply copy the author's words.

Rephrase them in your own words. You remember your own thoughts and words much better than someone else's, and subconsciously tend to associate the important details to the core concepts.

4. **Ask Why?** Pull apart written material paragraph by paragraph and don't forget the captions under the illustrations.

Example: If the heading is "Stream Erosion", flip it around to read, "Why do streams erode?" Then answer the questions.

If you train your mind to think in a series of questions and answers, not only will you learn more, but it also helps to lessen the test anxiety because you are used to answering questions.

5. **Read for reinforcement and future needs**. Even if you only have 10 minutes, put your notes or a book in your hand. Your mind is similar to a computer; you have to input data in order to have it processed. *By reading, you are creating the neural connections for future retrieval.* The more times you read something, the more you reinforce the learning of ideas.

Even if you don't fully understand something on the first pass, *your mind stores much of the material for later recall.*

6. **Relax to learn so go into exile.** Our bodies respond to an inner clock called biorhythms. Burning the midnight oil works well for some people, but not everyone.

If possible, set aside a particular place to study that is free of distractions. Shut off the television, cell phone, and pager and exile your friends and family during your study period.

If you really are bothered by silence, try background music. Light classical music at a low volume has been shown to aid in concentration over other types. Music that evokes pleasant emotions without lyrics are highly suggested. Try just about anything by Mozart. It relaxes you.

7. Use arrows not highlighters. At best, it's difficult to read a page full of yellow, pink, blue, and green streaks. Try staring at a neon sign for a while and you'll soon see that the horde of colors obscure the message.

A quick note, a brief dash of color, an underline, and an arrow pointing to a particular passage is much clearer than a horde of highlighted words.

8. Budget your study time. Although you shouldn't ignore any of the material, *allocate your available study time in the same ratio that topics may appear on the test.*

TEACHER CERTIFICATION STUDY GUIDE

Testing Tips:

1. Get smart, play dumb. Don't read anything into the question. Don't assume that the test writer is looking for something else than what is asked. Stick to the question as written and don't read extra things into it.

2. Read the question and all the choices *twice* before answering the question. You may miss something by not carefully reading, and then re-reading both the question and the answers.

If you really don't have a clue as to the right answer, leave it blank on the first time through. Go on to the other questions, as they may provide a clue as to how to answer the skipped questions.

If later on, you still can't answer the skipped ones . . . **Guess.** The only penalty for guessing is that you *might* get it wrong. Only one thing is certain; if you don't put anything down, you will get it wrong!

3. Turn the question into a statement. Look at the way the questions are worded. The syntax of the question usually provides a clue. Does it seem more familiar as a statement rather than as a question? Does it sound strange?

By turning a question into a statement, you may be able to spot if an answer sounds right, and it may trigger memories of material you have read.

4. Look for hidden clues. It's actually very difficult to compose multiple-foil (choice) questions without giving away part of the answer in the options presented.

In most multiple-choice questions, you can often readily eliminate one or two of the potential answers. This leaves you with only two real possibilities and automatically your odds go to Fifty-Fifty for very little work.

5. Trust your instincts. For every fact that you have read, you subconsciously retain something of that knowledge. On questions that you aren't certain about, go with your basic instincts. **Your first impression on how to answer a question is usually correct.**

6. Mark your answers directly on the test booklet. Don't bother trying to fill in the optical scan sheet on the first pass through the test.

Just be very careful not to miss-mark your answers when you eventually transcribe them to the scan sheet.

7. Watch the clock! You have a set amount of time to answer the questions. Don't get bogged down trying to answer a single question at the expense of 10 questions you can more readily answer.

FOUNDATION LEV. MATH. x

ALGEBRA (SMR Domain 1)

Algebraic Structures (SMR 1.1)

Skill a. Apply basic properties of real and complex numbers in constructing mathematical arguments (e.g., if a < b and c < 0, then ac > bc)

Basic Properties of Real and Imaginary/Complex Numbers

Real Numbers

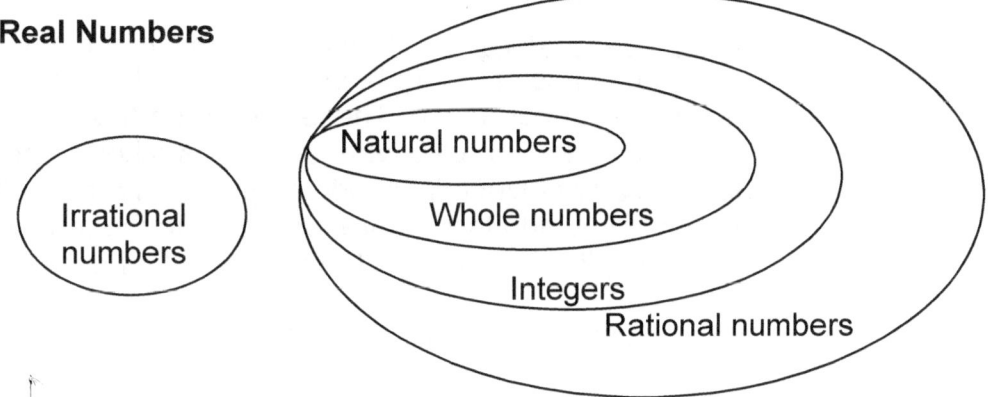

For a listing of mathematical symbols, go to:
http://en.wikipedia.org/wiki/Math_symbols

Real numbers are denoted by $\mathbb{R}$ and are numbers that can be shown by an infinite decimal representation such as 3.286275347.... The real numbers include rational numbers such as 42 and −23/129, and irrational numbers, such as the $\sqrt{2}$ and π, which can be represented as points along an infinite number line. Real numbers are also known as, "the unique complete Archimedean *ordered field*." Real numbers are differentiated from imaginary numbers.

Real numbers and their properties:

Real numbers have the two primary properties of being an ordered field, and having the least upper bound property. The First Property says that real numbers comprise an *ordered field* (with addition and multiplication as well as division by nonzero numbers), that can be ordered on a number line in a way that works with addition and multiplication.

Example: O is an **ordered field** if the order satisfies the following properties:

- if $a \leq b$ then $a + c \leq b + c$
- if $0 \leq a$ and $0 \leq b$ then $0 \leq a\,b$

It then follows that for every a, b, c, d in O:

- Either $-a \leq 0 \leq a$ or $a \leq 0 \leq -a$.
- We can add inequalities:

Example: If $a \leq b$ and $c \leq d$, then $a + c \leq b + d$

- We are allowed to "multiply inequalities with positive elements": If $a \leq b$ and $0 \leq c$, then $ac \leq bc$.

The <u>Second Property</u> of real numbers says that if a nonempty set of real numbers has an upper bound (e.g. $\leq$ or less than or = to) then it has a least upper bound. These two properties together define the real numbers completely, and allow its other properties to be inferred: every polynomial of odd degree with real coefficients has a real root. If you add the square root of −1 to the real numbers, you have a complex number and the result is algebraically closed.

Real numbers are classified as follows:

A. Natural numbers, denoted by $\mathbb{N}$: The counting numbers, 1, 2, 3,...

Algebraic properties of natural numbers (also discussed in section 0005, Natural numbers):

	Addition	multiplication
<u>closure</u>:	$a + b$ is a natural number	$a \times b$ is a natural number
<u>associativity</u>:	$a + (b + c) = (a + b) + c$	$a \times (b \times c) = (a \times b) \times c$
<u>commutativity</u>:	$a + b = b + a$	$a \times b = b \times a$
existence of an <u>identity element</u>:	$a + 0 = a$	$a \times 1 = a$
<u>distributivity</u>:		$a \times (b + c) = (a \times b) + (a \times c)$
No <u>zero divisors</u>:		if $ab = 0$, then either $a = 0$ or $b = 0$ (or both)

B. Whole numbers: The counting numbers along with zero, 0, 1, 2...

C. Integers denoted by $\mathbb{Z}$: The counting numbers, their negatives, and zero, ..., ⁻1, 0, 1,...

D. Rationals denoted by $\mathbb{Q}$: All of the fractions that can be formed from the whole numbers. Zero cannot be the denominator. In decimal form, these numbers will either be terminating or repeating decimals. Simplify square roots to determine if the number can be written as a fraction.

E. Irrationals denoted by *i*: Real numbers that cannot be written as a fraction. The decimal forms of these numbers are neither terminating nor repeating. <u>Examples:</u> $\pi, e, \sqrt{2}$, etc.

The relative size of real numbers expressed as fractions, decimals, percents and scientific notation:
Compare the relative size of real numbers expressed in a variety of forms, including fractions, decimals, percents, and scientific notation:

To convert a fraction to a decimal, simply divide the numerator (top) by the denominator (bottom). Use long division if necessary.

If a decimal has a fixed number of digits, the decimal is said to be terminating. To write such a decimal as a fraction, first determine what place value the farthest right digit is in, for example: tenths, hundredths, thousandths, ten thousandths, hundred thousands, etc. Then drop the decimal and place the string of digits over the number given by the place value.

If a decimal continues forever by repeating a string of digits, the decimal is said to be repeating. To write a repeating decimal as a fraction, follow these steps:

1. Let x = the repeating decimal
   (e.g. x=0.716716716...)
2. Multiply x by the multiple of ten that will move the decimal just to the right of the repeating block of digits.
   (e.g. 1000x=716.716716...)
3. Subtract the first equation from the second.
   (e.g. 1000x-x=716.716.716...-0.716716...)
4. Simplify and solve this equation. The repeating block of digits will subtract out.
   (e.g. 999x = 716 so x = $\frac{716}{999}$)

The solution will be the fraction for the repeating decimal.

FOUNDATION LEV. MATH.

A **decimal** can be converted to a **percent** by multiplying by 100%, or merely moving the decimal point two places to the right. A **percent** can be converted to a **decimal** by dividing by 100%, or moving the decimal point two places to the left.

Examples: Convert the following decimals into percents.

    0.375 = 37.5%
    0.7 = 70%
    0.04 = 4 %
    3.15 = 315 %

Examples: Convert the following percents into decimals.

    84% = 0.84
    3% = 0.03
    60% = 0.6
    110% = 1.1
    $\frac{1}{2}$% = 0.5% = 0.005

A **percent** can be converted to a **fraction** by placing it over 100 and reducing to simplest terms.

Examples: Convert the following percents into fractions.
    32% = $\frac{32}{100}$ = $\frac{8}{25}$
    6% = $\frac{6}{100}$ = $\frac{3}{50}$
    111% = $\frac{111}{100}$ = $1\frac{11}{100}$
    = $\frac{10}{100}$ = $\frac{1}{10}$

To find the **decimal** equivalent of a **fraction**, use the denominator to divide the numerator. Note decimal comes from deci or part of ten.

Example: Find the decimal equivalent of $\frac{7}{10}$.

$$\begin{array}{r} 0.7 \\ 10\overline{)7.0} \\ \underline{70} \\ 00 \end{array}$$

Since 10 cannot divide into 7 evenly, put a decimal point in the answer row on top; put a zero behind 7 to make it 70. Continue the division process. If a remainder occurs, put a zero by the last digit of the remainder and continue the division.

Thus $\dfrac{7}{10} = 0.7$

It is a good idea to write a zero before the decimal point so that the decimal point is emphasized.

Example: Find the decimal equivalent of $\dfrac{7}{125}$.

$$\begin{array}{r} 0.056 \\ 125\overline{)7.000} \\ \underline{625} \\ 750 \\ \underline{750} \\ 0 \end{array}$$

A **decimal** can be converted into a **fraction** by multiplying by 1 in the form of a fraction (e.g. $\dfrac{10}{10}, \dfrac{100}{100}, \dfrac{1000}{1000}$) to get rid of the decimal point.

Example: Convert 0.056 to a fraction.

Multiplying 0.056 by $\dfrac{1000}{1000}$ to get rid of the decimal point

$$0.056 \times \dfrac{1000}{1000} = \dfrac{56}{1000} = \dfrac{7}{125}$$

The **percentage** of a number can be found by converting the percentage into decimal form and then multiplying the decimal by the number.

Example: Find 23% of 1000.

$23\% = 0.23$

$0.23 \times 1000 = 230$

$= 0.0625 = 0.0625 \times \dfrac{10000}{10000} = \dfrac{625}{10000} = \dfrac{1}{16}$

Scientific notation is a more convenient method for writing very large and very small numbers. It employs two factors. The first factor is a number between -10 and 10. The second factor is a power of 10. This notation is a shorthand way to express large numbers (like the weight of 100 freight cars in kilograms) or small numbers (like the weight of an atom in grams).

Recall:
$10^n = (10)^n$ Ten multiplied by itself n times.
$10^6 = 1,000,000$ (mega)
$10^3 = 10 \times 10 \times 10 = 1000$ (kilo)
$10^2 = 10 \times 10 = 100$ (hecto)
$10^1 = 10$ (deca)
$10^0 = 1$ Any nonzero number raised to power of zero is 1.
$10^{-1} = 1/10$ (deci)
$10^{-2} = 1/100$ (centi)
$10^{-3} = 1/1000$ (milli)
$10^{-6} = 1/1,000,000$ (micro)

Scientific notation format. Convert a number to a form of $b \times 10^n$ where -10<b<10 and n is an integer.

Example: 356.73 can be written in various forms.

$$356.73 = 3567.3 \times 10^{-1} \quad (1)$$
$$= 35673 \times 10^{-2} \quad (2)$$
$$= 35.673 \times 10^1 \quad (3)$$
$$= 3.5673 \times 10^2 \quad (4)$$
$$= 0.35673 \times 10^3 \quad (5)$$

Only (4) is written in proper scientific notation format.

Example: Write 46,368,000 in scientific notation.

1) Introduce a decimal point. 46,368,000 = 46,368,000.0

2) Move the decimal place to **left** until only one nonzero digit is in front of it, in this case between the 4 and 6.

3) Count the number of digits the decimal point moved, in this case 7. This is the nth the power of ten and is **positive** because the decimal point moved **left**.
Therefore, $46{,}368{,}000 = 4.6368 \times 10^7$

Example: Write 0.00397 in scientific notation.

1) Decimal point is already in place.

2) Move the decimal point to the **right** until there is only one nonzero digit in front of it, in this case between the 3 and 9.

3) Count the number of digits the decimal point moved, in this case 3. This is the nth the power of ten and is **negative** because the decimal point moved **right**.
Therefore, $0.00397 = 3.97 \times 10^{-3}$.

Example: Evaluate $\dfrac{3.22 \times 10^{-3} \times 736}{0.00736 \times 32.2 \times 10^{-6}}$

Since we have a mixture of large and small numbers, convert each number to scientific notation:

$736 = 7.36 \times 10^2$

$0.00736 = 7.36 \times 10^{-3}$

$32.2 \times 10^{-6} = 3.22 \times 10^{-5}$ thus, we have,

$\dfrac{3.22 \times 10^{-3} \times 7.36 \times 10^2}{7.36 \times 10^{-3} \times 3.22 \times 10^{-5}}$

$= \dfrac{3.22 \times 7.36 \times 10^{-3} \times 10^{2}}{7.36 \times 3.22 \times 10^{-3} \times 10^{-5}}$

$= \dfrac{3.22 \times 7.36}{7.36 \times 3.22} \times \dfrac{10^{-1}}{10^{-8}}$

$= \dfrac{3.22 \times 7.36}{3.22 \times 7.36} \times 10^{-1} \times 10^{8}$

$= \dfrac{23.6992}{23.6992} \times 10^{7}$

$= 1 \times 10^{7} = 10{,}000{,}000$

Algebraic Structures (SMR 1.1)

Skill b. Know that the rational numbers and real numbers can be ordered and that the complex numbers cannot be ordered, but that any polynomial equation with real coefficients can be solved in the complex field

Imaginary and complex numbers and their properties: We just reviewed real numbers. Real numbers can be ordered but complex numbers cannot be ordered. **Complex numbers denoted by $\mathbb{C}$:** $\mathbb{C}$ means $\{a+bi : a,b \in \mathbb{R}\}$ ($\in$ means "element of"). In other words, complex numbers are an extension of real numbers made by attaching an imaginary number *i*, which satisfies: $i^2 = -1$. Complex numbers are of the form *a + bi*, where *a* and *b* are *real* numbers and $i = \sqrt{-1}$. "a" and "b" are the real part of the complex number while 'i' is the imaginary part. When *i* appears in a fraction, the fraction is usually simplified so that *i* is not in the denominator.

The complex plane and complex numbers as ordered pairs: Every complex number $a + bi$ can be shown as a pair of 2 real numbers. For the real part *a* and the imaginary part *bi*, *b* is also real.

Example: *3i* has a real part *0* and imaginary part *3* and 4 has a real part 4 and an imaginary part 0. As another way of writing complex numbers, we can write them as ordered pairs:

Complex #	Ordered pair
$3 + 2i$	(3, 2)
$\sqrt{3} + \sqrt{3}i$	$(\sqrt{3} + \sqrt{3})$
$7i$	(0, 7)
$\dfrac{6+2i}{7}$	$\left(\dfrac{6}{7}, \dfrac{2}{7}\right)$

A visual representation of imaginary numbers:
When i^2 appears in a problem, it can be replaced by -1 since
$i^2 = -1$, $x^2 = -1$

FOUNDATION LEV. MATH.

How do we turn a 1 into a -1? We can work with what is called a complex plane and visually see how it can be done. Instead of an x and a y-axis, we have an axis that represents the dimension of real numbers and an axis that represents the imaginary dimension. If we rotate x 180° in a counterclockwise direction, we can change 1 into -1, which is the same as multiplying 1 by i.

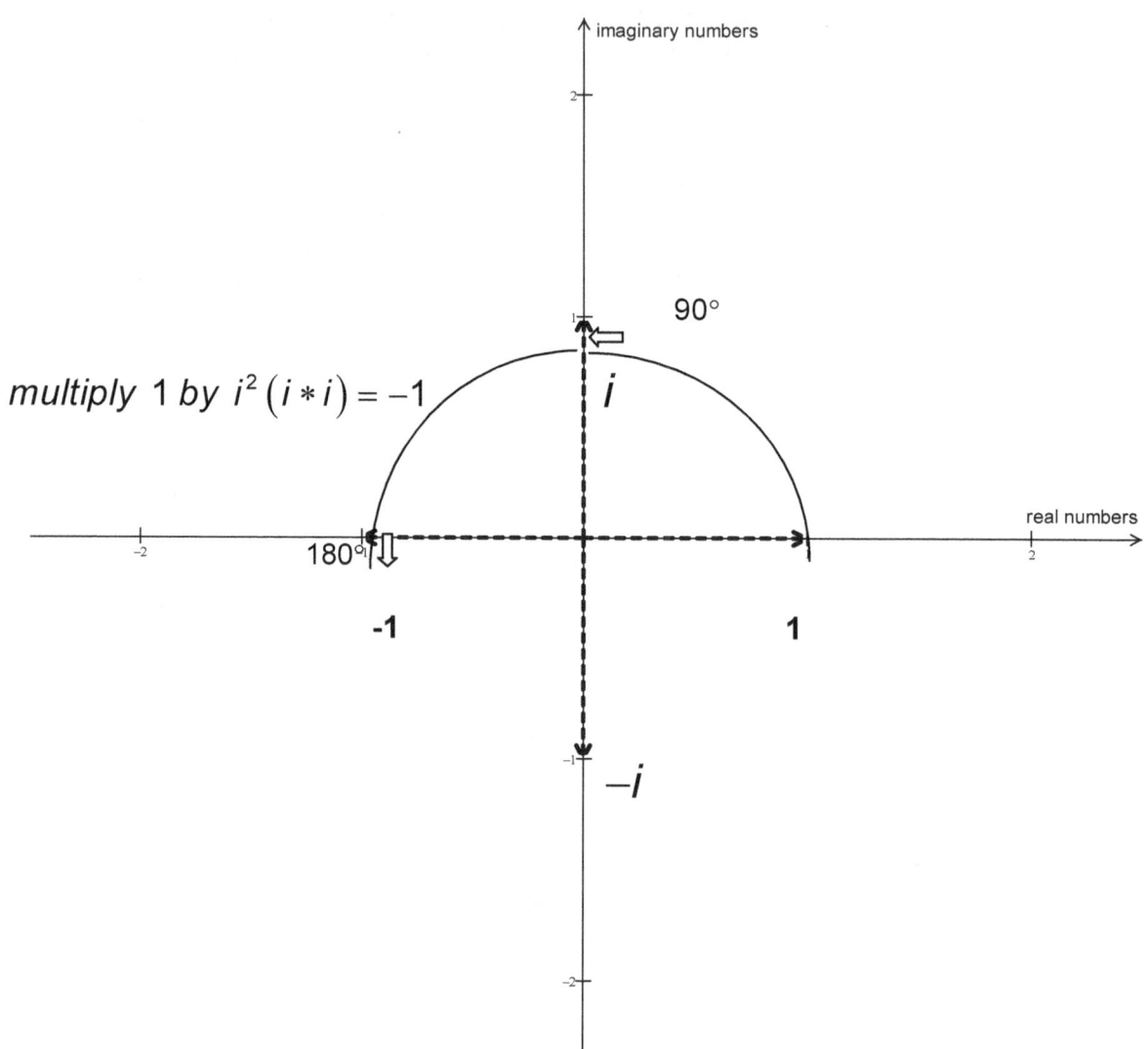

We could also rotate clockwise 180° to turn -1 into 1. This is a multiplication by i^2.

If we multiply by $-i$ once, we turn 1 into $-i$ and $-i$ into -1. Therefore, there are *two* square roots of -1: i and $-i$.

Therefore, i (or -i) is what real numbers turn into when rotated 180° and two rotations in either direction is -1: it brings us back to the dimension of real positive and negative numbers.

Operations involving polynomial equations in a complex field:
To add or subtract complex numbers, add or subtract the real parts. Then add or subtract the imaginary parts and keep the **i** (just like combining like terms).

Examples: Add $(2 + 3i) + (^-7 - 4i)$.

$2 + {}^-7 = {}^-5 \qquad 3i + {}^-4i = {}^-i$ so,

$(2 + 3i) + (^-7 - 4i) = {}^-5 - i$

Subtract $(8 - 5i) - (^-3 + 7i)$
$8 - 5i + 3 - 7i = 11 - 12i$

To multiply 2 complex numbers, F.O.I.L. (F=first terms, O= outer terms, I= inner terms and L = last terms) the 2 complex factors together. Replace i^2 with $a\ ^-1$ and finish combining like terms. Answers should have the form $a + b\ i$.

Multiply the 1st terms to get 48

Example: Multiply $(8 + 3i)(6 - 2i)$ use F.O.I.L. (First, Outer, Inner, Last).

Multiply the outer terms to get -16*i* and so on....

$48 - 16i + 18i - 6i^2 \qquad$ Let $i^2 = {}^-1$.

$48 - 16i + 18i - 6(^-1)$

$48 - 16i + 18i + 6$

$54 + 2i \qquad\qquad$ This is the answer.

Example: Multiply $(5 + 8i)^2$ ←Write this out twice.
$(5 + 8i)(5 + 8i) \qquad$ F.O.I.L. this
$25 + 40i + 40i + 64i^2 \qquad$ Let $i^2 = {}^-1$.
$25 + 40i + 40i + 64(^-1)$
$25 + 40i + 40i - 64$
$^-39 + 80i \qquad\qquad$ This is the answer.

When dividing 2 complex numbers, you must eliminate the complex number in the denominator. If the complex number in the denominator is of the form $b\ i$, multiply both the numerator and denominator by **i**. Remember to replace i^2 with $a\ ^-1$ and then continue simplifying the fraction.

FOUNDATION LEV. MATH. 11

Example:

$$\frac{2+3i}{5i} \quad \text{Multiply this by } \frac{i}{i}$$

$$\frac{2+3i}{5i} \times \frac{i}{i} = \frac{(2+3i)\,i}{5i \cdot i} = \frac{2i + 3i^2}{5i^2} = \frac{2i + 3(^-1)}{^-5} = \frac{^-3 + 2i}{^-5} = \frac{3 - 2i}{5}$$

If the complex number in the denominator is of the form $a + bi$, multiply both the numerator and denominator by **the conjugate of the denominator** (see more about the conjugate in SMR1.2, section b). The conjugate of a complex number is the number with the sign of its imaginary part reversed. The conjugate of $2 - 3i$ is $2 + 3i$. The conjugate of $^-6 + 11i$ is $^-6 - 11i$. Multiply together the factors on the top and bottom of the fraction. Remember to replace i^2 with a $^-1$, combine like terms, and then continue simplifying the fraction.

Example:

$$\frac{4+7i}{6-5i} \quad \text{Multiply numerator and denominator by } 6+5i,$$

the conjugate of the denominator.

$$\frac{(4+7i)}{(6-5i)} \times \frac{(6+5i)}{(6+5i)} = \frac{24 + 20i + 42i + 35i^2}{36 + 30i - 30i - 25i^2} = \frac{24 + 62i + 35(^-1)}{36 - 25(^-1)} = \frac{^-11 + 62i}{61}$$

Example:

$$\frac{24}{^-3 - 5i} \quad \text{Multiply numerator and denominator by } -3+5i,$$

the conjugate of the denominator.

$$\frac{24}{^-3-5i} \times \frac{^-3+5i}{^-3+5i} = \frac{^-72 + 120i}{9 - 25i^2} = \frac{^-72 + 120i}{9 + 25} = \frac{^-72 + 120i}{34} = \frac{^-36 + 60i}{17}$$

Solving polynomial equations in the complex field:

$4x^2 - 2x + 7 = 0$ This is not a perfect square

$x^2 - \frac{1}{2}x + \frac{7}{4} = 0$ Divide by 4, the coefficient of the quadratic term

$x^2 - \frac{1}{2}x = -\frac{7}{4}$ Put in the form $x^2 + bx$

$x^2 - \frac{1}{2}x + \frac{1}{16} = -\frac{7}{4} + \frac{1}{16}$ To complete the square, divide $b(2)$ by 2 and

then square the result: $\left(-\frac{1}{2} \div 2\right)^2 = \frac{1}{16}$

$\left(x^2 - \frac{1}{4}\right)^2 = -\frac{27}{16}$ Factor the left side so you have a perfect square, simplify the right

$\left(x - \frac{1}{4}\right) = \sqrt{-\frac{27}{16}}$ Use the Square Root Property

$x - \frac{1}{4} = \pm \frac{3i\sqrt{3}}{4}$ Simplify the right side, $\sqrt{-1} = i$

$x = \frac{1}{4} \pm \frac{3i\sqrt{3}}{4}$ Add $\frac{1}{4}$ to each side to solve for x

The solution is $x = \left\{\frac{1}{4} + \frac{3i\sqrt{3}}{4}, \frac{1}{4} - \frac{3i\sqrt{3}}{4}\right\}$ an imaginary solution with complex numbers.

Check the solution by graphing and notice that there are no real solutions for the equation as it has no roots (x-intercepts). Imaginary solutions must be check by substituting the answers back into the original equation.

For more on solving polynomials in the complex field, see Skill SMR1.2.b

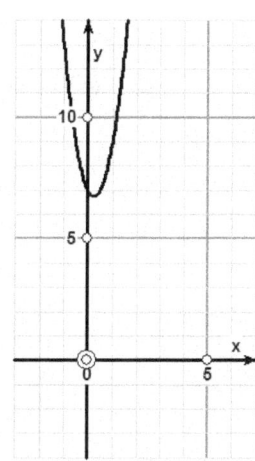

quadratic equation with no real roots

FOUNDATIO

Algebraic Structures (SMR 1.1)

Skill c. Know why the real and complex numbers are each a field, and that particular rings are not fields (e.g., integers, polynomial rings, matrix rings)

Fields and Rings:

A. Fields: A set of elements (usually numbers) that may be combined under the operations of addition and multiplication so that it constitutes an additive group, the nonzero elements form a multiplicative group, and multiplication distributes over addition. The set of real numbers and the set of complex numbers are both examples of fields. A field is a ring where multiplication is commutative (in the U.S. and Russia, but not in France and other places in Europe), commutative meaning if $a(b) = c$ then, $b(a) = c$.

$\mathbb{Z}$ (integers) is a ring that is not a field in that it does not have the multiplicative inverse:

For all a in $\mathbb{F}$, $a(a^{-1}) = a^{-1}(a) = 1$, this is what multiplicative inverse means. For integers, which includes the negative numbers, the multiplicative inverse does not apply:

$$0(0^{-1}) \neq 1.$$

B. Ring: An algebraic structure in which addition and multiplication are defined and have properties listed below. A ring is a generalization of the set of integers, which are one example of a ring. If a ring also has the commutative property of multiplication (with zero removed) it is a field. Other examples include the polynomials and matrices.

A ring is a set R equipped with two binary operations + and ·, called *addition* and *multiplication*:

Multiplication distributes over addition:

$a \cdot (b + c) = (a \cdot b) + (a \cdot c)$

$(a + b) \cdot c = (a \cdot c) + (b \cdot c)$ Distributive Property of Multiplication

FOUNDATION LEV. MATH.

$(R, +)$

$(a + b) + c = a + (b + c)$ Associative Property of Addition

$a + b = b + a$ Commutative Property of Addition

$0 + a = a + 0 = a$ Additive Identity

$\forall a \;\exists (-a)$ such that $a + -a = -a + a = 0$

$(R, *)$

$1 \cdot a = a \cdot 1 = a$ Multiplicative Identity

$(a \cdot b) \cdot c = a \cdot (b \cdot c)$ Associative Property of Multiplication

$0a = a0 = 0$

$(-1)a = -a$

$(-a)b = a(-b) = -(ab)$

$(ab)^{-1} = b^{-1} a^{-1}$ if both a and b are invertible

Summary of Field Axioms:

Name	Addition	Multiplication
Commutativity	$a + b = b + a$	$ab = ba$
Associativity	$(a+b)+c = a+(b+c)$	$(ab)c = a(bc)$
Distributivity	$a(b+c) = ab + bc$	$(a+b)c = ac + bc$
Identity	$a + 0 = a = 0 + a$	$a \cdot 1 = a = 1 \cdot a$
Inverses	$a + (-a) = 0 = (-a) + a$	$a(a^{-1}) = 1 = a^{-1}$ if $a \neq 0$

Polynomial Equations and Inequalities (SMR 1.2)

Skill a. **Know why graphs of linear inequalities are half planes and be able to apply this fact (e.g. linear programming)**

Linear Inequalities:

To graph **an inequality**, solve the inequality for y. This gets the inequality in the **slope intercept form**, (for example: $y < mx + b$). The point (0,b) is the y-intercept and m is the line's slope.

- If the inequality solves to $x >, \geq, <$ or $\leq$ any number, then the graph includes a **vertical line**.

- If the inequality solves to $y >, \geq, <$ or $\leq$ any number, then the graph includes a **horizontal line**.

- When graphing a linear inequality, the line will be dotted if the inequality sign is $<$ or $>$. If the inequality sign is either $\geq$ or $\leq$, the line on the graph will be a solid line. Shade above the line when the inequality sign is $\geq$ or $>$. Shade below the line when the inequality sign is $<$ or $\leq$. For inequalities of the forms $x >$ number, $x \leq$ number, $x <$ number, or $x \geq$ number, draw a vertical line (solid or dotted). Shade to the right for $>$ or $\geq$. Shade to the left for $<$ or $\leq$.

Remember: Dividing or multiplying by a negative number will reverse the direction of the inequality sign.

Use these rules to graph and shade each inequality. The solution to a system of linear inequalities consists of the part of the graph where the shaded areas for all the inequalities in the system overlap. For instance, if the graph of one inequality was shaded with red, and the graph of another inequality was shaded with blue, then the overlapping area would be shaded purple. The points in the purple area would be the solution set of this system.

Example: Solve by graphing:

$x + y \leq 6$
$x - 2y \leq 6$

Solving the inequalities for y, they become:

$y \leq {}^-x + 6$ (y intercept of 6 and slope = $^-1$)

$y \geq 1/2\, x - 3$ (y intercept of $^-3$ and slope = $1/2$)
A graph with shading is shown below:

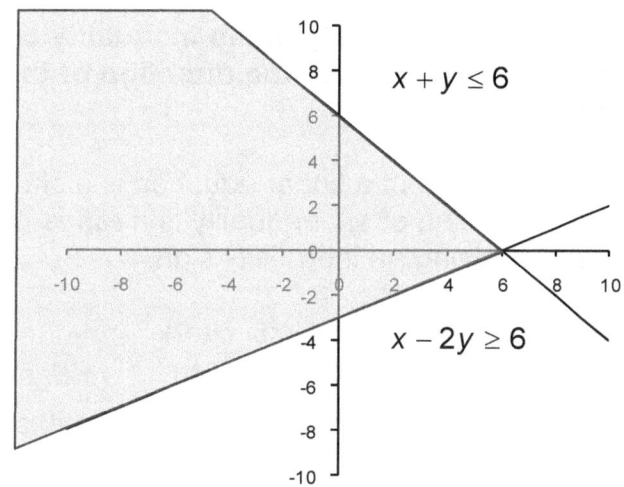

To solve an **equation or inequality**, follow these steps:

STEP   1. If there are parentheses, use the distributive property to eliminate them.

STEP   2. If there are fractions, determine their LCD (least common denominator). Multiply every term of the equation by the LCD. This will cancel out all of the fractions making it easier to solve the equation or inequality.

STEP   3. If there are decimals, find the largest decimal. Multiply each term by a power of 10(10, 100, 1000,etc.) with the same number of zeros as the length of the decimal. This will eliminate all decimals while solving the equation or inequality.

STEP   4. Combine like terms on each side of the equation or inequality.

STEP   5. If there are variables on both sides of the equation, add or subtract one of those variable terms to move it to the other side. Combine like terms.

STEP   6. If there are constants on both sides, add or subtract one or more of those constants to both sides. Combine like terms.

STEP 7. If there is a coefficient in front of the variable, divide both sides by this number to get the answer to the equation. However, remember:

Dividing or multiplying an inequality by a negative number will reverse the direction of the inequality sign.

STEP 8. The solution of a linear equation is a single number. The solution of an inequality is a range of values shown using an inequality sign.

Example: Solve:
$3(2x+5) - 4x = 5(x+9)$
$6x + 15 - 4x = 5x + 45$ ref. step 1
$2x + 15 = 5x + 45$ ref. step 4
$^-3x + 15 = 45$ ref. step 5
$^-3x = 30$ ref. step 6
$x = {^-}10$ ref. step 7

Example: Solve:
$1/2(5x + 34) = 1/4(3x - 5)$
$5/2 x + 17 = 3/4 x - 5/4$ ref. step 1
LCD of 5/2, 3/4, and 5/4 is 4.
Multiply by the LCD of 4.
$4(5/2 x + 17) = (3/4 x - 5/4)4$ ref. step 2
$10x + 68 = 3x - 5$
$7x + 68 = {^-}5$ ref. step 5
$7x = {^-}73$ ref. step 6
$x = {^-}73/7$ or $^-10\ 3/7$ ref. step 7

FOUNDATION LEV. MATH.

Check:

$$\frac{1}{2}\left[5\frac{-73}{7}+34\right]=\frac{1}{4}\left[3\left(\frac{-73}{7}\right)-5\right]$$

$$\frac{-73(5)}{14}+17=\frac{3(-73)}{28}-\frac{5}{4}$$

$$\frac{-73(5)+17(14)}{14}=\frac{3(-73)}{28}-\frac{5}{4}$$

$$\frac{-73(5)+17(14)}{14}=\frac{3(-73)-35}{28}$$

$$\left(\frac{-365+238}{28}\right)\times 2=\frac{-219-35}{28}$$

$$\frac{-254}{28}=\frac{-254}{28}$$

Example: Solve: $6x + 21 < 8x + 31$

$$-2x + 21 < 31 \quad \text{ref. step 5}$$
$$-2x < 10 \quad \text{ref. step 6}$$
$$x > -5 \quad \text{ref. step 7}$$

Note that the inequality sign has changed.

Linear Programming and inequalities can be used to solve various types of word problems and can be used in a practical way solving real-world problems. It is often used in various industries, ecological sciences and governmental organizations to determine or project production costs, the amount of pollutants dispersed into the air, etc. The key to most linear programming problems is to organize the information in the word problem into a chart or graph of some type.

Example: A printing manufacturer makes 2 types of printers, a Printmaster and a Speedmaster printer. The Printmaster takes up 10^3 feet of space, weighs 5.000 pounds and the Speedmaster takes up 5^3 feet of space and weighs 600 pounds. The total available space for storage before shipping is $2,000^3$ feet and the weight limit for the space is 300,000 pounds. The profit on the Printmaster is $50,000 and the profit on the Speedmaster is $30,000. How many of each machine should be sold to maximize profitability and what is the maximum possible profit?

First, let x represent the number of Printmaster sold and y represent the number of Speedmaster sold. Therefore,

the equation for space is $10x + 5y \leq 2000$, which simplifies to: $2x + y \leq 400$, which in terms of y is $y \leq -2x + 400$, and since you can't have a negative number of printers, $x \geq 0, y \geq 0$. The equation for weight is $5000x + 600y \leq 300000$, which simplifies to: $50x + 6y \leq 3000$.

Substitute in x=0 and y=0 in both equations to find where each linear equation meets the x and y-axis and you get the points (0,400) and (200,0) for space and the points (60,0) and (0,500) for weight.

By using substitution, we can solve the system of equations for space and weight:

$50x + 6(-2x + 400) \leq 3000$

$50x - 12x + 2400 \leq 3000$

$38x \leq 600$

$x \leq 15.9$ Substitute 15.9 back into one of the equations for x to solve for y:

$2(15.9) + y \leq 400$

$31.8 + y \leq 400$

$y \leq 378.2$

The equation for profit is 50,000x + 30,000y and to find the maximum values, make a table using the information you found (numbers found above were rounded to whole numbers):

Vertexes	50,000x	30,000y	50,000x + 30,000y
(0,0)	0	0	0
(0,400)	0	12,000,000	12,000,000
(16,378)	900,000	11,340,000	12,240,000
(60,0)	300,000	0	300,000

You can see from the table that the maximum profit is reached when 16 Printmaster (x) are sold and 378 Speedmaster (y) are sold to get a maximum profit of $12,240,000.

This can be shown visually in a graph. Below is a graph of the linear inequality for space and for weight, and their point of intersection, which is the point (16,378), which tells you the number of each printer that needs to be sold for maximum profitability based on the weight and space constraints.

Graph the inequalities:

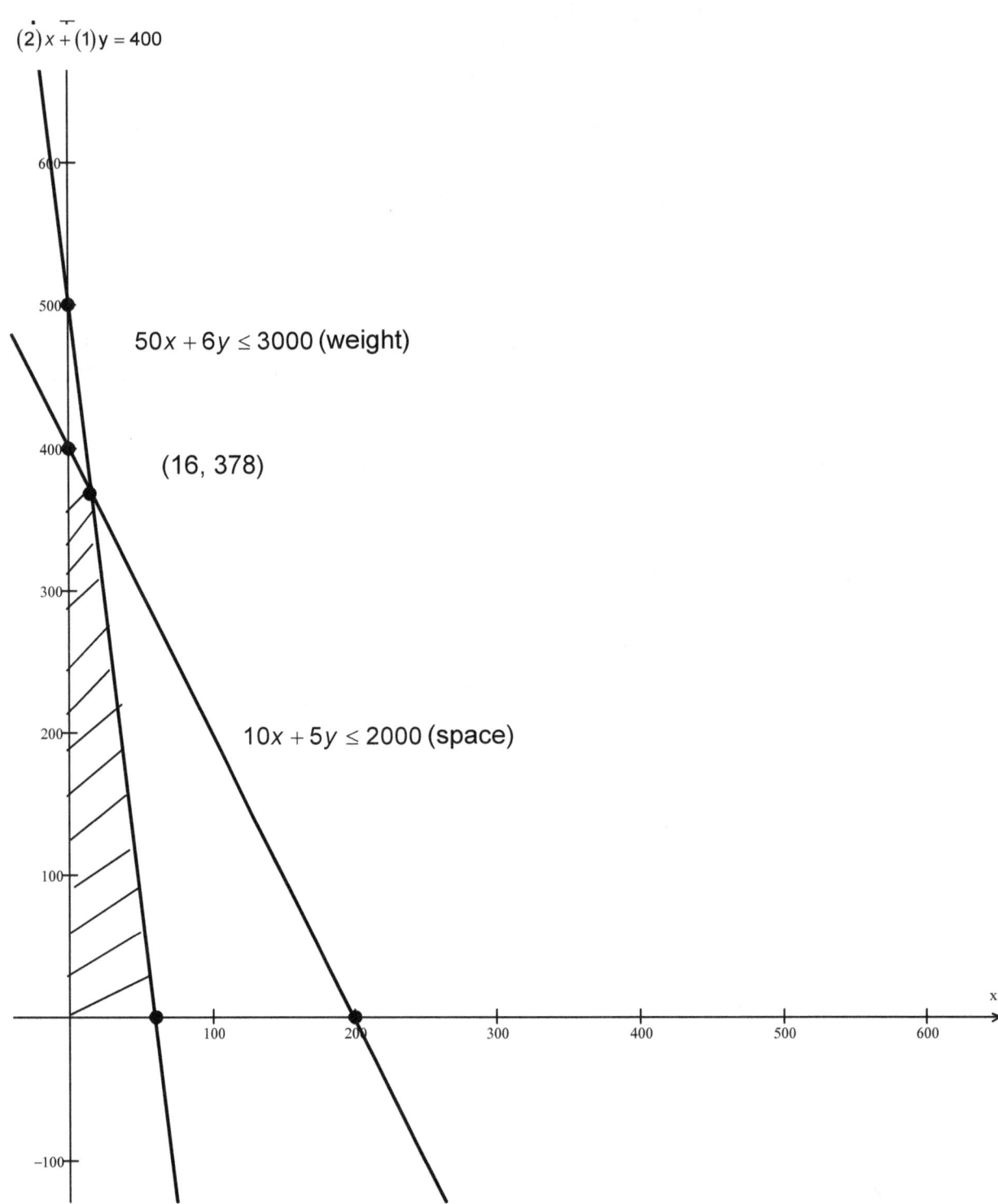

Example: The YMCA wants to sell raffle tickets to raise at least $32,000. If they must pay $7,250 in expenses and prizes out of the money collected from the tickets, how many tickets worth $25 each must they sell?

Solution: Since they want to raise **at least $32,000**, that means they would be happy to get $32,000 **or more**. This requires an inequality.

Let x = number of tickets sold
Then $25x$ = total money collected for x tickets

Total money minus expenses is greater than $32,000.

$$25x - 7250 \geq 32000$$
$$25x \geq 39250$$
$$x \geq 1570$$

If they sell **1,570 tickets or more**, they will raise AT LEAST $32,000.

Example: Sharon's Bike Shoppe can assemble a 3-speed bike in 30 minutes or a 10-speed bike in 60 minutes. The profit on each bike sold is $60 for a 3 speed or $75 for a 10-speed bike. How many of each type of bike should they assemble during an 8-hour day (480 minutes) to make the maximum profit? Total daily profit must be at least $300.

Let x = number of 3 speed bikes
y = number of 10 speed bikes

Since there are only 480 minutes to use each day,

$30x + 60y \leq 480$ is the first inequality.

Since the total daily profit must be at least $300,

$60x + 75y \geq 300$ is the second inequality.

$30x + 60y \leq 480$ solves to $y \leq 8 - 1/2\, x$
$60y \leq -30x + 480$
$$y \leq -\frac{1}{2}x + 8$$

$60x + 75y \geq 300$ solves to $y \geq 4 - 4/5\,x$

$$75y + 60x \geq 300$$
$$75y \geq -60x + 300$$
$$y \geq -\frac{4}{5}x + 4$$

<u>Example:</u> Graph these 2 inequalities:

$$y \leq 8 - 1/2\,x$$
$$y \geq 4 - 4/5\,x$$

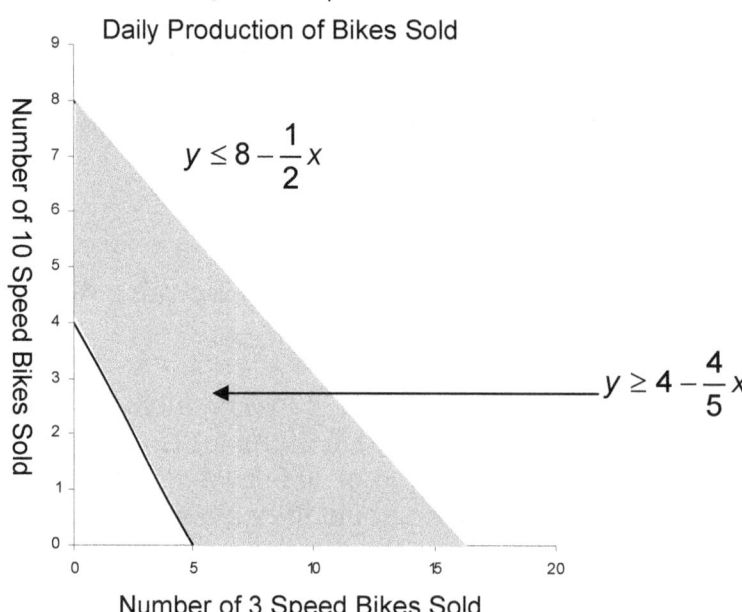

Realize that $x \geq 0$ and $y \geq 0$, since the number of bikes assembled cannot be a negative number. Graph these as additional constraints on the problem. The number of bikes assembled must always be an integer value, so points within the shaded area of the graph must have integer values. The maximum profit will occur at or near a corner of the shaded portion of this graph. Those points occur at (0,4), (0,8), (16,0), or (5,0). Since profits are $60/3-speed or $75/10-speed, the profit would be :

    (0,4) $60(0) + 75(4) = 300$

    (0,8) $60(0) + 75(8) = 600$

    (16,0) $60(16) + 75(0) = 960$ ← Maximum profit

    (5,0) $60(5) + 75(0) = 300$

The maximum profit would occur if 16 3-speed bikes were made daily.

Polynomial Equations and Inequalities (SMR 1.2)

Skill b. Prove and use the following:
The Rational Root Theorem for polynomials with integer coefficients
The Factor Theorem
The Conjugate Roots Theorem for polynomial equations with real coefficients
The Quadratic Formula for real and complex quadratic polynomials
The Binomial Theorem

Polynomials: To understand the theorems that follow, you must have some knowledge of polynomials. You may have dealt with expressions like $2x^2$ or $5x$ or $6x$. Polynomials can be a single expression or sums of these expressions and every part of the polynomial is called a "term." The terms can have variables in them and exponents but there are no fractional exponents, no square roots of exponents and no variables in the denominator.

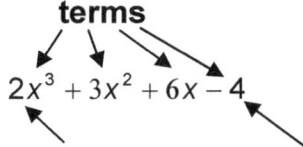

Leading term   constant term (has no variable and ∴ never changes and is the y-intercept).

Polynomials written *in standard form* ($ax^2 + bx + c = 0$) have the terms written in decreasing value according to the value of the exponent, like above. This particular polynomial shown above is a "degree 3" polynomial because the exponent of the 1st term is 3. A special case of a polynomial is the quadratic equation, which is degree 2: $x^2 + 4x + 4 = 0$. There are many ways to solve for *x* in polynomials and quadratics, but sometimes the only way to solve for *x* in a quadratic equation is to use the quadratic formula:

$$x = \frac{-b \pm \sqrt{b^2 - 4ac}}{2a}$$

There is much more on quadratic equations later in this section.

The Rational Root Theorem – this theorem is also known as the Rational Zero Theorem and offers a list of all possible rational roots or zeros of the polynomial equation (all coefficients are integers):

$$a_n x^n + a_{n-1} x^{n-1} + a_{n-2} x^{n-2} + \ldots a_2 x^2 + a_1 x + a_0 = 0$$

A root or a zero is a solution for x in the polynomial equation and is where the graph of the polynomial crosses the x-axis and y is zero. Every rational solution, zero or root of x can be written as $x = \pm \dfrac{p}{q}$ where p is an integer factor of the constant term a_0 and q is an integer factor of the leading coefficient a_n.

The Rational Root Theorem proof is on the next page.

The Rational Root Theorem Proof: Every rational solution, zero or root of x can be written as $x = \pm \frac{p}{q}$ where p is an integer factor of the constant term c_0 and q is an integer factor of the leading coefficient c_n

and where $c_0 b^n$ is divisible by a:

$p(x) \in \mathbb{Z}[x]$ where $\mathbb{Z}$ represents integers. Let n be a positive integer with deg $p(x) = n$. Let $c_0, \ldots, c_n$ such that $p(x) = c_n x^n + c_{n-1} x^{n-1} + \ldots c_1 x + c_0$.

Let $a, b \in \mathbb{Z}$ with the $\gcd(a,b) = 1$ and $b > 0$ such that $\frac{a}{b}$ is a root of $p(x)$.

Then $0 = p\left(\frac{a}{b}\right) = c_n \left(\frac{a}{b}\right)^n + c_{n-1} \left(\frac{a}{b}\right)^{n-1} + \ldots + c_1 \left(\frac{a}{b}\right) + c_0$

$= c_n \left(\frac{a^n}{b^n}\right) + c_{n-1} \left(\frac{a^{n-1}}{b^{n-1}}\right) + \ldots + c_1 \left(\frac{a}{b}\right) + c_0$. Multiply by b^n and order:

$c_n a^n + c_{n-1} a^{n-1} b + \ldots + c_1 a b^{n-1} + c_0 b^n = 0$

$c_0 b^n = -c_n a^n - c_{n-1} a^{n-1} b - \ldots - c_1 a b^{n-1}$

$c_0 b^n = a(-c_n a^{n-1} - -c_{n-1} a^{n-2} b - \ldots - c_1 b^{n-1})$ ∴ (therefore) $\frac{c_0 b^n}{a}$ and since the $\gcd(a,b) = 1$, then $\frac{c_0}{a}$

Also, $c_n a^n + c_{n-1} a^{n-1} b + \ldots + c_1 a b^{n-1} + c_0 b^n = 0$

$c_n a^n = -c_{n-1} a^{n-1} b - \ldots - c_1 a b^{n-1} - c_0 b^n$

$c_n a^n = b(-c_{n-1} a^{n-1} - \ldots - c_1 a b^{n-2} - c_0 b^{n-1})$ ∴ $\frac{c_n a^n}{b}$ and $\frac{c_n}{b}$.

Example: $3x^3 - 7x^2 + 3x - 4 = 0$ Every rational solution of this polynomial must be among the numbers represented by:

$\pm \frac{1,2,4}{1,3}$ this leads to the possible answers of

$1, -1, 2, -2, 4, -4, \frac{2}{3}, -\frac{2}{3}, \frac{4}{3}, -\frac{4}{3}$

Since the polynomial given above is of degree 3 (the exponent of the first term is 3), then there cannot be more than 3 roots or zeros for this equation.

Example: $2x^2 + x - 3 = 0$ and $x = \pm \dfrac{p}{q} = \pm \dfrac{1,3}{1,2}$

this leads to possible answers of 1, -1, 3, -3, $\dfrac{1}{2}$, $-\dfrac{1}{2}$, $\dfrac{3}{2}$, $-\dfrac{3}{2}$ and since this polynomial, a quadratic equation, is of degree 2, there are only 2 roots or zeros.

The Factor Theorem: The factor theorem establishes the relationship between the factors and the zeros or roots of a polynomial and is useful for finding the factors of higher degree polynomials. It states that a polynomial $f(x)$ has a factor $x - a$ if and only if $f(a) = 0$.

Factor Theorem Proof:
A polynomial $f(x)$ has a factor $x - a$ if and only if $f(a) = 0$.
Proof: If $f(x)$ is divided by $(x - a)$, then $R = f(a)$ by virtue of the Remainder Theorem.

$f(x) = (x - a) * q + f(a)$
Dividend = Divisor * quotient + Remainder Division Algorithm
$f(a) = 0$ is a given, $\therefore f(x) = (x - a) * q(x)$ which implies that $(x - a)$ is a factor of $f(x)$.

Conversely, we can show that $(x - a)$ is a factor of $f(x)$, then $f(a) = 0$.
$f(x) = (x - a) * q(x) + R$
If $(x - a)$ is a factor, then the remainder, $R = 0$ as $(x - a)$ divides into $f(x)$ evenly.
Since $R = f(a)$, by the Remainder Theorem $f(a) = 0$.

Example:
Find the factors of the polynomial $x^3 + 2x^2 - x - 2$
We use trial and error to find the first factor and when we find one and substitute it into the equation above and the equation is equal to zero, we know we have found a factor. Is $(x-2)$ a factor?

To find out, substitute 2 into the above equation

$(x-2) = 0$
$x = 2$
$2^3 + 2(2^2) - 2 - 2 = 8 + 8 - 4 = 12$.

We now know that $(x-2)$ is not a factor because when we substituted in 2 for x, we got 12 as a solution, not zero.
Let's try the polynomial factor $(x+2)$ or $x = -2$:
$(-2)^3 + 2(-2)^2 - (-2) - 2 = -8 + 8 + 2 - 2 = 0$. The equation is equal to zero so that we now know we have a factor and $x = -2$ is a root or zero. To find the remaining roots, we can divide our original polynomial by the factor we found.
$\frac{x^3 + 2x^2 - x - 2}{x+2} = x^2 - 1$ which factors to: $(x+1)(x-1)$. We now have the 3 factors of $x^3 + 2x^2 - x - 2$: $(x+2)$, $(x+1)$ and $(x-1)$.
We also have the roots or zeros of $x^3 + 2x^2 - x - 2$: (-2, -1, 1).

The Complex Conjugate Root Theorem states that if P is a polynomial function with real number coefficients and $a + bi$ (b is not zero) is a root of $P(x) = 0$, then $a - bi$ is also a root of P.

It follows that since complex factors come in pairs (an even number), when these factors are multiplied, the product is a quadratic polynomial with real coefficients.

The Complex Conjugate Root Theorem proof:
Given the following polynomial,

The complex conjugate is being taken as follows:
$$f(x) = a_0 + a_1 x + a_2 x^2 + \ldots + a_n x^n$$
and given that all numbers a_n are real. $f(x) = 0$,
$$\therefore a_0 + a_1 x + a_2 x^2 + \ldots + a_n x^n = 0.$$
Given all coefficients are real, taking the complex conjugate of the polynomial, it follows that
$$\overline{(a, x^r)} = a_r \overline{x}^r \text{ and } a_0 + a_1 \overline{x} + a_1 \overline{x}^2 + \ldots + a_n \overline{x}^n = \overline{0} = 0$$
and $\therefore$ for any root ζ, its complex conjugate $\overline{\zeta}$ is also a root.

Example: Find the complex roots of $4x^3 + 15x - 36 = 0$ which is already in the standard for $ax^2 + bx + c = 0$.
The equation is in order with powers of x from highest to lowest. Note that there are no common factors. The equation is degree 3, so there will be 3 roots or zeros. There is one variation in sign meaning that there will be one real root according to Descartes' Rule of Signs. According to the Rational Root Theorem, $x = \pm \frac{p}{q}$, we have numerous possibilities for roots as the numbers 1, 2, 3, 4, 6, 9, 12, 18 and 36 (factors of all of the coefficients, p), all divided by 4, 2 and 1 (factors of the coefficient a, q). We already have determined that there are no negative roots and that other two roots are the pair of complex conjugates. So let's start with $x = +\frac{p}{q} = \frac{1}{1}$ or 1,

Synthetic division can be used to find the value of a function at any value of x and can be useful in finding the zeros or roots of a polynomial. To do this, divide the value of x into the coefficients of the function (remember that coefficients of missing terms, like x^2 below, must be included).

```
1 | 4   0   15   -36
  |     4    4    19
  ----------------------
    4   4   19   -17   ←——— The value of the
                                function
```
We didn't get zero as a remainder, so 1 is not a root.

Let's try 2:

$$\begin{array}{r|rrrr} 2 & 4 & 0 & 15 & -36 \\ & & 8 & 16 & 62 \\ \hline & 8 & 8 & 31 & 26 \end{array}$$ ← The value of the function

We didn't get zero as a remainder, so 2 is not a root, but $f(1) = -17$ and $f(2) = 26$, so the zero or root lies somewhere between $x = 1$ and $x = 2$, and the only possible root we could choose from the list of possibilities above would be $\frac{3}{2}$:

$$\begin{array}{r|rrrr} \frac{3}{2} & 4 & 0 & 15 & -36 \\ & & 6 & 9 & 36 \\ \hline & 4 & 6 & 24 & 0 \end{array}$$ ← The value of the function

We found that $\frac{3}{2}$ works and is a root as the remainder is 0.

Next, we divide our original polynomial by $\left(x - \frac{3}{2}\right)$ to reduce the polynomial to a 2nd degree equation, which is a quadratic:

$$\frac{4x^3 + 15x - 36}{x - \frac{3}{2}} = 2x^2 + 3x + 12 = 0.$$

We know from Descartes' Rule of Signs that there is only one real root, so there is no sense in trying to factor this quadratic equation. We will have to used the Quadratic Formula to find the complex roots

$$x = \frac{-b \pm \sqrt{b^2 - 4ac}}{2a}.$$

$$x = \frac{-3 \pm \sqrt{9 - 4(2)(12)}}{2(2)} = \frac{-3 \pm \sqrt{-87}}{4} = -\frac{3}{4} + \left(\frac{\sqrt{-87}}{4}\right)i$$

and $-\frac{3}{4} - \left(\frac{\sqrt{-87}}{4}\right)i$

Example:
$x^2 - 6x + 13 = 0$, using the quadratic formula, we substitute in and find:

$$x = \frac{6 \pm \sqrt{36 - 4(13)}}{2} = \frac{6 \pm \sqrt{-16}}{2} = \frac{6 \pm \sqrt{-1}\sqrt{16}}{2} = \frac{6 \pm 4i}{2} = 3 + 2i, 3 - 2i$$

In both cases, we found the pair of complex numbers that are factors of the above polynomials. Any polynomial equation of degree *n* has exactly *n* zeros if we allow complex numbers and we can solve previously unsolvable polynomials by simply defining the $\sqrt{-1} = i$.

The Quadratic Formula for real and complex quadratic polynomials:

A **quadratic equation** is written in the form $ax^2 + bx + c = 0$. One method of solving it is by **factoring** the quadratic expression and applying the condition that at least one of the factors must equal zero in order for the whole expression to be zero.

TEACHER CERTIFICATION STUDY GUIDE

The Quadratic Formula proof:

$$ax^2 + bx + c = 0$$

$$x^2 + \frac{b}{a}x + \frac{c}{a} = 0$$

$$x^2 + \frac{b}{a}x = -\frac{c}{a}$$

$$x^2 + \frac{b}{a}x + \left(\frac{b}{2a}\right)^2 = -\frac{c}{a} + \left(\frac{b}{2a}\right)^2 \quad \text{(complete the square)}$$

$$x^2 + \frac{b}{a}x + \frac{b^2}{4a^2} = -\frac{c}{a} + \frac{b^2}{4a^2}$$

$$\left(x + \frac{b}{2a}\right)\left(x + \frac{b}{2a}\right) = -\frac{c}{a}\left(\frac{4a}{4a}\right) + \frac{b^2}{4a^2} \quad \text{(factor left side; use LCD on right)}$$

$$\left(x + \frac{b}{2a}\right)^2 = \frac{b^2 - 4ac}{4a^2}$$

$$\sqrt{\left(x + \frac{b}{2a}\right)^2} = \pm\sqrt{\frac{b^2 - 4ac}{4a^2}}$$

$$x + \frac{b}{2a} = \pm\frac{\sqrt{b^2 - 4ac}}{2a} \quad \text{now solve for x:}$$

$$x + \frac{b}{2a} - \frac{b}{2a} = \pm\frac{\sqrt{b^2 - 4ac}}{2a} - \frac{b}{2a}$$

$$x = -b \pm \frac{\sqrt{b^2 - 4ac}}{2a} \quad \text{and you now have the Quadratic Formula}$$

Example:

Solve the equation.

$x^2 + 10x - 24 = 0$
$(x + 12)(x - 2) = 0$ Factor.
$x + 12 = 0$ or $x - 2 = 0$ Set each factor equal to 0.
$x = {}^-12 \quad x = 2$ Solve.

Check:
$x^2 + 10x - 24 = 0$
$({}^-12)^2 + 10({}^-12) - 24 = 0 \quad\quad (2)^2 + 10(2) - 24 = 0$
$144 - 120 - 24 = 0 \quad\quad\quad\quad\quad 4 + 20 - 24 = 0$
$0 = 0 \quad\quad\quad\quad\quad\quad\quad\quad\quad\quad 0 = 0$

FOUNDATION LEV. MATH.

A quadratic equation can also be solved by **completing the square**.

Example:

Solve the equation.

$x^2 - 6x + 8 = 0$

$x^2 - 6x = {}^-8$	Move the constant to the right side.
$x^2 - 6x + 9 = {}^-8 + 9$	Add the square of half the coefficient of x to both sides.
$(x - 3)^2 = 1$	Write the left side as a perfect square.
$x - 3 = \pm\sqrt{1}$	Take the square root of both sides.
$x - 3 = 1 \quad x - 3 = {}^-1$	Solve.
$x = 4 \quad\quad x = 2$	

Check:

$x^2 - 6x + 8 = 0$

$4^2 - 6(4) + 8 = 0 \quad\quad 2^2 - 6(2) + 8 = 0$

$16 - 24 + 8 = 0 \quad\quad 4 - 12 + 8 = 0$

$0 = 0 \quad\quad\quad\quad\quad\quad 0 = 0$

Graphing parabolic equations:

The general technique for graphing quadratics is the same as for graphing linear equations. Graphing a quadratic equation, however, results in a parabola instead of a straight line.

FORM OF EQUATION $\quad y = a(x - h)^2 + k \quad\quad x = a(y - k)^2 + h$

IDENTIFICATION $\quad x^2$ term, y not squared $\quad y^2$ term, x not squared

SKETCH OF GRAPH

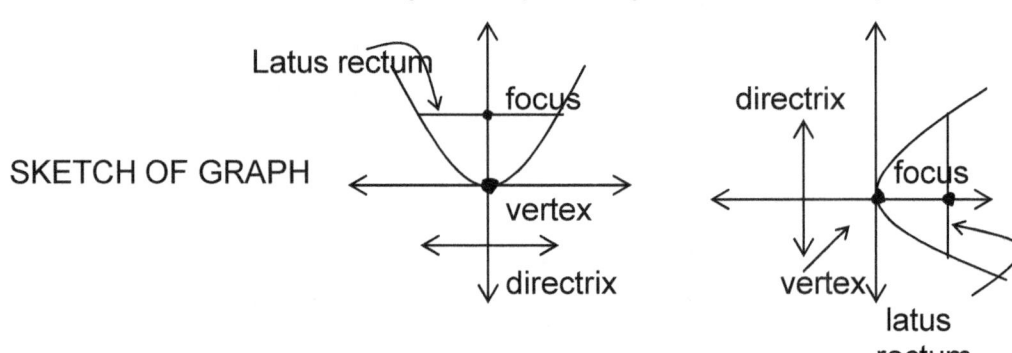

	$x = h$	$y = k$
AXIS OF SYMMETRY	-A line through the vertex and focus upon which the parabola is symmetric.	
VERTEX	(h, k)	(h, k)
FOCUS	$(h, k + 1/4a)$	$(h + 1/4a, k)$
DIRECTRIX	$y = k - 1/4a$	$x = h - 1/4a$
DIRECTION OF OPENING	up if $a > 0$, down if $a < 0$	right if $a > 0$, left if $a < 0$
LENGTH OF LATUS RECTUM	$|1/a|$	$|1/a|$

Example:

1. Find all identifying features of $y = {}^-3x^2 + 6x - 1$.

First, the equation must be put into the general form $y = a(x-h)^2 + k$.

$y = {}^-3x^2 + 6x - 1$ 1. Begin by completing the square.
$= {}^-3(x^2 - 2x + 1) - 1 + 3$
$= {}^-3(x-1)^2 + 2$ 2. Using the general form of the equation begin to identify known variables.

$a = {}^-3 \quad h = 1 \quad k = 2$

axis of symmetry: $x = 1$
vertex: $(1, 2)$
focus: $(1, 1\frac{1}{4})$
directrix: $y = 2\frac{3}{4}$
direction of opening: down since $a < 0$
length of latus rectum: $1/3$

Example:

Graph $y = 3x^2 + x - 2$.

x	$y = 3x^2 + x - 2$
$^-2$	8
$^-1$	0
0	$^-2$
1	2
2	12

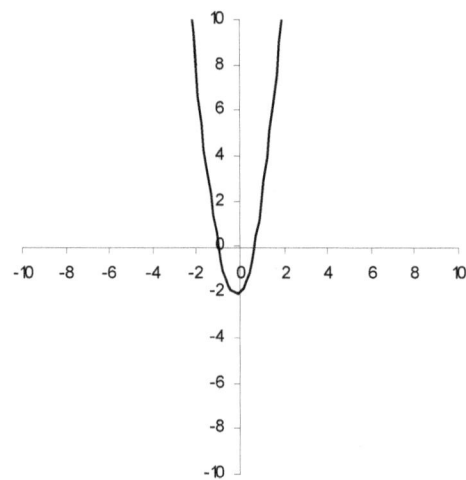

To solve **a quadratic equation** using the **quadratic formula**, make sure that your equation is in the form $ax^2 + bx + c = 0$. Substitute these values into the formula:

$$x = \frac{-b \pm \sqrt{b^2 - 4ac}}{2a}$$

Simplify the result to find the answers. (Remember, there could be 2 real answers, one real answer, or 2 complex answers that include "i").

Example:

Solve the equation.

$3x^2 = 7 + 2x$

$a = 3 \quad b = {}^-2 \quad c = {}^-7$

$$x = \frac{-({}^-2) \pm \sqrt{({}^-2)^2 - 4(3)({}^-7)}}{2(3)}$$

$$x = \frac{2 \pm \sqrt{4 + 84}}{6}$$

$$x = \frac{2 \pm \sqrt{88}}{6}$$

$$x = \frac{2 \pm 2\sqrt{22}}{6}$$

$$x = \frac{1 \pm \sqrt{22}}{3}$$

Example: Solve and graph: $y > x^2 + 4x - 5$.

The axis of symmetry is located at $x = {}^-b/2a$. Substituting 4 for b, and 1 for a, this formula becomes:

$$x = {}^-(4)/2(1) = {}^-4/2 = {}^-2$$

Find coordinates of points to each side of $x = {}^-2$.

x	y
${}^-5$	0
${}^-4$	${}^-5$
${}^-3$	${}^-8$
${}^-2$	${}^-9$
${}^-1$	${}^-8$
0	${}^-5$
1	0

Graph these points to form a parabola. Draw out as a dotted line. Since a greater than sign is used, shade above and inside the parabola.

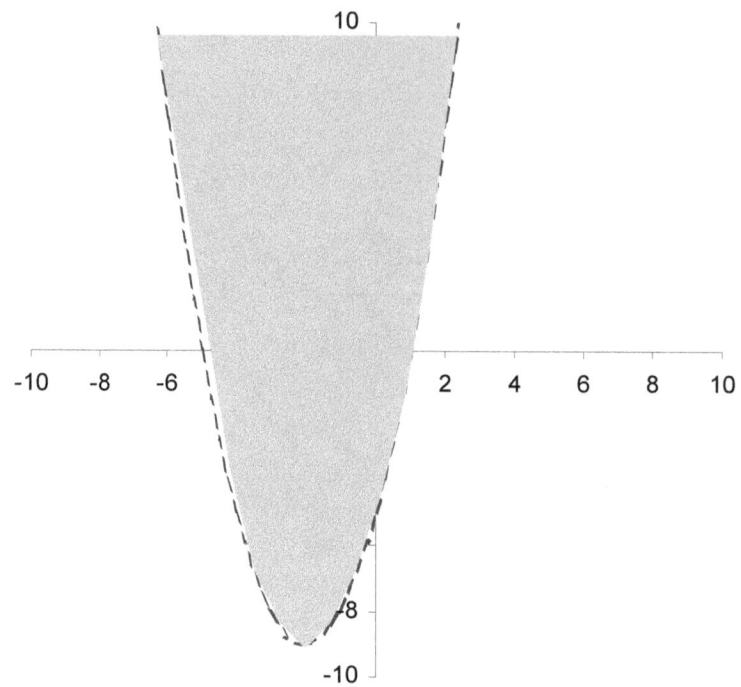

To solve a quadratic inequality (with x^2), solve for y. The axis of symmetry is located at $x = {}^-b/2a$. Find coordinates of points to each side of the axis of symmetry. Graph the parabola as a dotted line if the inequality sign is either $<$ or $>$. Graph the parabola as a dotted line if the inequality sign is either $\leq$ or $\geq$.

Shade above (or inside) the parabola if the sign is $\geq$ or $>$.
Shade below (or outside) the parabola if the sign is $\leq$ or $<$.

Example: Solve: $8x^2 - 10x - 3 = 0$

In this equation $a = 8$, $b = {}^-10$, and $c = {}^-3$.
Substituting these into the quadratic equation, it becomes:

$$x = \frac{{}^-({}^-10) \pm \sqrt{({}^-10)^2 - 4(8)({}^-3)}}{2(8)} = \frac{10 \pm \sqrt{100 - 96}}{16}$$

$$x = \frac{10 \pm \sqrt{196}}{16} = \frac{10 \pm 14}{16} = 24/16 = 3/2 \text{ or } {}^-4/16 = {}^-1/4$$

Check:
$x = -\dfrac{1}{4}$

$\dfrac{1}{2} + \dfrac{10}{4} - 3 = 0$ Both Check

$3 - 3 = 0$

Follow these steps to write **a quadratic equation** from its roots:

1. Add the roots together to get their **sum**. Multiply the roots together to get their **product**.
2. A quadratic equation can be written using the sum and product like this:

$$x^2 + (\text{opposite of the sum})x + \text{product} = 0$$

3. If there are any fractions in the equation, multiply every term by the common denominator to eliminate the fractions. This is the quadratic equation.
4. If a quadratic equation has only 1 root, use it twice and follow the first 3 steps above.

Example:
Find a quadratic equation with roots of 4 and ⁻9.

Solutions:
The sum of 4 and ⁻9 is ⁻5. The product of 4 and ⁻9 is ⁻36.
The equation would be:

$$x^2 + (\text{opposite of the sum})x + \text{product} = 0$$
$$x^2 + 5x - 36 = 0$$

Example:
Find **a quadratic equation with roots** of $5 + 2i$ and $5 - 2i$.

Solutions:
The sum of $5 + 2i$ and $5 - 2i$ is 10. The product of $5 + 2i$ and $5 - 2i$ is $25 - 4i^2 = 25 + 4 = 29$.

The equation would be:

$$x^2 + (\text{opposite of the sum})x + \text{product} = 0$$
$$x^2 - 10x + 29 = 0$$

Example:
Find a quadratic equation with roots of $2/3$ and $^-3/4$.

Solutions:
The sum of $2/3$ and $^-3/4$ is $^-1/12$. The product of $2/3$ and $^-3/4$ is $^-1/2$.

The equation would be:
$$x^2 + (\text{opposite of the sum})x + \text{product} = 0$$
$$x^2 + 1/12\, x - 1/2 = 0$$

Common denominator = 12, so multiply by 12.

$$12(x^2 + 1/12\, x - 1/2 = 0$$
$$12x^2 + 1x - 6 = 0$$
$$12x^2 + x - 6 = 0$$

Practice problems:
1. Find a quadratic equation with a root of 5.
2. Find a quadratic equation with roots of $8/5$ and $^-6/5$.
3. Find a quadratic equation with roots of 12 and $^-3$.

To factor the **sum or the difference of perfect cubes**, follow this procedure:

a. Factor out any greatest common factor (GCF).

b. Make a parentheses for a binomial (2 terms) followed by a trinomial (3 terms).

c. The sign in the first parentheses is the same as the sign in the problem. The difference of cubes will have a "-" sign in the first parentheses. The sum of cubes will use a "+".

d. The first sign in the second parentheses is the opposite of the sign in the first parentheses. The second sign in the other parentheses is always a "+".

e. Determine what would be cubed to equal each term of the problem. Put those expressions in the first parentheses.

f. To make the 3 terms of the trinomial, think square - product - square. Looking at the binomial, square the first term. This is the trinomial's first term. Looking at the binomial, find the product of the two terms, ignoring the signs. This is the trinomial's second term. Looking at the binomial, square the third term. This is the trinomial's third term. Except in rare instances, the trinomial does not factor again.

FOUNDATION LEV. MATH.

TEACHER CERTIFICATION STUDY GUIDE

Factor completely:

1.
$16x^3 + 54y^3$
$2(8x^3 + 27y^3)$ ← GCF
$2(\ +\ )(\ -\ +\ )$ ← signs
$2(2x+3y)(\ \ -\ \ +\ \ )$ ← what is cubed to equal $8x^3$ or $27y^3$
$2(2x+3y)(4x^2 - 6xy + 9y^2)$ ← square-product-square

2.
$64a^3 - 125b^3$
$(\ -\ )(\ +\ +\ )$ ← signs
$(4a-5b)(\ \ +\ \ +\ \ )$ ← what is cubed to equal $64a^3$ or $125b^3$
$(4a-5b)(16a^2 + 20ab + 25b^2)$ ← square-product-square

3. $27x^{27} + 343y^{12} = (3x^9 + 7y^4)(9x^{18} - 21x^9 y4 + 49y^8)$
Note: The coefficient 27 is different from the exponent 27.

Practice problems:
1. $216x^3 - 125y^3$
2. $4a^3 - 32b^3$
3. $40x^{29} + 135x^2 y^3$

To **factor a polynomial**, follow these steps:

a. **Factor out any GCF** (greatest common factor)

b. For a binomial (2 terms), check to see if the problem is the **difference of perfect squares**. If both factors are perfect squares, then it factors this way:
$$a^2 - b^2 = (a-b)(a+b)$$

If the problem is not the difference of perfect squares, then check to see if the problem is either the sum or difference of perfect cubes.

$x^3 - 8y^3 = (x-2y)(x^2 + 2xy + 4y^2)$ ← difference

$64a^3 + 27b^3 = (4a+3b)(16a^3 - 12ab + 9b^2)$ ← sum

** The sum of perfect squares does NOT factor.

FOUNDATION LEV. MATH.

c. Trinomials could be perfect squares. Trinomials can be factored into 2 binomials (un-FOILing). Be sure the terms of the trinomial are in descending order. If last sign of the trinomial is a "+", then the signs in the parentheses will be the same as the sign in front of the second term of the trinomial. If the last sign of the trinomial is a "-", then there will be one "+" and one "-" in the two parentheses. The first term of the trinomial can be factored to equal the first terms of the two factors. The last term of the trinomial can be factored to equal the last terms of the two factors. Work backwards to determine the correct factors to multiply together to get the correct center term.

Examples:

1. $4x^2 - 25y^2$
2. $6b^2 - 2b - 8$
3. Find a factor of $6x^2 - 5x - 4$
   a. $(3x+2)$ b. $(3x-2)$ c. $(6x-1)$ d. $(2x+1)$

Answers:

1. No GCF; this is the difference of perfect squares.

$$4x^2 - 25y^2 = (2x - 5y)(2x + 5y)$$

1. GCF of 2; Try to factor into 2 binomials:

$$6b^2 - 2b - 8 = 2(3b^2 - b - 4)$$

Signs are one "+", one "−". $3b^2$ factors into $3b$ and b. Find factors of 4: 1 & 4; 2 & 2.

$$6b^2 - 2b - 8 = 2(3b^2 - b - 4) = 2(3b - 4)(b + 1)$$

3. If an answer choice is correct, find the other factor:

   a. $(3x+2)(2x-2) = 6x^2 - 2x - 4$
   b. $(3x-2)(2x+2) = 6x^2 + 2x - 4$
   c. $(6x-1)(x+4) = 6x^2 + 23x - 4$
   d. $(2x+1)(3x-4) = 6x^2 - 5x - 4$ ← correct factors

The binomial expansion theorem is another method used to find the coefficients of $(x+y)^3$. Although Pascal's Triangle is easy to use for small values of n, it can become cumbersome to use with larger values of n. See the following website for an explanation of the various mathematical symbols used below:
http://en.wikipedia.org/wiki/Math_symbols

Binomial Theorem:

For any positive value of n,
$$(x+y)^n = x^n + \frac{n!}{(n-1)!1!}x^{n-1}y + \frac{n!}{(n-2)!2!}x^{n-2}y^2 + \ldots + \frac{n!}{1!(n-1)!}x\,y^{n-1} + y^n$$

Example: $(x+y)^3 = (x+y)(x+y)(x+y)$ and if we multiply, we will find that we have $2^3 = 8$ terms (multiplication of n binomials yields 2^n terms):
$x^3 + yx^2 + yx^2 + yx^2 + yx + yx + yx + y^3 = x^3 + 3yx^2 + 3y^2x + y^3$.
The binomial theorem gives us how many terms there are of each type.

If we expand a binomial expression of increasing powers, we have a series of polynomials that have a pattern:
$(x+y)^0 = 1$
$(x+y)^1 = 1x + 1y$
$(x+y)^2 = 1x^2 + 2xy + 1y^2$
$(x+y)^3 = 1x^3 + 3x^2y + 3xy^2 + 1y^3$
$(x+y)^4 = 1x^4 + 4x^3y + 4xy^3 + 6x^2y^2 + 1y^4$
$(x+y)^5 = 1x^5 + 5x^4y + 5xy^4 + 10x^3y^2 + 10x^2y^3 + 1y^5$

Example:
1. Expand $(3x+y)^5$

$$(3x)^5 + \frac{5!}{4!1!}(3x)^4 y^1 + \frac{5!}{3!2!}(3x)^3 y^2 + \frac{5!}{2!3!}(3x)^2 y^3 + \frac{5!}{1!4!}(3x)^1 y^4 + y^5 =$$

$$243x^5 + 405x^4y + 270x^3y^2 + 90x^2y^3 + 15xy^4 + y^5$$

FOUNDATION LEV. MATH.

Any term of a binomial expansion can be written individually. For example, the seventh term of $(x+y)^n$, would be raised to the 6th power and since the sum of exponents on x and y must equal seven, then the x must be raised to the $n-6$ power.

The formula to find the rth term of a binomial expansion is:
$$\frac{n!}{[n-(r-1)]!(r-1)!} x^{n-(r-1)} y^{r-1}$$

where $r=$ the number of the desired term and $n=$ the power of the binomial

Example:

1. Find the third term of $(x+2y)^{11}$

$x^{n-(r-1)}$	y^{r-1}	Find x and y exponents.
$x^{11-(3-1)}$	y^{3-1}	
x^9	y^2	$y=2y$
$\frac{11!}{9!2!}(x^9)(2y)^2$		Substitute known values.
$220x^9y^2$		Solution.

TEACHER CERTIFICATION STUDY GUIDE

Polynomial Equations and Inequalities (SMR 1.2)

Skill c. **Analyze and solve polynomial equations with real coefficients using the Fundamental Theorem of Algebra**

The Fundamental Theorem of Algebra is about solving equations and says that "every polynomial equation over the field of complex numbers of degree higher than 1 has a complex solution." It follows from the theorem that is the degree of a polynomial is odd, then it must have at least one real root.

Polynomial equations are in the form

$$P(x) = a_n x^n + a_{n-1} x^{n-1} + a_{n-2} x^{n-2} + \ldots a_2 x^2 + a_1 x + a_0 = 0$$

Where n is the degree of the polynomial P and a_n is non-zero coefficient and x is the unknown.

The number "a" is a solution to P(x) = 0, for substituting "a" for "x" gives its identity: P(a) = 0.

Start with natural numbers (1,2,3,...), and the equation x + a = b. For example, x + 4 = 12 has a solution x = 12 - 4 = 8. In addition, x + 4 = 10 has a solution x = 10 - 4 = 6. Further, x + 10 = 4 has a solution x = 4 - 10 = **?**. What does 4-10 mean in the natural numbers? No number exists such that when added to 10 gives 4. This would mean that the set of natural numbers is not *algebraically closed*. However, negative numbers help take care of this problem:

Example:

$x + a = b$ where a and b are $\in$ (an element of a set) N: a, b $\in$ N, has the solution $x \in$ Z (Z is the set of integer numbers which include negative numbers).

Negative numbers bring us closer to a solution and true statement: Any equation $x + a = b$, where a, b $\in$ Z, has a solution, $x \in Z$, so that the equation has a solution even if the variables or their coefficients are negative.

FOUNDATION LEV. MATH.

Example:

Other equations over I: 4x - 8 = 0. x = 8/4 = 2. However, 4x + 32 = 0. x = -32/4 = -8, and 3x - 13 = 0. x = 13/3 = what?. Is there an integer that when multiplied by 3 yields 13? No, I is not algebraically closed either. Nevertheless, the introduction of rational numbers Q brings us closer to solving the problem:

Again, note the symbol $\in$ indicates "an element of", $\subset$ indicates "subset of."

An equation $ax + b = 0$, where $a, b \in Z$, has a solution $x \in Q$.

When the coefficients are rational, the equation still has a rational solution. However, Q is still not algebraically closed. For there are equations with rational coefficients (e.g., $x^2 = \sqrt{3}$) that have no rational solution. This brings us to the set R, real numbers. R is a big field but is still not algebraically closed: the equation $x^2 + 2 = 0$ with real coefficients has no real solution. So eventually, we arrive at C, the complex number field. Polynomial equations with real coefficients unsolvable among reals will have complex solutions and every polynomial equation with complex coefficients has at least one complex solution and therefore the field of complex numbers is algebraically closed.

Again, synthetic division can be used to find the value of a function at any value of x and can be useful in finding the zeros or roots of a polynomial. To do this, divide the value of x into the coefficients of the function (remember that coefficients of missing terms, like x^2 below, must be included). The remainder of the synthetic division is the value of the function. If $f(x) = x^3 - 6x + 4$, the possible zeros are ± 1, 2, 4 and to find the value of the function at x = 1, use synthetic division:

Note the 0 for the missing x^2 term.

```
2 | 1   0   -6    4
  |     2    4   -4
    ─────────────────
    1   2   -2    0  ←──── The value of the
                             function
```

Therefore, (2, 0) is a point of the graph and 2 is a zero or root as the value of the function has to be equal to zero for the value of x to be a root.

Divide $2x^3 - 6x - 104$ by 4. What is your conclusion?

$$\begin{array}{r|rrrr} 4 & 2 & 0 & -6 & -104 \\ & & 8 & 32 & 104 \\ \hline & 2 & 8 & 26 & 0 \end{array}$$ ← This is the remainder of the function.

Since the remainder is **0**, then **($x-4$)** is a factor and the 4 is a root or zero.

Once again, Descartes' Rule of Signs can help to determine how many positive real roots or how many negative real roots a function would have. Given any polynomial, be sure that the exponents on the terms are in descending order. Count the number of successive terms of the polynomial where there is a sign change. The number of positive roots will be equal to the number of sign changes or will be less than the number of sign changes by a multiple of 2. For example,

$$y = 2x^5 + 3x^4 - 6x^3 + 4x^2 + 8x - 9 \quad \text{has 3 sign changes.}$$
$$\rightarrow 1 \quad \rightarrow 2 \quad \rightarrow 3$$

That means that this equation will have either 3 positive roots or 1 positive root.

For the equation:

$$y = 4x^6 - 5x^5 + 6x^4 - 3x^3 + 2x^2 + 8x - 10 \quad \text{has 5 sign changes.}$$
$$\rightarrow 1 \quad \rightarrow 2 \quad \rightarrow 3 \quad \rightarrow 4 \quad \rightarrow 5$$

This equation will have either 5 positive roots (equal to the number of sign changes) or 3 positive roots (2 less) or only 1 positive root (4 less).

For the equation:

$$y = x^8 - 3x^5 - 6x^4 - 3x^3 + 2x^2 - 8x + 10 \quad \text{has 4 sign changes.}$$
$$\rightarrow 1 \quad \quad \rightarrow 2 \quad \rightarrow 3 \quad \rightarrow 4$$

This equation will have either 4 positive roots (equal to the number of sign changes) or 2 positive roots (2 less) or no positive roots (4 less).

The second part of Descartes' Rule of Signs also requires that terms be in descending order of exponents. Next look at the equation and change the signs of the terms that have an odd exponent. Then count the number of sign changes in successive terms of the new polynomial. The number of negative terms will be equal to the number of sign changes or will be less than the number of sign changes by a multiple of 2.

For example, given the equation:

$$y = 2x^5 + 3x^4 - 6x^3 + 4x^2 + 8x - 9$$

Change the signs of the terms with odd exponents.

$$y = {}^-2x^5 + 3x^4 + 6x^3 + 4x^2 - 8x - 9$$

Now count the number of sign changes in this equation.

$y = {}^-2x^5 + 3x^4 + 6x^3 + 4x^2 - 8x - 9$ has 2 sign
$\quad\quad\;\, \rightarrow 1 \quad\quad\quad\quad\quad \rightarrow 2 \quad\quad\quad\quad$ changes.

This tells you that there are 2 negative roots or 0 negative roots (2 less).

<u>Example</u>: Determine the number of positive or negative real roots for the equation:

$$y = x^3 + 9x^2 + 23x + 15$$

This equation is of degree 3, so it has, at most, 3 roots. Look at the equation. There are 0 sign changes. This means there are 0 positive roots. To check for negative roots, change the signs of the terms with odd exponents. The equation becomes:

$y = {}^-x^3 + 9x^2 - 23x + 15$ Now count sign changes.
$\quad\;\, \rightarrow 1 \;\rightarrow 2 \;\rightarrow 3 \quad$ There are 3 sign changes.

This means there are either 3 negative roots or only 1 negative root.

To find points on the graph of a polynomial, substitute desired values in place of x and solve for the corresponding y value of that point on the graph. A second way to do the same thing is to do a synthetic division, dividing by the x value of the desired point. The remainder at the end of the synthetic division is the y value of the point. Find a group of points to plot, graph and connect the points from left to right on the graph. The y intercept will always have a y value equal to the constant of the equation.

Given any polynomial, be sure that the exponents on the terms are in descending order. List out all of the factors of the first term's coefficient and of the constant in the last term. Make a list of fractions by putting each of the factors of the last term's coefficient over each of the factors of the first term. Reduce fractions when possible. Put a ± in front of each fraction. This list of fractions is a list of the only possible rational roots of a function. If the polynomial is of degree **n**, then at most n of these will actually be roots of the polynomial.

Example: List the possible rational roots for the function
$f(x) = x^2 - 5x + 4$.

$$\pm \frac{\text{factors of 4}}{\text{factors of 1}} = \pm 1, 2, 4 \leftarrow 6 \text{ possible rational roots}$$

Example: List the possible rational roots for the function
$f(x) = 6x^2 - 5x - 4$.

Make fractions of the following form to find POSSIBLE rational roots:

$$\text{rational roots} = \pm \frac{\text{factors of 4}}{\text{factors of 6}} = \pm \frac{1,2,4}{1,2,3,6} =$$

$$\pm \frac{1}{2}, \frac{1}{3}, \frac{1}{6}, \frac{2}{3}, \frac{4}{3}, 1, 2, 4 \text{ are the only 16 rational numbers that could be roots.}$$

Since this equation is of degree 2, there are, at most, 2 rational roots. (They happen to be 4/3 and ⁻1/2.)

Polynomial Equation word problems:

Word problems that have more than one unknown quantity can sometimes be written as a system of equations. This system can then be solved using **substitution**, the **addition-subtraction method**, or **determinants**.

Example: Farmer Greenjeans bought 4 cows and 6 sheep for $1700. Mr. Ziffel bought 3 cows and 12 sheep for $2400. If all the cows were the same price and all the sheep were another price, find the price charged for a cow or for a sheep.

Let x = price of a cow
Let y = price of a sheep

Then Farmer Greenjeans' equation would be: $4x + 6y = 1700$
Mr. Ziffel's equation would be: $3x + 12y = 2400$

To solve by **addition-subtraction**:

Multiply the first equation by $^-2$: $\quad ^-2(4x + 6y = 1700)$
Keep the other equation the same: $\quad (3x + 12y = 2400)$
By doing this, the equations can be added to each other to eliminate one variable and solve for the other variable.

$$^-8x - 12y = ^-3400$$
$$3x + 12y = 2400 \quad \text{Add these equations.}$$
$$^-5x = ^-1000$$

$x = 200 \leftarrow$ the price of a cow was $200.
Solving for y, $y = 150 \leftarrow$ the price of a sheep was $150.

To solve by **substitution**:

Solve one of the equations for a variable in terms of the other variable. The goal here, as in the previous method, is to get an equation that contains only one unknown variable so that we can solve for it. (Try to get an equation without fractions if possible.) Substitute this expression into the equation that you have not yet used. Solve the resulting equation for the value of the remaining variable.

$$4x + 6y = 1700$$
$$3x + 12y = 2400 \leftarrow \text{Solve this equation for } x$$

This gives us
$x = 800 - 4y$

Now substitute $800 - 4y$ in place of x in the OTHER equation.

$4x + 6y = 1700$ is now written as
4(800 - 4y) + 6y = 1700
3200 − 16y + 6y = 1700
3200 − 10y = 1700
-10y = -1500
$y = 150$, or $150 is the price of a sheep.

Substituting 150 back into an equation for y, find x.
$4x + 6(150) = 1700$
$4x + 900 = 1700$
$4x = 800$
$x = 200$, i.e. $200 is the price of a cow.

To solve by **determinants**:

Let x = price of a cow
Let y = price of a sheep

Then Farmer Greenjeans' equation would be: $4x + 6y = 1700$
Mr. Ziffel's equation would be: $3x + 12y + 2400$

The solution for x or y is expressed as a ratio of two determinants. As shown below, the bottom determinant contains the x and y coefficients. The top determinant is almost the same as this bottom determinant. The only difference is that when you are solving for x, the x coefficients are replaced with the constants on the right hand side of the equations. Likewise, when you are solving for y, the y coefficients are replaced with the constants on the right hand side of the equations.

Using the fact that the value of a 2 by 2 determinant, $\begin{vmatrix} a & b \\ c & d \end{vmatrix}$, is found by $ad - bc$, we can write the solutions of x and y as:

$$x = \frac{\begin{vmatrix} 1700 & 6 \\ 2400 & 12 \end{vmatrix}}{\begin{vmatrix} 4 & 6 \\ 3 & 12 \end{vmatrix}} = \frac{1700(12) - 6(2400)}{4(12) - 6(3)} = \frac{20400 - 14400}{48 - 18} = \frac{6000}{30} = 200$$

$$x = \frac{\begin{vmatrix} 4 & 1700 \\ 3 & 2400 \end{vmatrix}}{\begin{vmatrix} 4 & 6 \\ 3 & 12 \end{vmatrix}} = \frac{2400(4) - 3(1700)}{4(12) - 6(3)} = \frac{9600 - 5100}{48 - 18} = \frac{4500}{30} = 150$$

Word problems with 3 unknowns can also be written as a system of equations. This system can then be solved using **substitution**, the **addition-subtraction method**, or **determinants**.

Example: Mrs. Allison bought 1 pound of potato chips, a 2-pound beef roast, and 3 pounds of apples for a total of $ 8.19. Mr. Bromberg bought a 3-pound beef roast and 2 pounds of apples for $ 9.05. Kathleen Kaufman bought 2 pounds of potato chips, a 3-pound beef roast, and 5 pounds of apples for $ 13.25. Find the per pound price of each item.

Let x = price of a pound of potato chips
Let y = price of a pound of roast beef
Let z = price of a pound of apples

Mrs. Allison's equation would be: $1x + 2y + 3z = 8.19$
Mr. Bromberg's equation would be: $3y + 2z = 9.05$
K. Kaufman's equation would be: $2x + 3y + 5z = 13.25$

To solve by **substitution**:

Take the first equation and solve it for x. (This was chosen because x is the easiest variable to get alone in this set of equations.) This equation would become:

$$x = 8.19 - 2y - 3z$$

Substitute this expression into the other equations in place of the variable x:

$$3y + 2z = 9.05 \leftarrow \text{equation 2}$$
$$2(8.19 - 2y - 3z) + 3y + 5z = 13.25 \leftarrow \text{equation 3}$$

Simplify the equation by combining like terms:

$$3y + 2z = 9.05 \leftarrow \text{equation 2}$$
$$^-1y - 1z = {}^-3.13 \leftarrow \text{equation 3}$$

Solve equation 3 for either y or z:
$$y = 3.13 - z$$

Substitute this into equation 2 for y:
$$3(3.13 - z) + 2z = 9.05 \leftarrow \text{equation 2}$$
$$^-1y - 1z = {}^-3.13 \leftarrow \text{equation 3}$$

Combine like terms in equation 2:

$$9.39 - 3z + 2z = 9.05$$
$$z = .34 \text{ (per pound price of apples)}$$

Substitute .34 for z in equation 3 to solve for y:
$$y = 3.13 - z$$
$$= 3.13 - .34$$
$$y = 2.79 \text{ (per pound price of roast beef)}$$

Substituting .34 for z and 2.79 for y in one of the original equations, solve for x:

$$1x + 2y + 3z = 8.19$$
$$1x + 2(2.79) + 3(.34) = 8.19$$
$$x + 5.58 + 1.02 = 8.19$$
$$x + 6.60 = 8.19$$
$$x = 1.59 \text{ (per pound of potato chips)}$$

To solve by **addition-subtraction**:

Choose a variable to eliminate. Since the second equation is already missing an x, let's eliminate x from equations 1 and 3.

1) $1x + 2y + 3x = 8.19$ ← Multiply by $^-2$ below.
2) $3y + 2z = 9.05$
3) $2x + 3y + 5z = 13.25$

$^-2(1x + 2y + 3z = 8.19)$ = $^-2x - 4y - 6z = {}^-16.38$
Keep equation 3 the same: $2x + 3y + 5z = 13.25$

By doing this, the equations $^-y - z = {}^-3.13$ ← equation 4
can be added to each other to
eliminate one variable.

The equations left to solve are equations 2 and 4:
   $^-y - z = {}^-3.13$ ← equation 4
   $3y + 2z = 9.05$ ← equation 2

Multiply equation 4 by 3: $3(^-y - z = {}^-3.13)$
Keep equation 2 the same: $3y + 2z = 9.05$

$^-3y - 3z = {}^-9.39$
$\underline{3y + 2z = 9.05}$ Add these equations.
     $^-1z = {}^-.34$
        $z = .34$ ← the per pound price of apples
solving for y, $y = 2.79$ ← the per pound roast beef price
solving for x, $x = 1.59$ ← the per pound potato chips price

To solve by **determinants**:

Let x = price of a pound of potato chips
Let y = price of a pound of roast beef
Let z = price of a pound of apples

1) $1x + 2y + 3z = 8.19$
2) $3y + 2z = 9.05$
3) $2x + 3y + 5z = 13.25$

FOUNDATION LEV. MATH.

TEACHER CERTIFICATION STUDY GUIDE

The solution for x, y or z is expressed as a ratio of two 3 by 3 determinants. As shown below, the bottom determinant contains the x, y and z coefficients. The top determinant is almost the same as this bottom determinant. The only difference is that when you are solving for x, the x coefficients are replaced with the constants on the right hand side of the equations. Likewise, when you are solving for y or z, the y or z coefficients are replaced with the constants on the right hand side of the equations.

The value of a 3 by 3 determinant,

$$\begin{vmatrix} a & b & c \\ d & e & f \\ g & h & i \end{vmatrix}$$

is found by the following steps:

Copy the first two columns to the right of the determinant:

$$\begin{vmatrix} a & b & c \\ d & e & f \\ g & h & i \end{vmatrix} \begin{matrix} a & b \\ d & e \\ g & h \end{matrix}$$

Multiply the diagonals from top left to bottom right, and add the terms together.

$$\begin{vmatrix} a^* & b^\circ & c^\bullet \\ d & e^* & f^\circ \\ g & h & i^* \end{vmatrix} \begin{matrix} a & b \\ d^\bullet & e \\ g^\circ & h^\bullet \end{matrix} = a^*e^*i^* + b^\circ f^\circ g^\circ + c^\bullet d^\bullet h^\bullet$$

Then multiply the diagonals from bottom left to top right, and add the terms together.

$$\begin{vmatrix} a & b & c^* \\ d & e^* & f^\circ \\ g^* & h^\circ & i^\bullet \end{vmatrix} \begin{matrix} a^\circ & b^\bullet \\ d^\bullet & e \\ g & h \end{matrix} = g^*e^*c^* + h^\circ f^\circ a^\circ + i^\bullet d^\bullet b^\bullet$$

FOUNDATION LEV. MATH.

Subtract the first diagonal total from the second diagonal total:

$$(a*e*i* + b°f°g° + c^\bullet a^\bullet h^\bullet) - (g*e*c* + h°f°a° + i^\bullet a^\bullet b^\bullet)$$

This gives the value of the determinant. To find the value of a variable, divide the value of the top determinant by the value of the bottom determinant.

1) $1x + 2y + 3z = 8.19$
2) $3y + 2z = 9.05$
3) $2x + 3y + 5z = 13.25$

Solve: $x = \dfrac{\begin{vmatrix} 8.19 & 2 & 3 \\ 9.05 & 3 & 2 \\ 13.25 & 3 & 5 \end{vmatrix}}{\begin{vmatrix} 1 & 2 & 3 \\ 0 & 3 & 2 \\ 2 & 3 & 5 \end{vmatrix}}$

Multiply the diagonals from top left to bottom right, and add the terms together.

$\begin{vmatrix} 8.19^* & 2° & 3^\bullet \\ 9.05 & 3^* & 2° \\ 13.25 & 3 & 5^* \end{vmatrix} \begin{matrix} 8.19 & 2 \\ 9.05^\bullet & 3 \\ 13.25° & 3^\bullet \end{matrix}$

$= (8.19^*)(3^*)(5^*) + (2°)(2°)(13.25°) + (3^\bullet)(9.05^\bullet)(3^\bullet)$

Then multiply the diagonals from bottom left to top right, and add the terms together.

$\begin{vmatrix} 8.19 & 2 & 3^* \\ 9.05 & 3^* & 2° \\ 13.25^* & 3° & 5^\bullet \end{vmatrix} \begin{matrix} 8.19° & 2^\bullet \\ 9.05^\bullet & 3 \\ 13.25 & 3 \end{matrix}$

$= (13.25^*)(3^*)(3^*) + (3°)(2°)(8.19°) + (5^\bullet)(9.05^\bullet)(2^\bullet)$

Subtract the first diagonal total from the second diagonal total:

$$(8.19^*)(3^*)(5^*) + (2°)(2°)(13.25°) + (3^\bullet)(9.05^\bullet)(3^\bullet)$$
$$- \underline{(13.25^*)(3^*)(3^*) + (3°)(2°)(8.19°) + (5^\bullet)(9.05^\bullet)(2^\bullet)}$$
$$^-1.59$$

Use the same multiplying and subtraction procedure for the bottom determinant to get $^-1$ as an answer. Now divide:

$$x = \frac{^-1.59}{^-1} = \$1.59/\text{lb of potato chips}$$

$$y = \frac{\begin{vmatrix} 1 & 8.19 & 3 \\ 0 & 9.05 & 2 \\ 2 & 13.25 & 5 \end{vmatrix}}{\begin{vmatrix} 1 & 2 & 3 \\ 0 & 3 & 2 \\ 2 & 3 & 5 \end{vmatrix}} = \frac{-2.79}{-1} = \$2.79/\text{lb of roast beef}$$

NOTE: The bottom determinant always has the same value for each variable.

$$z = \frac{\begin{vmatrix} 1 & 2 & 8.19 \\ 0 & 3 & 9.05 \\ 2 & 3 & 13.25 \end{vmatrix}}{\begin{vmatrix} 1 & 2 & 3 \\ 0 & 3 & 2 \\ 2 & 3 & 5 \end{vmatrix}} = \frac{^-.34}{-1} = \$.34/\text{lb of apples}$$

Example: The Simpsons went out for dinner. All 4 of them ordered the Aardvark steak dinner. Bert paid for the 4 meals and included a tip of $12 for a total of $84.60. How much was an Aardvark steak dinner?

Let $x =$ the price of one Aardvark dinner
So $4x =$ the price of 4 Aardavark dinners
$4x = 84.60 - 12$
$4x = 72.60$
$x = \dfrac{72.60}{4} = \$18.15$ The price of one Aardvark dinner.

Some word problems can be solved using a system of equations (see previous section SMR 1.2 skill "a" on linear programming for more examples) or inequalities. Watch for words like greater than, less than, at least, or no more than which indicate the need for inequalities.

Example: John has 9 coins, which are either dimes or nickels that are worth $.65. Determine how many of each coin he has.

Let $d =$ number of dimes.
Let $n =$ number of nickels.
The number of coins total 9.
The value of the coins equals 65.

Then: $n + d = 9$
$5n + 10d = 65$

Multiplying the first equation by $^-5$, it becomes:
$^-5n - 5d = {}^-45$
$\underline{5n + 10d = 65}$
$5d = 20$

$d = 4$
n = 9-d=5

Therefore, there are 4 dimes and 5 nickels.

Functions (SMR 1.3)

Skill a. Analyze and prove general properties of functions (i.e., domain and range, one-to-one, onto inverses, composition, and differences between relations and functions)

Functions and their properties:

If two things vary directly, as one gets larger, the other also gets larger. If one gets smaller, then the other gets smaller too. If x and y vary directly, there should be a constant, c, such that $y = cx$. Something can also vary directly with the square of something else, $y = cx^2$.

-If two things vary inversely, as one gets larger, the other one gets smaller instead. If x and y vary inversely, there should be a constant, c, such that $xy = c$ or $y = c/x$. Something can also vary inversely with the square of something else, $y = c/x^2$.

Example: If $30 were paid for 5 hours work, how much would be paid for 19 hours work?

This is direct variation and $30 = 5c, so the constant is 6 ($6/hour). So $y = 6(19)$ or y = $114.

This could also be done as a proportion:

$$\frac{\$30}{5} = \frac{y}{19}$$

$$5y = 570$$
$$y = 114$$

A **relation** is any set of ordered pairs.

The **domain** of a relation is the set made of all the first coordinates of the ordered pairs.

The **range** of a relation is the set made of all the second coordinates of the ordered pairs.

A **function** is a relation in which different ordered pairs have different first coordinates. (No x values are repeated).

On a graph, use the **vertical line test** to look for a function. If any vertical line intersects the graph of a relation in more than one point, then the relation is not a function.

A **mapping** is a diagram with arrows drawn from each element of the domain to the corresponding elements of the range. If 2 arrows are drawn from the same element of the domain, then it is not a function.

Example: Determine the domain and range of this mapping.

domain: {4, –5}

range: {6, 8, 11}

There are two methods of finding the values of a function. To find the value of a function when $x = 3$, first substitute 3 in place of every variable x. Then simplify the expression following the order of operations.

Example: For the function $f(x) = x^3 - 6x + 4$ find f(3)

Substitute 3 for x.
$f(3) = 3^3 - 6(3) + 4 = 27 - 18 + 4 = 13$.
So (3, 13) is a point on the graph of f(x).

Determine the domain and range
of this mapping.

ANSWERS

domain: {4, -5 }

range: {6, 8, 11}

FOUNDATION LEV. MATH.

Practice problems:

1. Determine which of these are functions:
   a. $\{(1,^-4),(27,1)(94,5)(2,^-4)\}$
   b. $f(x) = 2x - 3$
   c. $A = \{(x,y) \mid xy = 24\}$
   d. $y = 3$
   e. $x = {}^-9$
   f. $\{(3,2),(7,7),(0,5),(2,^-4),(8,^-6),(1,0),(5,9),(6,^-4)\}$

2. Determine the domain and range of this graph.

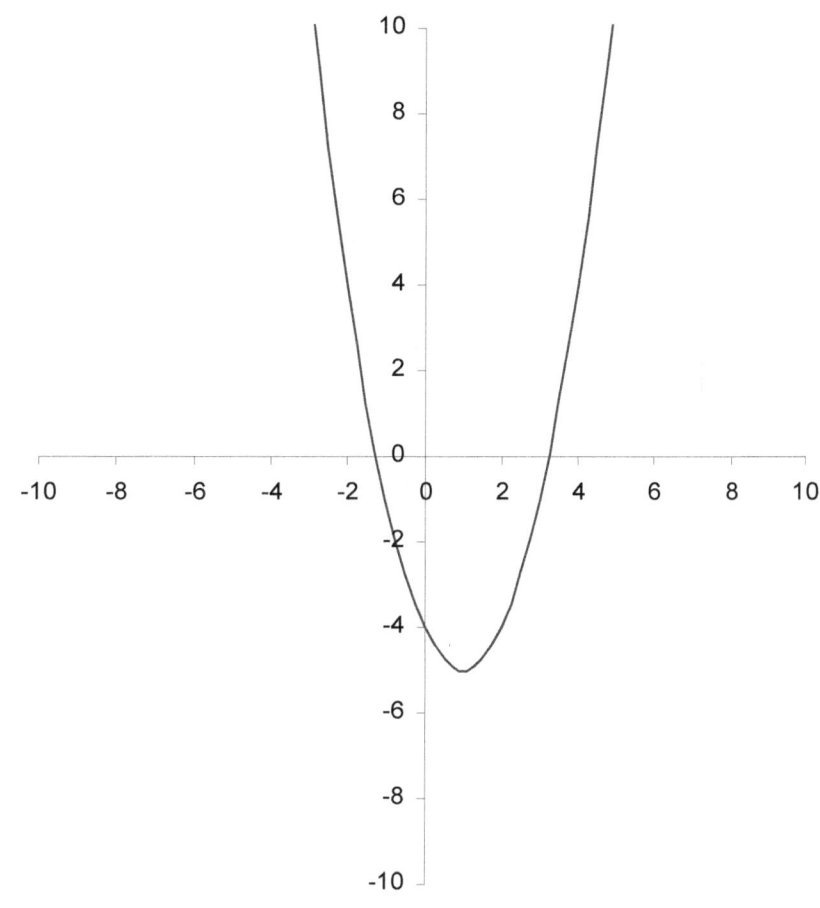

Practice problems:

1. If $A = \{(x,y) \mid y = x^2 - 6\}$, find the domain and range.

2. Give the domain and range of set B if:

   $B = \{(1, {}^-2),(4, {}^-2),(7, {}^-2),(6, {}^-2)\}$

3. Determine the domain of this function:

   $f(x) = \dfrac{5x + 7}{x^2 - 4}$

4. Determine the domain and range of these graphs.

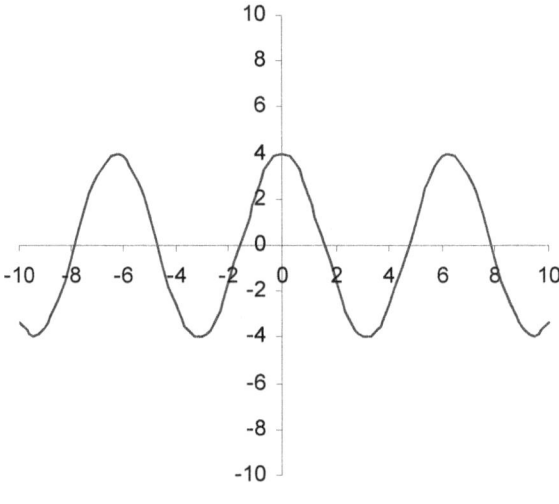

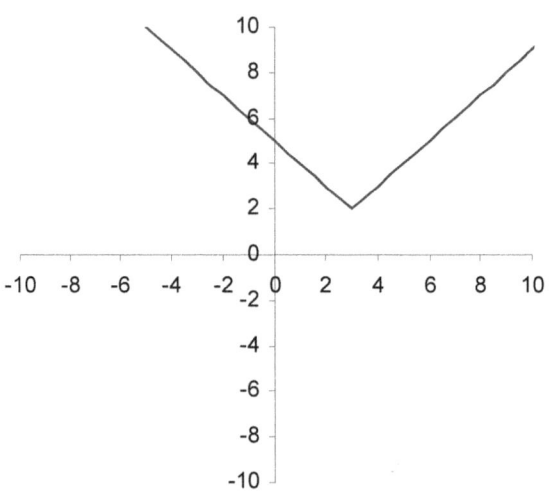

5. If $E = \{(x,y) \mid y = 5\}$, find the domain and range.

6. Determine the ordered pairs in the relation shown in this mapping.

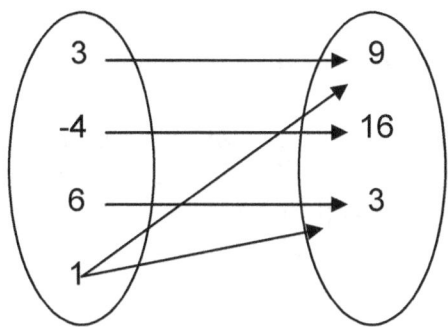

Functions (SMR 1.3)

Skill b. Analyze properties of polynomial, rational, radical, and absolute value functions in a variety of ways (e.g., graphing, solving problems)

The Degree of a Polynomial:

The degree of an equation that has not more than one variable in each term is the exponent of the highest power to which that variable is raised in the equation.

Examples:

The equation $4x - 10 = 0$ is a FIRST-DEGREE equation, since x is raised only to the first power.

A SECOND-DEGREE equation is $5x^2 - 4x - 6 = 0$ since the term with the highest exponent is $5X^2$.

The equation, $2x^3 - 5x^2 + x = 0$ is a THIRD DEGREE equation since the highest exponent is in the term $2x^3$.

The equation $5x - 6y = 25$ is of the FIRST DEGREE as the two variables, x and y are both raised to the first power.

If a term has more than one variable, as in $2xy = 6$, it is necessary to add the exponents of the variables within the term to get the degree of the equation. Since $1 + 1 = 2$, the equation $2xy = 6$ is of the SECOND DEGREE.

A **first-degree equation** in the form $ax + by = c$ is the graph of a line.

To graph this equation, find either one point and the slope of the line or find two points. To find a point and slope, solve the equation for y. This gets the equation in **slope intercept form**, $y = mx + b$.

The point $(0,b)$ is the y-intercept and m is the line's slope. To find any 2 points, substitute any 2 numbers for x and solve for y. To find the intercepts, substitute 0 for x and then 0 for y.

Remember: lines with a positive slope will go up to the right. Negative slope lines go up to the left.

FOUNDATION LEV. MATH.

If the equation solves to **x = any number**, then the graph is a **vertical line** and has a slope is undefined.

If the equation solves to **y = any number**, then the graph is a **horizontal line** and it's slope is zero.

To find the y intercept, substitute 0 for x and solve for y. This is the y intercept. The y intercept is also the value of b in $y = mx + b$.

To find the x intercept, substitute 0 for y and solve for x. This is the x intercept.

1. Find the slope and intercepts of $3x + 2y = 14$.

$$3x + 2y = 14$$
$$2y = {}^-3x + 14$$
$$y = {}^-2/3\ x + 7$$

The slope of the line is $^-2/3$, the value of m.
The y intercept of the line is 7.

The intercepts can also be found by substituting 0 in place of the other variable in the equation.

To find the y intercept:	To find the x intercept:
let $x = 0$; $3(0) + 2y = 14$	let $y = 0$; $3x + 2(0) = 14$
$0 + 2y = 14$	$3x + 0 = 14$
$2y = 14$	$3x = 14$
$y = 7$	$x = 14/3$
(0,7) is the y intercept.	(14/3, 0) is the x intercept.

Practice problems:

Find the slope and the y-intercepts (if they exist) for these equations:

1. $5x + 7y = {}^-70$
2. $x - 2y = 14$
3. $5x + 3y = 3(5 + y)$
4. $2x + 5y = 15$

Linear Inequalities

When graphing a linear inequality, the line will be dotted if the inequality sign is $<$ or $>$. If the inequality signs are either $\geq$ or $\leq$, the line on the graph will be a solid line. Shade above the line when the inequality sign is $\geq$ or $>$. Shade below the line when the inequality sign is $<$ or $\leq$. Inequalities of the form $x >, x \leq, x <,$ or $x \geq$ number, draw a vertical line (solid or dotted). Shade to the right for $>$ or $\geq$. Shade to the left for $<$ or $\leq$. Remember: **Dividing or multiplying by a negative number will reverse the direction of the inequality sign.**

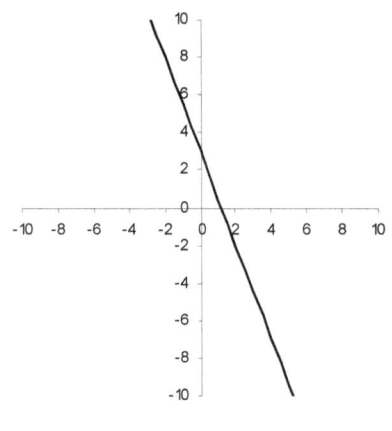
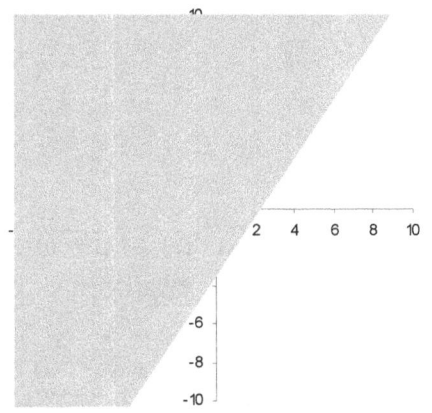

$5x + 2y = 6$

$y = {}^-5/2\, x + 3$

$3x - 2y \geq 6$

$y \leq 3/2\, x - 3$

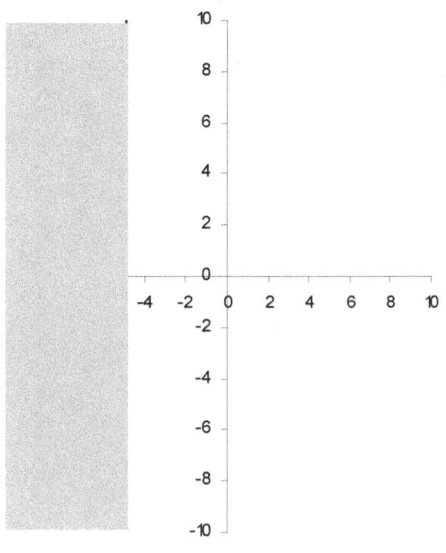

$3x + 12 < -3$

$x < {}^-5$

There are 2 easy ways to find the values of a function. First to find the value of a function when $x = 3$, substitute 3 in place of every letter x. Then simplify the expression following the order of operations. For example, if $f(x) = x^3 - 6x + 4$, then to find f(3), substitute 3 for x. The equation becomes $f(3) = 3^3 - 6(3) + 4 = 27 - 18 + 4 = 13$. So (3, 13) is a point of the graph or f(3) = 13.

A second way to find the value of a function is to use synthetic division as shown above in 0002 Polynomial Equations and Inequalities (SMR 1.2):.
To find the value of a function when $x = 3$, divide 3 into the coefficients of the function. (Remember that coefficients of missing terms, like x^2, must be included). The remainder is the value of the function.
If $f(x) = x^3 - 6x + 4$, then to find f(3) using synthetic division:

Note the 0 for the missing x^2 term.

```
  |1   0  ⁻6   4
 3|    3   9   9
   1   3   3  13  ← this is the value of the function.
```

Therefore, (3, 13) is a point of the graph.

Example: Find values of the function at integer values from $x = -3$ to $x = 3$ if $f(x) = x^3 - 6x + 4$.

If $x = {}^-3$:

$$f({}^-3) = ({}^-3)^3 - 6({}^-3) + 4$$
$$= ({}^-27) - 6({}^-3) + 4$$
$$= {}^-27 + 18 + 4 = {}^-5$$

synthetic division:

$$\begin{array}{r|rrrr} {}^-3 & 1 & 0 & {}^-6 & 4 \\ & & {}^-3 & 9 & {}^-9 \\ \hline & 1 & {}^-3 & 3 & {}^-5 \end{array}$$ ← this is the value of the function if $x = {}^-3$.
Therefore, $({}^-3, {}^-5)$ is a point of the graph.

If $x = {}^-2$:

$$f({}^-2) = ({}^-2)^3 - 6({}^-2) + 4$$
$$= ({}^-8) - 6({}^-2) + 4$$
$$= {}^-8 + 12 + 4 = 8$$ ← this is the value of the function if $x = {}^-2$.
Therefore, $({}^-2, 8)$ is a point of the graph.

If $x = {}^-1$:

$$f({}^-1) = ({}^-1)^3 - 6({}^-1) + 4$$
$$= ({}^-1) - 6({}^-2) + 4$$
$$= {}^-1 + 6 + 4 = 9$$

synthetic division:

$$\begin{array}{r|rrrr} {}^-1 & 1 & 0 & {}^-6 & 4 \\ & & {}^-1 & 1 & 5 \\ \hline & 1 & {}^-1 & {}^-5 & 9 \end{array}$$ ← this is the value if the function if $x = {}^-1$.
Therefore, $({}^-1, 9)$ is a point of the graph.

FOUNDATION LEV. MATH.

If $x = 0$:

$$f(0) = (0)^3 - 6(0) + 4$$
$$= 0 - 6(0) + 4$$
$$= 0 - 0 + 4 = 4 \leftarrow \text{this is the value of the function if } x = 0.$$
Therefore, $(0, 4)$ is a point of the graph.

If $x = 1$:

$$f(1) = (1)^3 - 6(1) + 4$$
$$= (1) - 6(1) + 4$$
$$= 1 - 6 + 4 = {}^-1$$

synthetic division:

$$\begin{array}{r|rrrr} & 1 & 0 & {}^-6 & 4 \\ 1 & & 1 & 1 & {}^-5 \\ \hline & 1 & 1 & {}^-5 & {}^-1 \end{array}$$

$1 \quad 1 \quad {}^-5 \quad {}^-1 \leftarrow$ this is the value of the function of $x = 1$.
Therefore, $(1, {}^-1)$ is a point of the graph.

If $x = 2$:

$$f(2) = (2)^3 - 6(2) + 4$$
$$= 8 - 6(2) + 4$$
$$= 8 - 12 + 4 = 0$$

synthetic division:

$$\begin{array}{r|rrrr} & 1 & 0 & {}^-6 & 4 \\ 2 & & 2 & 4 & {}^-4 \\ \hline & 1 & 2 & {}^-2 & 0 \end{array}$$

$1 \quad 2 \quad {}^-2 \quad 0 \leftarrow$ this is the value of the function if $x = 2$.
Therefore, $(2, 0)$ is a point of the graph.

If $x = 3$:

$$f(3) = (3)^3 - 6(3) + 4$$
$$= 27 - 6(3) + 4$$
$$= 27 - 18 + 4 = 13$$

synthetic division:

$$3 \begin{array}{|rrrr} 1 & 0 & -6 & 4 \\ & 3 & 9 & 9 \\ \hline 1 & 3 & 3 & 13 \end{array}$$ ← this is the value of the function if $x = 3$.

Therefore, $(3, 13)$ is a point of the graph.

The following points are points on the graph:

X	Y
-3	-5
-2	8
-1	9
0	4
1	-1
2	0
3	13

Note the change in sign of the y value between $x = -3$ and $x = -2$. This indicates there is a zero between $x = -3$ and $x = -2$. Since there is another change in sign of the y value between $x = 0$ and $x = -1$, there is a second root there. When $x = 2$, $y = 0$ so $x = 2$ is an exact root of this polynomial.

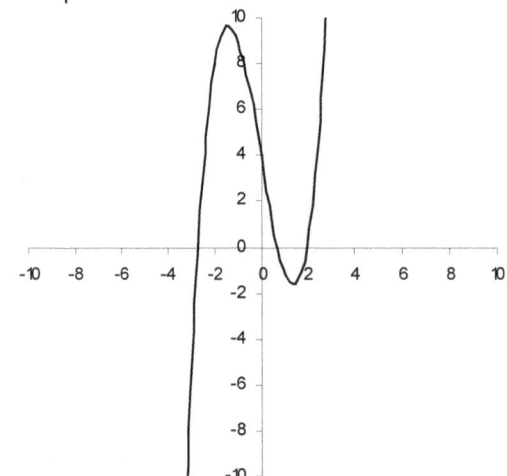

Example: Find values of the function at $x = -5, 2,$ and 17 if $f(x) = 2x^5 - 4x^3 + 3x^2 - 9x + 10$.

If $x = -5$:

$$\begin{aligned} f(-5) &= 2(-5)^5 - 4(-5)^3 + 3(-5)^2 - 9(-5) + 10 \\ &= 2(-3125) - 4(-125) + 3(25) - 9(-5) + 10 \\ &= -6250 + 500 + 75 + 45 + 10 = -5620 \end{aligned}$$

synthetic division:

$$\begin{array}{r|rrrrrr} -5 & 2 & 0 & ^-4 & 3 & ^-9 & 10 \\ & & ^-10 & 50 & ^-230 & 1135 & ^-5630 \\ \hline & 2 & ^-10 & 46 & ^-227 & ^-1126 & ^-5620 \end{array}$$

← this is the value of the function if $x = {}^-5$.

Therefore, $({}^-5, {}^-5620)$ is a point of the graph.

If $x = 2$:

$$f(2) = 2(2)^5 - 4(2)^3 + 3(2)^2 - 9(2) + 10$$
$$= 2(32) - 4(8) + 3(4) - 9(2) + 10$$
$$= 64 - 32 + 12 - 18 + 10 = 36$$

synthetic division:

$$\begin{array}{r|rrrrrr} 2 & 2 & 0 & ^-4 & 3 & ^-9 & 10 \\ & & 4 & 8 & 8 & 22 & 26 \\ \hline & 2 & 4 & 4 & 11 & 13 & 36 \end{array}$$

← this is the value of the function if $x = 2$.

Therefore, $(2, 36)$ is a point of the graph.

If $x = 17$:

$$f(17) = 2(17)^5 - 4(17)^3 + 3(17)^2 - 9(17) + 10$$
$$= 2(1419857) - 4(4913) + 3(289) - 9(17) + 10$$
$$= 2839714 - 19652 + 867 - 153 + 10 = 2820786$$

synthetic division:

$$\begin{array}{r|rrrrrr} 17 & 2 & 0 & ^-4 & 3 & ^-9 & 10 \\ & & 34 & 578 & 9758 & 165937 & 2820776 \\ \hline & 2 & 34 & 574 & 9761 & 165928 & 2820786 \end{array}$$

← this is the value of the function if $x = 17$.

Therefore, $(17, 2820786)$ is a point of the graph.

The Greatest Integer Function or **Step Function** has the equation: $f(x) = j[rx - h] + k$ or $y = j[rx - h] + k$. (h,k) is the location of the left endpoint of one step. j is the vertical jump from step to step. r is the reciprocal of the length of each step. If (x,y) is a point of the function, then when x is an integer, its y value is the same integer. If (x,y) is a point of the function, then when x is not an integer, its y value is the first integer less than x. Points on $y = [x]$ would include:

$(3,3), (^-2, ^-2), (0,0), (1.5,1), (2.83,2), (^-3.2, ^-4), (^-.4, ^-1)$.

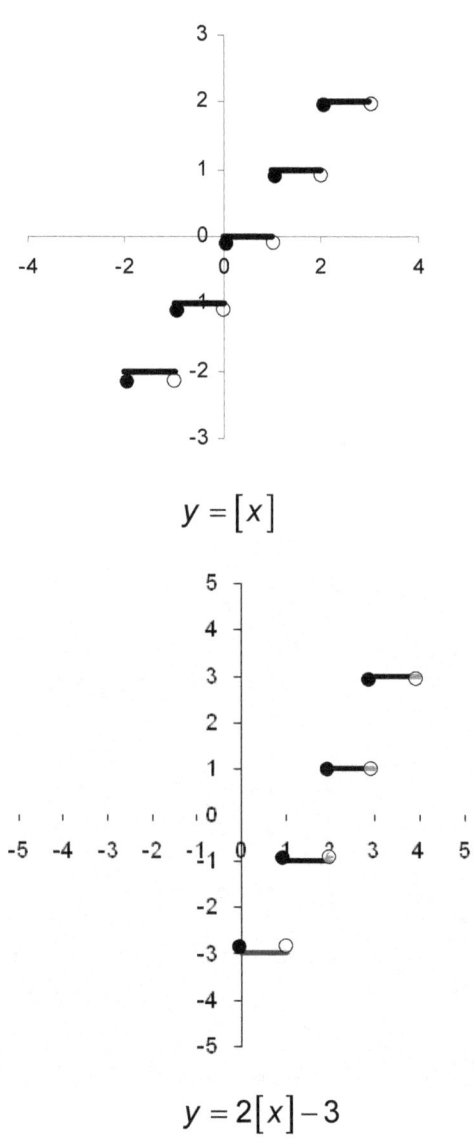

$y = [x]$

$y = 2[x] - 3$

Rational functions and expressions: a rational expression can be written as the ration of 2 polynomial expressions and a rational function is simply a function that gets its value from the rational expression. Examples of rational functions (and their associated expressions) are:

$$r(x) = \frac{x^2 + 2x + 4}{x - 3} \text{ and } r(x) = \frac{x}{x - 3},$$

which is clearly the ratio of 2 polynomials. The following is a rational expression:

$$\frac{1}{x + \frac{2}{x}}$$

(it is not in standard form but can be converted to standard form by multplying by $\frac{x}{x}) = \frac{x}{2x + 1}$

Polynomial expressions can be evaluated using addition, subtraction and multiplication but rational expressions may require division for evaluation. Rational expressions work just like fractions and can be changed into other equivalent fractions by either reducing them or by changing them to have a common denominator. When dividing any number of terms by a single term, divide or reduce their coefficients. Then subtract the exponent of a variable on the bottom from the exponent of the same variable from the numerator.

To reduce a rational expression with more than one term in the denominator, the expression must be factored first. Factors that are the same will cancel and each becomes a 1. Factors that have exactly the opposite signs of each other, such as $(a - b)$ and $(b - a)$, will cancel and one factor becomes a 1 and the other becomes a $^-1$.

To make a fraction have a common denominator, factor the fraction. Determine what factors are missing from that particular denominator, and multiply both the numerator and the denominator by those missing fractions. This gives a new fraction, which now has the common denominator.

Examples:
Simplify these fractions:

1. $\dfrac{24x^3y^6z^3}{8x^2y^2z} = 3xy^4z^2$

2. $\dfrac{3x^2 - 14xy - 5y^2}{x^2 - 25y^2} = \dfrac{(3x+y)(x-5y)}{(x+5y)(x-5y)} = \dfrac{3x+y}{x+5y}$

3. Re-write this fraction with a denominator of $(x+3)(x-5)(x+4)$.

$$\dfrac{x+2}{x^2+7x+12} = \dfrac{x+2}{(x+3)(x+4)} = \dfrac{(x+2)(x-5)}{(x+3)(x+4)(x-5)}$$

In order **to add or subtract** rational expressions, they must have a common denominator. If they don't have a common denominator, then factor the denominators to determine what factors are missing from each denominator to make the LCD. Multiply both numerator and denominator by the missing factor(s). Once the fractions have a common denominator, add or subtract their numerators, but keep the common denominator the same. Factor the numerator if possible and reduce if there are any factors that can be cancelled.

In order **to multiply** rational expressions, they do not have to have a common denominator. If you factor each numerator and denominator, you can cancel out any factor that occurs in both the numerator and denominator. Then multiply the remaining factors of the numerator together. Last, multiply the remaining factors of the denominator together.

In order **to divide** rational expressions, the problem must be re-written as the first fraction multiplied times the inverse of the second fraction. Once the problem has been written as a multiplication, factor each numerator and denominator. Cancel out any factor that occurs in both the numerator and denominator. Then multiply the remaining factors of the numerator together. Last, multiply the remaining factors of the denominator together.

Example:

1. $\dfrac{5}{x^2-9} - \dfrac{2}{x^2+4x+3} = \dfrac{5}{(x-3)(x+3)} - \dfrac{2}{(x+3)(x+1)} =$

$\dfrac{5(x+1)}{(x+1)(x-3)(x+3)} - \dfrac{2(x-3)}{(x+3)(x+1)(x-3)} = \dfrac{3x+11}{(x-3)(x+3)(x+1)}$

2. $\dfrac{x^2-2x-24}{x^2+6x+8} \times \dfrac{x^2+3x+2}{x^2-13x+42} = \dfrac{(x-6)(x+4)}{(x+4)(x+2)} \times \dfrac{(x+2)(x+1)}{(x-7)(x-6)} = \dfrac{x+1}{x-7}$

To solve an **equation with rational expressions**, find the least common denominator of all the fractions. Multiply each term by the LCD of all fractions. This will cancel out all of the denominators and give an equivalent algebraic equation that can be solved. Solve the resulting equation. Once you have found the answer(s), substitute them back into the original equation to check them. Sometimes there are solutions that do not check in the original equation. These are extraneous solutions, which are not correct and must be eliminated. If a problem has more than one potential solution, each solution must be checked separately.

> **NOTE: What this really means is that you can simply substitute the answers from any multiple choice question back into the question to determine which answer choice is correct.**

Example:

1. $\dfrac{72}{x+3} = \dfrac{32}{x+3} + 5$ LCD $= x+3$, so multiply by this.

$(x+3) \times \dfrac{72}{x+3} = (x+3) \times \dfrac{32}{x+3} + 5(x+3)$

$72 = 32 + 5(x+3) \rightarrow 72 = 32 + 5x + 15$

$72 = 47 + 5x \quad \rightarrow 25 = 5x$

$5 = x$ (This checks too).

FOUNDATION LEV. MATH.

2. $\dfrac{12}{2x^2-4x} + \dfrac{13}{5} = \dfrac{9}{x-2}$ Factor $2x^2-4x = 2x(x-2)$.

LCD $= 5 \times 2x(x-2)$ or $10x(x-2)$

$10x(x-2) \times \dfrac{12}{2x(x-2)} + 10x(x-2) \times \dfrac{13}{5} = \dfrac{9}{x-2} \times 10x(x-2)$

$60 + 2x(x-2)(13) = 90x$

$26x^2 - 142x + 60 = 0$

$2(13x^2 - 71x + 30) = 0$

$2(x-5)(13x-6)$ so $x = 5$ or $x = 6/13$ ← both check

Practice problems:

1. $\dfrac{x+5}{3x-5} + \dfrac{x-3}{2x+2} = 1$

2. $\dfrac{2x-7}{2x+5} = \dfrac{x-6}{x+8}$

A rational function is given in the form $f(x) = p(x)/q(x)$. In the equation, $p(x)$ and $q(x)$ both represent polynomial functions where $q(x)$ does not equal zero. The branches of rational functions approach asymptotes. Setting the denominator equal to zero and solving will give the value(s) of the vertical asymptotes(s) since the function will be undefined at this point. If the value of $f(x)$ approaches b as the $|x|$ increases, the equation $y = b$ is a horizontal asymptote. To find the horizontal asymptote it is necessary to make a table of values for x that are to the right and left of the vertical asymptotes. The pattern for the horizontal asymptotes will become apparent as the $|x|$ increases.

If there are more than one vertical asymptotes, remember to choose numbers to the right and left of each one in order to find the horizontal asymptotes and have sufficient points to graph the function.

Example:

1. Graph $f(x) = \dfrac{3x+1}{x-2}$.

$x - 2 = 0$
$x = 2$

x	f(x)
3	10
10	3.875
100	3.07
1000	3.007
1	⁻4
⁻10	2.417
⁻100	2.93
⁻1000	2.99

1. Set denominator = 0 to find the vertical asymptote.

2. Make a table choosing numbers to the right and left of the vertical asymptote.

3. The pattern shows that as the $|x|$ increases f(x) approaches the value 3, therefore a horizontal asymptote exists at $y = 3$

Sketch the graph.

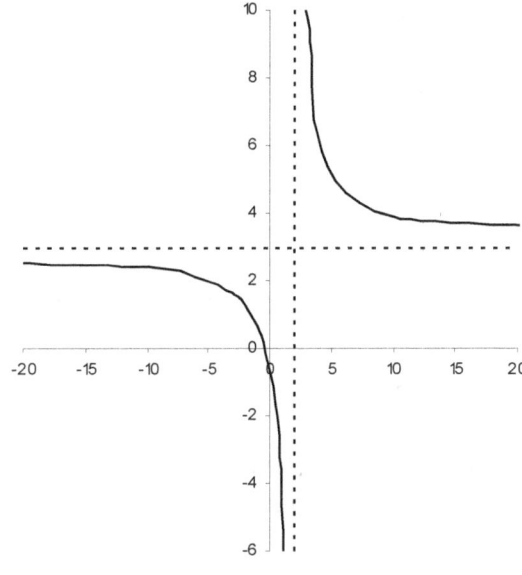

Radical Functions

To **simplify a radical**, follow these steps:

First, factor the number or coefficient completely.

For square roots, group like-factors in groups of 2. For cube roots, group like-factors in groups of 3. For n^{th} roots, group like-factors in groups of n.

Now, for each of those groups, put one of that number outside the radical. Multiply these numbers by any number already in front of the radical. Any factors that were not combined in groups should be multiplied back together and left inside the radical.

The index number of a radical is the little number on the front of the radical. For a cube root, the index is a 3. If no index appears, then the index is a 2 (for square roots).

For variables inside the radical, divide the index number of the radical into each exponent. The quotient (the answer to the division) is the new exponent to be written on the variable outside the radical. The remainder from the division is the new exponent on the variable remaining inside the radical sign. If the remainder is zero, then the variable no longer appears inside the radical sign.

Note: Remember that the square root of a negative number can be done by replacing the negative sign inside the square root sign with an "i" in front of the radical (to indicate an imaginary number). Then simplify the remaining positive radical by the normal method. Include the "i" outside the radical as part of the answer.

$$\sqrt{-18} = i\sqrt{18} = i\sqrt{3 \cdot 3 \cdot 2} = 3i\sqrt{2}$$

Remember that if the index number is an odd number, you can still simplify the radical to get a negative solution.

Examples:

1. $\sqrt{50a^4b^7} = \sqrt{5 \cdot 5 \cdot 2 \cdot a^4b^7} = 5a^2b^3\sqrt{2b}$
2. $7x\sqrt[3]{16x^5} = 7x\sqrt[3]{2 \cdot 2 \cdot 2 \cdot 2 \cdot x^5} = 7x \cdot 2x\sqrt[3]{2x^2} = 14x^2\sqrt[3]{2x^2}$

Practice problems:

1. $\sqrt{72a^9}$
2. $\sqrt{-98}$
3. $\sqrt[3]{-8x^6}$
4. $2x^3y\sqrt[4]{243x^6y^{11}}$

The **conjugate of a binomial** is the same expression as the original binomial with the sign between the 2 terms changed.

$\quad$ The conjugate of $3+2\sqrt{5}$ is $3-2\sqrt{5}$.
$\quad$ The conjugate of $\sqrt{5}-\sqrt{7}$ is $\sqrt{5}+\sqrt{7}$.
$\quad$ The conjugate of $^-6-\sqrt{11}$ is $^-6+\sqrt{11}$.

To multiply binomials including radicals, "FOIL" the binomials together. (that is, distribute each term of the first binomial times each term of the second binomial). Multiply what is in front of the radicals together. Multiply what is inside of the two radicals together. Check to see if any of the radicals can be simplified. Combine like terms, if possible.

When one binomial is divided by another binomial, multiply both the numerator and denominator by the conjugate of the denominator. "FOIL" or distribute one binomial through the other binomial. Simplify the radicals, if possible, and combine like terms. Reduce the resulting fraction if every term is divisible outside the radical signs by the same number.

<u>Examples:</u>

1. $(5+\sqrt{10})(4-3\sqrt{2}) = 20 - 15\sqrt{2} + 4\sqrt{10} - 3\sqrt{20} =$
$\quad 20 - 15\sqrt{2} + 4\sqrt{10} - 6\sqrt{5}$

2. $(\sqrt{6}+5\sqrt{2})(3\sqrt{6}-8\sqrt{2}) = 3\sqrt{36} - 8\sqrt{12} + 15\sqrt{12} - 40\sqrt{4} =$
$\quad 3\cdot 6 - 8\cdot 2\sqrt{3} + 15\cdot 2\sqrt{3} - 40\cdot 2 = 18 - 16\sqrt{3} + 30\sqrt{3} - 80 = {}^-62 + 14\sqrt{3}$

3. $\dfrac{1-\sqrt{2}}{3+5\sqrt{2}} = \dfrac{1-\sqrt{2}}{3+5\sqrt{2}} \cdot \dfrac{3-5\sqrt{2}}{3-5\sqrt{2}} = \dfrac{3-5\sqrt{2}-3\sqrt{2}+5\sqrt{4}}{9-25\sqrt{4}} = \dfrac{3-5\sqrt{2}-3\sqrt{2}+10}{9-50} =$
$\quad \dfrac{13-8\sqrt{2}}{^-41}$ or $-\dfrac{13-8\sqrt{2}}{41}$ or $\dfrac{^-13+8\sqrt{2}}{41}$

FOUNDATION LEV. MATH.

Practice problems:

1. $(3+2\sqrt{6})(4-\sqrt{6})$
2. $(\sqrt{5}+2\sqrt{15})(\sqrt{3}-\sqrt{15})$
3. $\dfrac{6+2\sqrt{3}}{4-\sqrt{6}}$

Before you can **add or subtract square roots**, the numbers or expressions inside the radicals must be the same. First, simplify the radicals, if possible. If the numbers or expressions inside the radicals are the same, add or subtract the numbers (or like expressions) in front of the radicals. Keep the expression inside the radical the same. Be sure that the radicals are as simplified as possible.

Note: If the expressions inside the radicals are not the same, and cannot be simplified to become the same, then they cannot be combined by addition or subtraction.

To multiply 2 square roots together, follow these steps:

1. Multiply what is outside the radicals together.
2. Multiply what is inside the radicals together.
3. Simplify the radical if possible. Multiply whatever is in front of the radical times the expression that is coming out of the radical.

To divide one square root by another, follow these steps:

1. Work separately on what is inside or outside the square root sign.
2. Divide or reduce the coefficients outside the radical.
3. Divide any like variables outside the radical.
4. Divide or reduce the coefficients inside the radical.
5. Divide any like variables inside the radical.
6. If there is still a radical in the denominator, multiply both the numerator and denominator by the radical in the denominator. Simplify both resulting radicals and reduce again outside the radical (if possible).

Examples:

1. $6\sqrt{7} + 2\sqrt{5} + 3\sqrt{7} = 9\sqrt{7} + 2\sqrt{5}$ These cannot be combined further.

2. $5\sqrt{12} + \sqrt{48} - 2\sqrt{75} = 5\sqrt{2 \cdot 2 \cdot 3} + \sqrt{2 \cdot 2 \cdot 2 \cdot 2 \cdot 3} - 2\sqrt{3 \cdot 5 \cdot 5} =$
   $5 \cdot 2\sqrt{3} + 2 \cdot 2\sqrt{3} - 2 \cdot 5\sqrt{3} = 10\sqrt{3} + 4\sqrt{3} - 10\sqrt{3} \quad\quad = 4\sqrt{3}$

3. $(6\sqrt{15x})(7\sqrt{10x}) = 42\sqrt{150x^2} = 42\sqrt{2 \cdot 3 \cdot 5 \cdot 5 \cdot x^2} = 42 \cdot 5x\sqrt{2 \cdot 3} = 210x\sqrt{6}$

4. $\dfrac{105x^8 \sqrt{18x^5 y^6}}{30x^2 \sqrt{27x^2 y^4}} = \dfrac{7x^6 (x^2)(y^3)\sqrt{2x}}{2(x)(y^2)\sqrt{3}} = \dfrac{7x^7 y \sqrt{2x}}{2\sqrt{3}}$

   $= \dfrac{7x^7 y \sqrt{2x}}{2\sqrt{3}} \cdot \dfrac{\sqrt{3}}{\sqrt{3}} = \dfrac{7x^7 y \sqrt{6x}}{6}$

Practice problems:

1. $6\sqrt{24} + 3\sqrt{54} - \sqrt{96}$
2. $(2x^2 y\sqrt{18x})(7xy^7 \sqrt{4x})$
3. $\dfrac{125a^5 \sqrt{56a^4 b^7}}{40a^2 \sqrt{40a^2 b^8}}$
4. $2\sqrt{3} + 4\sqrt{5} + 6\sqrt{25} - 7\sqrt{9} + 2\sqrt{5} - 8\sqrt{20} - 6\sqrt{16} - 7\sqrt{3}$

To solve **a radical equation**, follow these steps:

1. Get a radical alone on one side of the equation.
2. Raise both **sides** of the equation to the power equal to the index number. **Do not raise them to that power term by term, but raise the entire side to that power**. Combine any like terms.
3. If there is another radical still in the equation, repeat steps one and two (i.e. get that radical alone on one side of the equation and raise both sides to a power equal to the index). Repeat as necessary until the radicals are all gone.
4. Solve the resulting equation.
5. Once you have found the answer(s), substitute them back into the original equation to check them. Sometimes there are solutions that do not check in the original equation. These are extraneous solutions, which are not correct and must be eliminated. If a problem has more than one potential solution, each solution must be checked separately.

NOTE: What this really means is that you can simply just substitute the answers from any multiple choice test back into the question to determine which answer choice is correct.

Examples:

1. $\sqrt{2x+1} + 7 = x$
   $\sqrt{2x+1} = x - 7$
   $\left(\sqrt{2x+1}\right)^2 = (x-7)^2$ ← BOTH sides are squared.
   $2x + 1 = x^2 - 14x + 49$
   $0 = x^2 - 16x + 48$
   $0 = (x-12)(x-4)$
   $x = 12, x = 4$

When you check these answers in the original equation, 12 checks; however, **4 does not check in the original equation**. Therefore, the only answer is x = 12.

2. $\sqrt{3x+4} = 2\sqrt{x-4}$
   $\left(\sqrt{3x+4}\right)^2 = \left(2\sqrt{x-4}\right)^2$
   $3x + 4 = 4(x-4)$
   $3x + 4 = 4x - 16$
   $20 = x$ ← This checks in the original equaion.

3. $\sqrt[4]{7x-3} = 3$
   $\left(\sqrt[4]{7x-3}\right)^4 = 3^4$
   $7x - 3 = 81$
   $7x = 84$
   $x = 12$ ← This checks out with the original equation.

4. $\sqrt{x} = {}^-3$

$\left(\sqrt{x}\right)^2 = \left({}^-3\right)^2$

$x = 9$ ← This does NOT check in the original equation. Since there is no other answer to check, the correct answer is the empty set or the null set or $\varnothing$.

Practice problem:

Solve and check.

1. $\sqrt{6x - 2} = 5\sqrt{x - 13}$

Absolute Value Equations:

To solve an **absolute value equation,** follow these steps:

1. Get the absolute value expression alone on one side of the equation.

2. Split the absolute value equation into 2 separate equations without absolute value bars. In one equation, the expression inside the absolute value bars is equal to the expression on the other side of the original equation. In the other equation, the expression inside the absolute value bars is equal to the negative of the expression on the other side of the original equation.

3. Now solve each of these equations.

4. **Check each answer by substituting them into the original equation** (with the absolute value symbol). There will be answers that do not check in the original equation. These answers are discarded as they are **extraneous solutions**. If all answers are discarded as incorrect, then the answer to the equation is $\varnothing$, which is the empty or null set. (0, 1, or 2 solutions could be correct.)

To solve an **absolute value inequality**, follow these steps:

1. Get the absolute value expression alone on one side of the inequality. Remember: **Dividing or multiplying by a negative number will reverse the direction of the inequality sign.**

2. Remember what the inequality sign is at this point.

3. Split the absolute value inequality into 2 separate inequalities. For the first inequality, rewrite the inequality without the absolute value bars and solve it. For the next inequality, write the expression inside the absolute value bars followed by the opposite inequality sign and then by the negative of the expression on the other side of the inequality. Now solve it.

4. If the inequality sign in step 2 is $<$ or $\leq$, the solution is expressed by connecting the solutions of the two inequalities in step 3 by the word **and**. The solution set consists of the points between the 2 numbers on the number line. If the inequality sign in step 2 is $>$ or $\geq$, the solution is expressed by connecting the solutions of the two inequalities in step 3 by the word **or**. The solution set consists of the points outside the 2 numbers on the number line.

If an expression inside an absolute value bar is compared to a negative number, the answer can also be either all real numbers or the empty set ($\varnothing$). For instance,

$$|x + 3| < {}^-6$$

would have the empty set as the answer, since an absolute value is always positive and will never be less than $^-6$. However,

$$|x + 3| > {}^-6$$

would have all real numbers as the answer, since an absolute value is always positive or at least zero, and will never be less than -6. In similar fashion,

$$|x + 3| = {}^-6$$

would never check because an absolute value will never give a negative value.

Example: Solve and check:

$$|2x - 5| + 1 = 12$$

FOUNDATION LEV. MATH.

$|2x-5|=11$ Get absolute value alone.

Rewrite as 2 equations and solve separately.

right hand side positive		right hand side negative
$2x - 5 = 11$		$2x - 5 = {}^-11$
$2x = 16$	and	$2x = {}^-6$
$x = 8$		$x = {}^-3$

Checks:
$$|2x - 5| + 1 = 12 \qquad\qquad |2x - 5| + 1 = 12$$
$$|2(8) - 5| + 1 = 12 \qquad |2(-3) - 5| + 1 = 12$$
$$|11| + 1 = 12 \qquad\qquad |-11| + 1 = 12$$
$$12 = 12 \qquad\qquad\qquad 12 = 12$$

This time both 8 and $^-3$ check.

Example: Solve and check:

$$2|x - 7| - 13 \geq 11$$

$$2|x - 7| \geq 24 \qquad \text{Get absolute value alone.}$$

$$|x - 7| \geq 12$$

Rewrite as 2 inequalities and solve separately.

right hand side positive		right hand side negative
$x - 7 \geq 12$	or	$x - 7 \leq {}^-12$
$x \geq 19$	or	$x \leq {}^-5$

Graphing Absolute Value Functions

The **absolute value function** for a 1st degree equation is of the form: $y = m(x - h) + k$. Its graph is in the shape of a $\vee$. The point (h,k) is the location of the maximum/minimum point on the graph. "$\pm m$" are the slopes of the 2 sides of the $\vee$. The graph opens up if m is positive and down if m is negative.

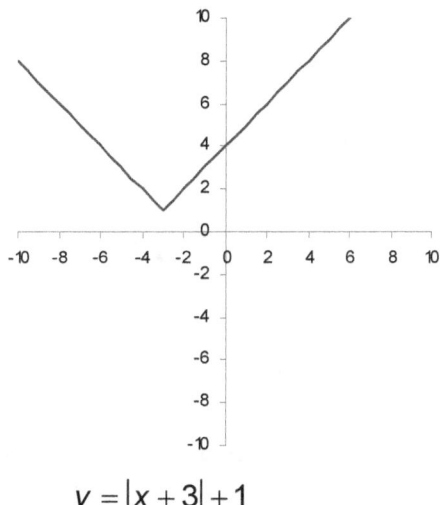

$$y = |x + 3| + 1$$

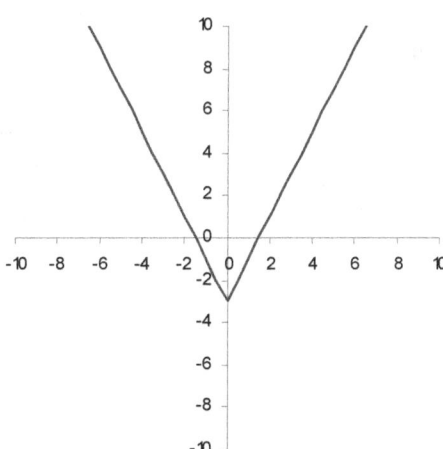

$$y = 2|x| - 3$$

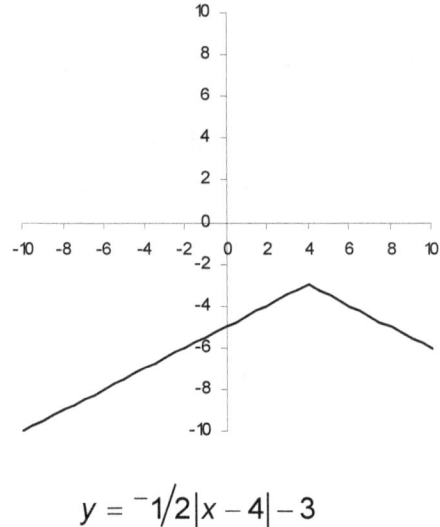

$$y = {}^-1/2|x-4| - 3$$

Note that on the first graph, the graph opens up since m is positive 1. It has ($^-$3,1) as its minimum point. The slopes of the 2 upward rays are $\pm$ 1.

The second graph also opens up since m is positive. (0,$^-$3) is its minimum point. The slopes of the 2 upward rays are $\pm$ 2.

The third graph is a downward $\wedge$ because m is $^-$1/2. The maximum point on the graph is at (4,$^-$3). The slopes of the 2 downward rays are $\pm$ 1/2.

The **identity function** is the linear equation $y = x$. Its graph is a line going through the origin (0,0) and through the first and third quadrants at a 45° degree angle.

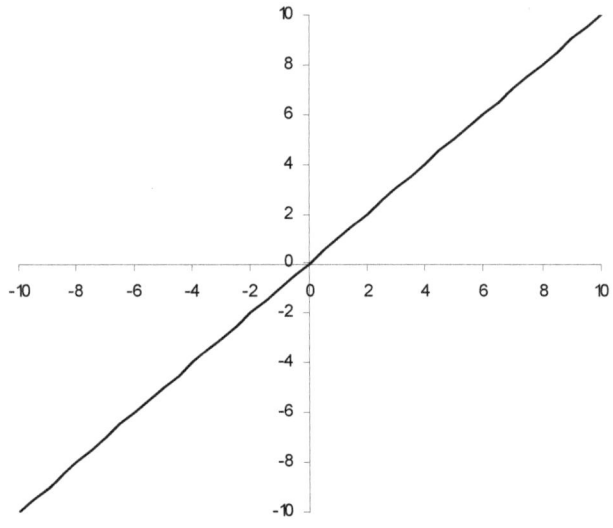

Note that both graphs should denote closed circles at the left side of each step, and open circles at the right side. In the graph of the first equation, the steps are going up as they move to the right. Each step is one space wide (inverse of r) with a solid dot on the left and a hollow dot on the right where the jump to the next step occurs. Each step is one square higher (j = 1) than the previous step. One step of the graph starts at (0,0) ← values of (h,k).

-In the second graph, the graph goes up to the right. One step starts at the point (0,3) ← values of (h,k). Each step is one square wide (r = 1) and each step is 2 squares higher than the previous step (j = 2).

Practice problems:
Graph the following equations:

1. $f(x) = x$
2. $y = {}^-|x - 3| + 5$
3. $y = 3[x]$
4. $y = \tfrac{2}{5}|x - 5| - 2$

Functions (SMR 1.3)

Skill c. Analyze properties of exponential and logarithmic functions in a variety of ways (e.g. graphing, solving problems)

When changing **common logarithms** to exponential form,

$$y = \log_b x \quad \text{if and only if} \quad x = b^y$$

Natural logarithms can be changed to exponential form by using,

$$\log_e x = \ln x \quad \text{or} \quad \ln x = y \text{ can be written as } e^y = x$$

Example:

Express in exponential form.

1. $\log_3 81 = 4$
   $x = 81 \quad b = 3 \quad y = 4$ Identify values.
   $81 = 3^4$ Rewrite in exponential form.

Solve by writing in exponential form.

1. $\log_x 125 = 3$

   $x^3 = 125$ Write in exponential form.
   $x^3 = 5^3$ Write 125 in exponential form.
   $x = 5$ Bases must be equal if exponents are equal.

Use a scientific calculator to solve.

2. Find $\ln 72$.
   $\ln 72 = 4.2767$ Use the $\ln x$ key to find natural logs.

3. Find $\ln x = 4.2767$ Write in exponential form.
   $e^{4.2767} = x$ Use the key (or 2nd $\ln x$) to find x. The small difference is due to rounding.
   $x = 72.002439$

To solve **logarithms or exponential functions** it is necessary to use several properties.

Multiplication Property $\quad \log_b mn = \log_b m + \log_b n$

Quotient Property $\quad \log_b \dfrac{m}{n} = \log_b m - \log_b n$

Powers Property $\quad \log_b n^r = r \log_b n$

Equality Property $\quad \log_b n = \log_b m$
if and only if $n = m$.

Change of Base Formula $\quad \log_b n = \dfrac{\log n}{\log b}$

$\log_b b^x = x \text{ and } b^{\log_b x} = x$

Example:

Solve for x.
1. $\log_6(x-5) + \log_6 x = 2$

$\log_6 x(x-5) = 2$ Use product property.
$\log_6 x^2 - 5x = 2$ Distribute.
$x^2 - 5x = 6^2$ Write in exponential form.
$x^2 - 5x - 36 = 0$ Solve quadratic equation.
$(x+4)(x-9) = 0$
$x = {}^-4 \quad x = 9$

***Be sure to check results. Remember x must be greater than zero in $\log x = y$.

Check: $\log_6(x-5) + \log_6 x = 2$

$\log_6({}^-4 - 5) + \log_6({}^-4) = 2$ Substitute the first answer ${}^-4$.

$\log_6({}^-9) + \log_6({}^-4) = 2$ This is undefined, x is less than zero.

$\log_6(9-5) + \log_6 9 = 2$ Substitute the second answer 9.

$\log_6 4 + \log_6 9 = 2$
$\log_6(4)(9) = 2$ Multiplication property.
$\log_6 36 = 2$
$6^2 = 36$ Write in exponential form.
$36 = 36$

Practice problems:

1. $\log_4 x = 2\log_4 3$

2. $2\log_3 x = 2 + \log_3(x-2)$

3. Use change of base formula to find $(\log_3 4)(\log_4 3)$.

Linear Algebra (SMR 1.4)

Skill a. **Understand and apply the geometric interpretation and basic operations of vectors in two and three dimensions, including their scalar multiples and scalar (dot) and cross products**

Vectors:

A vector is any quantity that has size or magnitude and direction. In a 2 dimensional x/y plane, we aren't usually looking for the exact position of a directional line segment $\vec{PQ}$, but we are concerned with the direction and length $\vec{PQ}$. These can be determined by the x and y components of $\vec{PQ}$, which leads us to vectors:

DEFINITION: The family of all directed line segments with the same components as $\vec{PQ}$ will be called the vector from P to Q. We say that $\vec{PQ}$ represents this vector.

Vectors are used to measure displacement of an object or force. Vector sums obey the same laws as real numbers.

Addition of vectors:
$$(a,b)+(c,d)=(a+c,b+d)$$

Addition Properties of vectors:
$a+b=b+a$
$a+(b+c)=(a+b)+c$
$a+0=a$
$a+(^-a)=0$

Subtraction of vectors:
$a-b=a+(^-b)$ therefore,
$a-b=(a_1,a_2)+(^-b_1,{}^-b_2)$ or
$a-b=(a_1,-b_1,a_2-b_2)$

FOUNDATION LEV. MATH.

Multiplication of vectors:

$$\vec{v} \bullet \vec{n} = \vec{n} \bullet \vec{v}, \quad \vec{v} \bullet \vec{v} = \|\vec{v}\|^2, \quad \vec{v} \bullet \vec{0} = 0$$

$$\vec{n}(\vec{v} + \vec{m}) = \vec{n} \bullet \vec{v} + \vec{n} \bullet \vec{m}, \text{ and } \vec{n}(\vec{v} \bullet \vec{m}) = \vec{m}(\vec{v} \bullet \vec{n}) = \vec{v}(\vec{n} \bullet \vec{m})$$

The sum A + B of vectors A and B is defined as follows. Let $\overrightarrow{QR}$ represent A and let $\overrightarrow{RS}$ represent B.

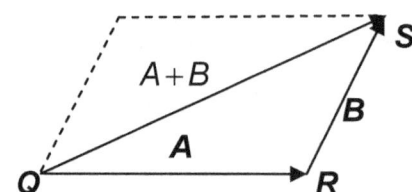

Then A + B is the vector represented by $\overrightarrow{QS}$. In other words, if A is the vector from Q to R and B is the vector from R to S, then A + B is the vector from Q to S.

Examples:

Use the Pythagorean Theorem to determine the magnitude of the *vector sum*.

Problem 1   Problem 2

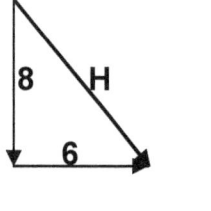 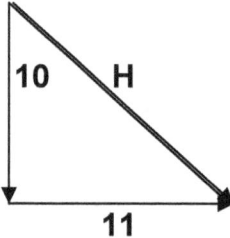

Problem 1 solution:

$$H^2 = 8^2 + 6^2 = \sqrt{100} = 10$$

Problem 2 solution:

$$H^2 = 10^2 + 11^2 = \sqrt{221} = 14.86$$

If $a = (4, {}^-1)$ and $b = ({}^-3, 6)$, find $a + b$ and $a - b$.

Using the rule for addition of vectors:

$$(4, ^-1) + (^-3, 6) = (4 + (^-3), ^-1 + 6)$$
$$= (1, 5)$$

Using the rule for subtraction of vectors:

$$(4, ^-1) - (^-3, 6) = (4 - (^-3), ^-1 - 6)$$
$$= (7, ^-7)$$

The dot product $a \cdot b$ is the multiplication of vectors:

$$a = (a_1, a_2) = a_1 i + a_2 j \quad \text{and} \quad b = (b_1, b_2) = b_1 i + b_2 j$$
$$a \cdot b = a_1 b_1 + a_2 b_2$$

$a \cdot b$ is read "*a* dot *b*". Dot products are also called scalar or inner products. When discussing dot products, it is important to remember that "*a* dot *b*" is not a vector, but a *real number*. Note that *i* is the unit vector in the x-direction and *j* is the unit vector in the y-direction.

Example:
$v = ai + bj$ and $z = ci + dj$ then the product of these 2 vectors would be: $v * z = a(c) + b(d)$

For 3 dimensional vectors if
$v = ai + bj + ck$ and $z = di + ej + fk$ then the product of these 2 vectors would be: $v * z = ad + be + cf$

Example: given 2 vectors, *v* and *z*:
$v = 3i + 2j$ and $z = 4i + j$ then the product of these 2 vectors would be: $v * z = 3(4) + 2(1) = 14$

Properties of the dot product:

$a \bullet a = |a|^2$

$a \bullet b = b \bullet a$

$a \bullet (b+c) = a \bullet b + a \bullet c$

$(ca) \bullet b = c(a \bullet b) = a \bullet (cb)$

$0 \bullet a = 0$

Examples:

Find the dot product.

1. $a = (5,2), b = (^-3,6)$
   $a \bullet b = (5)(^-3)+(2)(6)$
   $= {^-15} + 12$
   $= {^-3}$

2. $a = (5i + 3j), b = (4i - 5j)$
   $a \bullet b = (5)(4)+(3)(^-5)$
   $= 20 - 15$
   $= 5$

3. The magnitude and direction of a constant force are given by $a = 4i + 5j$. Find the amount of work done if the point of application of the force moves from the origin to the point $P(7,2)$.

The work W done by a constant force a as its point of application moves along a vector b is. $W = a \bullet b$

Sketch the constant force vector a and the vector b.

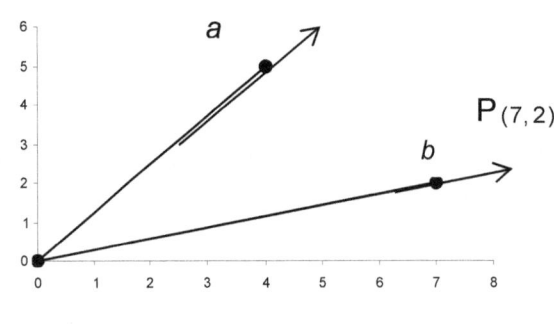

$b = (7,2) = 7i + 2j$

Use the definition of work done to solve.

$$W = a \bullet b$$
$$= (4i + 5j)(7i + 2j)$$
$$= (4)(7) + (5)(2)$$
$$= (28) + (10)$$
$$= 38$$

Occasionally, it is important to reverse the addition or subtraction process and express the single vector as the sum or difference of two other vectors. It may be critically important for a pilot to understand not only the air velocity but also the ground speed and the climbing speed.

Example:
A pilot is traveling at an air speed of 300 mph and a direction of 20 degrees. Find the horizontal vector (ground speed) and the climbing vector (climbing speed).

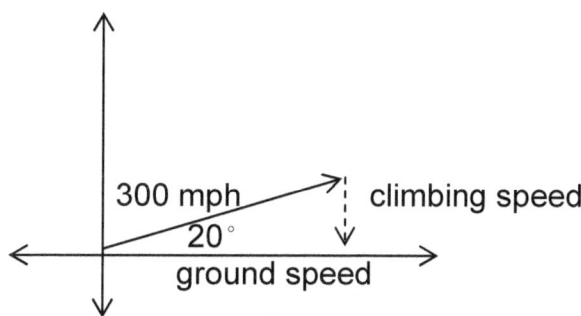

1. Draw sketch.
2. Use appropriate trigonometric ratio to calculate the component vectors.

To find the vertical vector:

$$\sin x = \frac{\text{opposite}}{\text{hypotenuse}}$$
$$x = 102.606$$

To find the horizontal vector:

$$\cos x = \frac{\text{adjacent}}{\text{hypotenuse}}$$
$$x = 281.908$$

Cross products of vectors:

The cross product between 2 vectors a and b is a 3rd vector. All vectors have 2 angles, θ and $2n-\theta$. The magnitude of the cross product is $|c| = |a \times b| = ab\sin\theta$ where θ is the smaller of the angles between the 2 vectors. An important characteristic of the direction of a cross product is that it has nothing to do with the angle θ, which is the enclosed angle of the 2 original vectors. This angle θ only affects the magnitude of the cross product, but not its direction. If n is the unit vector resulting from the above vector product, then

$$|c| = |a \times b| = ab\sin\theta n.$$

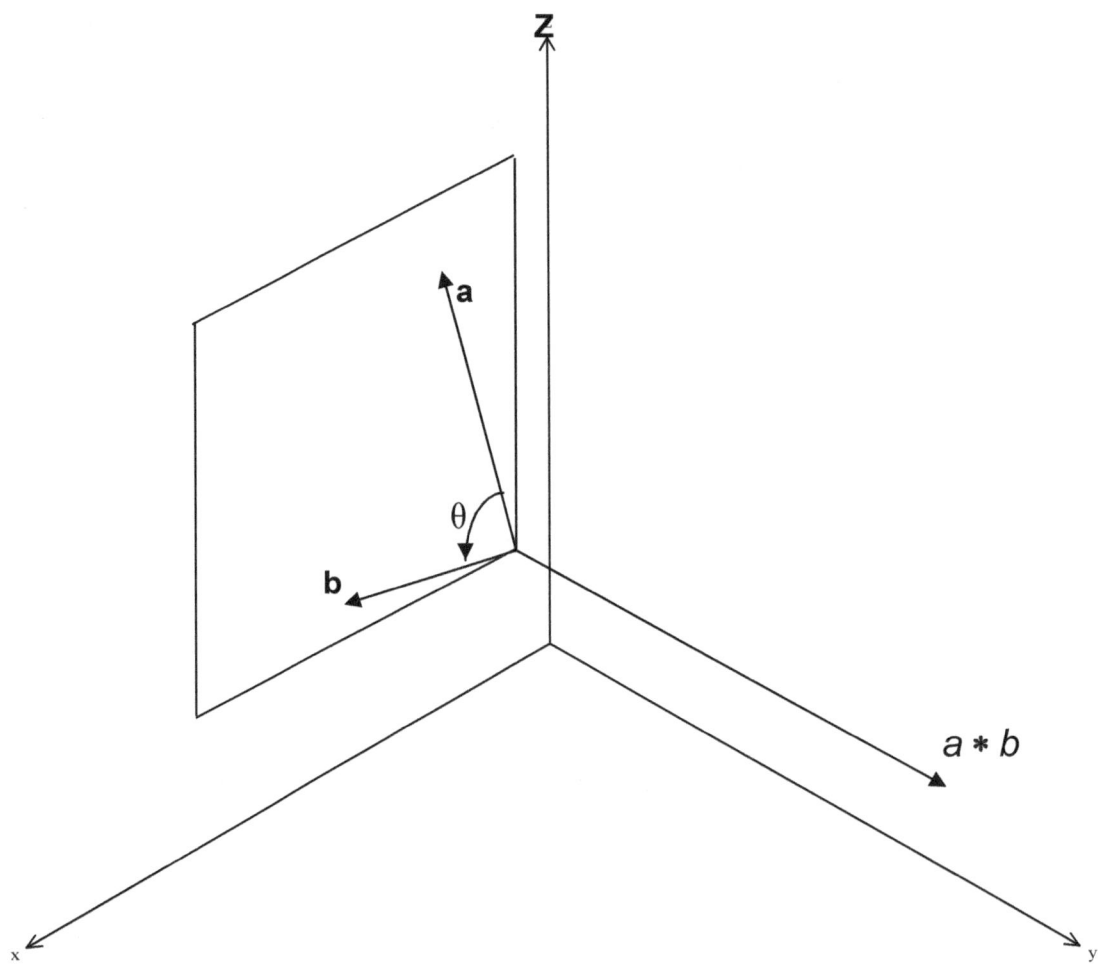

The rectangular coordinate system has 3 planes, all at right angles to each other. This coordinate systems makes it much easier to determine the direction of a vector product. But the actual direction of the vector isn't yet known. If we make it so that the vectors we're cross-multiplying lies within one of the 3 coordinate planes, the our cross product is situated to that it is perpendicular to the plane the vectors lie in as shown above and is parallel to the y-axis. But it could go in either direction on the y-axis and the way we determine its direction is to move from $\vec{A}$ to $\vec{B}$ within the plane formed by these 2 vectors. If the movement from $\vec{A}$ to $\vec{B}$ is clockwise, then the direction of the product vector is moving away from our perspective; if the movement is counterclockwise, as it is above, then the direction of the product vector is toward us, as shown above. Therefore, the direction of the cross product can be on a particular side of the coordinate plane, depending on whether the product is from $\vec{A}$ to $\vec{B}$ or if it is from $\vec{B}$ to $\vec{A}$. This means that vector products are not commutative like vector addition.

Vector Product Values

The actual value of a vector product is maximum for the maximum value of sine, which is $\sin 90° = 1$; therefore, the maximum value is: $(a \times b)_{max} = ab$ and the vector product for 0° and 180° $= \theta$ since the sine of both of these angles is zero. The cross-product of the same unit vector is equal to zero: $i \times i = j \times j = l \times l = m \times m = 0$

Vector cross products and geometry

Let u and v be vectors and consider the parallelogram that the 2 vectors will make. The area of the parallelogram will then be equal to $\|u * v\|$

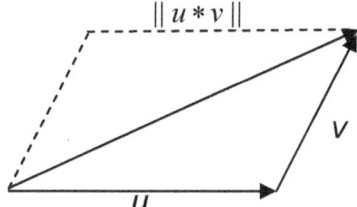

The *direction* of the vector cross product of $u * v$ is a right angle to the parallelogram and for
$i * j$, the magnitude is 1 and the direction is k, $\therefore i * j = k$

Linear Algebra (SMR 1.4)

Skill b. **Prove the basic properties of vectors (e.g., perpendicular vectors have zero dot product)**

The dot product of two perpendicular vectors is zero.

Proof: If the vector $\vec{a}$ makes an angle θ_1 with the x-axis and the vector $\vec{b}$ makes an angle θ_2 with the x-axis, we can express them in terms of their x and y components as:

$$\vec{a} = a\cos\theta_1 i + a\sin\theta_1 j$$
$$\vec{b} = b\cos\theta_2 i + b\sin\theta_2 j$$

Taking the dot product of the two vectors:

$$\vec{a} \bullet \vec{b} = ab\cos\theta_1\cos\theta_2 + ab\sin\theta_1\sin\theta_2 = ab\cos(\theta_1 - \theta_2)$$

If the vectors are perpendicular to each other, the angle between them $\theta_1 - \theta_2 = 90°$. Since $\cos 90° = 0$, $\vec{a} \bullet \vec{b} = 0$.

If the dot product of the same 2 vectors $\vec{V}$, equals zero, then $\vec{V} = 0$.
Proof: if $\vec{v} \bullet \vec{v} = 0$, then $\vec{v} = \vec{0}$.

$\vec{v} = (v_1, v_2, \ldots v_n)$, then find the dot product:

$$\vec{v} \bullet \vec{v} = (v_1, v_2, \ldots v_n)(v_1, v_2, \ldots v_n) =$$

$v_1^2 + v_2^2 + v_3^2 + \ldots v_n^2 = 0$ and because $v_n^2 \geq 0$ for all n, then the only way for the above sum to equal zero is if $v_n^2 = 0$, which in turn means that $v_n = 0$, and $\therefore \vec{v} = \vec{0}$.

Dot vectors obey the law of distributivity:

Proof: $\vec{v} \cdot (\vec{s} + \vec{m}) = \vec{v} \cdot \vec{s} + \vec{v} \cdot \vec{m}$

Start with 3 vectors: $\vec{v} = (v_1, v_2, \ldots v_n)$, $\vec{s} = (s_1, s_2, \ldots s_n)$ and $\vec{m}(m_1, m_2, \ldots m_n)$.

$$\begin{aligned}
\vec{v} \cdot (\vec{s} + \vec{m}) &= (v_1, v_2, \ldots v_n) \cdot [(s_1, s_2, \ldots s_n) + (m_1, m_2, \ldots m_n)] \\
&= (v_1, v_2, \ldots v_n) \cdot (s_1 + m_1, s_2 + m_2, \ldots s_n + m_n) \\
&= [v_1(s_1 + m_1), v_2(s_2 + m_2), \ldots v_n(s_n + m_n)] \\
&= v_1 s_1 + v_1 m_1, v_2 s_2 + v_2 m_2, \ldots v_n s_n + v_n m_n \\
&= (v_1 s_1, v_2 s_2, \ldots v_n s_n) + (v_1 m_1, v_2 m_2, \ldots v_n m_n) \\
&= (v_1, v_2, \ldots v_n) \cdot (s_1, s_2, \ldots s_n) + (v_1, v_2, \ldots v_n) \cdot (m_1, m_2, \ldots m_n) \\
&= \vec{v} \cdot \vec{s} + \vec{v} \cdot \vec{m}
\end{aligned}$$

Linear Algebra (SMR 1.4)

Skill c. **Understand and apply the basic properties and operations of matrices and determinants (e.g., to determine the solvability of linear systems of equations)**

Matrices:
A matrix is a square array of numbers called its entries or elements. The dimensions of a matrix are written as the number of rows (r) by the number of columns (r × c).

$\begin{vmatrix} 1 & 2 & 3 \\ 4 & 5 & 6 \end{vmatrix}$ is a 2 × 3 matrix (2 rows by 3 columns)

$\begin{vmatrix} 1 & 2 \\ 3 & 4 \\ 5 & 6 \end{vmatrix}$ is a 3 × 2 matrix (3 rows by 2 columns)

Associated with every square matrix is a number called the determinant.

Use these formulas to calculate determinants.

2 × 2 $\quad \begin{vmatrix} a & b \\ c & d \end{vmatrix} = ad - bc$

3 × 3
$\begin{vmatrix} a_1 & b_1 & c_1 \\ a_2 & b_2 & c_2 \\ a_3 & b_3 & c_3 \end{vmatrix} = (a_1 b_2 c_3 + b_1 c_2 a_3 + c_1 a_2 b_3) - (a_3 b_2 c_1 + b_3 c_2 a_1 + c_3 a_2 b_1)$

This is found by repeating the first two columns and then using the diagonal lines to find the value of each expression as shown below:

$\begin{vmatrix} a_1^* & b_1^\circ & c_1^\bullet \\ a_2 & b_2^* & c_2^\circ \\ a_3 & b_3 & c_3^* \end{vmatrix} \begin{matrix} a_1 & b_1 \\ a_2^\bullet & b_2 \\ a_3^\circ & b_3^\bullet \end{matrix}$

$= (a_1 b_2 c_3 + b_1 c_2 a_3 + c_1 a_2 b_3) - (a_3 b_2 c_1 + b_3 c_2 a_1 + c_3 a_2 b_1)$

FOUNDATION LEV. MATH.

Example:
1. Find the value of the determinant:

$$\begin{vmatrix} 4 & ^-8 \\ 7 & 3 \end{vmatrix} = (4)(3) - (7)(^-8)$$

Cross multiply and subtract.

$$12 - (^-56) = 68$$

Then simplify.

When given the following system of equations:

$$ax + by = e$$
$$cx + dy = f$$

The matrix equation is written in the form:

$$\begin{bmatrix} a & b \\ c & d \end{bmatrix} \begin{bmatrix} x \\ y \end{bmatrix} = \begin{bmatrix} e \\ f \end{bmatrix} \begin{bmatrix} a & b \\ c & d \end{bmatrix}$$

The solution is found using the inverse of the matrix of coefficients. Inverse of matrices can be written as follows:

$$A^{-1} = \frac{1}{\text{determinant of A}} \begin{vmatrix} d & -b \\ -c & a \end{vmatrix}$$

Example:
Write the matrix equation of the system.

$$3x - 4y = 2$$
$$2x + y = 5$$

$$\begin{bmatrix} 3 & -4 \\ 2 & 1 \end{bmatrix} \begin{bmatrix} x \\ y \end{bmatrix} = \begin{bmatrix} 2 \\ 5 \end{bmatrix}$$

Definition of matrix equation

$$\begin{bmatrix} x \\ y \end{bmatrix} = \frac{1}{11} \begin{bmatrix} 1 & 4 \\ -2 & 1 \end{bmatrix} \begin{bmatrix} 2 \\ 5 \end{bmatrix}$$

Multiply by the inverse of the coefficient matrix.

$$\begin{bmatrix} x \\ y \end{bmatrix} = \frac{1}{11} \begin{bmatrix} 22 \\ 11 \end{bmatrix}$$

Matrix multiplication.

$$\begin{bmatrix} x \\ y \end{bmatrix} = \begin{bmatrix} 2 \\ 1 \end{bmatrix}$$

Scalar multiplication.

The solution is (2,1).

Practice problems:

1. $x + 2y = 5$
   $3x + 5y = 14$

2. $^-3x + 4y - z = 3$
   $x + 2y - 3z = 9$
   $y - 5z = {}^-1$

Scalar multiplication is the product of the scalar (the outside number) and each element inside the matrix.

Sample problem:

Given: $A = \begin{bmatrix} 4 & 0 \\ 3 & -1 \end{bmatrix}$ Find 2A.

$2A = 2\begin{bmatrix} 4 & 0 \\ 3 & -1 \end{bmatrix}$

$\begin{bmatrix} 2(4) & 2(0) \\ 2(3) & 2(-1) \end{bmatrix}$ Multiply each element in the matrix by the scalar.

$\begin{bmatrix} 8 & 0 \\ 6 & -2 \end{bmatrix}$ Simplify.

Practice problems:

1. $-2\begin{bmatrix} 2 & 0 & 1 \\ -1 & -2 & 4 \end{bmatrix}$

2. $3\begin{bmatrix} 6 \\ 2 \\ 8 \end{bmatrix} + 4\begin{bmatrix} 0 \\ 7 \\ 2 \end{bmatrix}$

3. $2\begin{bmatrix} -6 & 8 \\ -2 & -1 \\ 0 & 3 \end{bmatrix}$

FOUNDATION LEV. MATH.

GEOMETRY (SMR Domain 2)

Parallelism (SMR 2.1)

Skill a. **Know the Parallel Postulate and its implications, and justify its equivalents (e.g., the Alternate Interior Angle Theorem, the angle sum of every triangle is 180 degrees)**

Definitions are explanations of all mathematical terms except those that are undefined.

Postulates are mathematical statements that are accepted as true statements without providing a proof.

Theorems are mathematical statements that can be proven to be true based on postulates, definitions, algebraic properties, given information, and previously proved theorems.

The **3 undefined terms of geometry** are point, line, and plane.

A plane is a flat surface that extends forever in two dimensions. It has no ends or edges. It has no thickness to it. It is usually drawn as a parallelogram that can be named either by 3 non-collinear points (3 points that are not on the same line) on the plane or by placing a letter in the corner of the plane that is not used elsewhere in the diagram.

A line extends forever in one dimension. It is determined and named by 2 points that are on the line. The line consists of every point that is between those 2 points as well as the points that are on the "straight" extension each way. A line is drawn as a line segment with arrows facing opposite directions on each end to indicate that the line continues in both directions forever.

A point is a position in space, on a line, or on a plane. It has no thickness and no width. Only 1 line can go through any 2 points. A point is represented by a dot named by a single letter.

Parallel and Perpendicular Lines

Parallel lines or planes do not intersect.

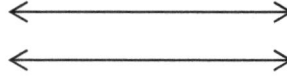

Perpendicular lines or planes form a 90 degree angle to each other.

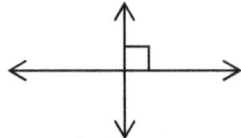

Every **angle** has exactly one ray, which bisects the angle. If a point on such a bisector is located, then the point is equidistant from the two sides of the angle. Distance from a point to a side is measured along a segment, which is perpendicular to the angle's side. The converse is also true. If a point is equidistant from the sides of an angle, then the point is on the bisector of the angle.

Every **segment** has exactly one line, which is both perpendicular to and bisects the segment. If a point on such a perpendicular bisector is located, then the point is equidistant to the endpoints of the segment. The converse is also true. If a point is equidistant from the endpoints of a segment, then that point is on the perpendicular bisector of the segment.

Classification of Angles and their Properties

The classifying of angles refers to the angle measure. The naming of angles refers to the letters or numbers used to label the angle.

Example:

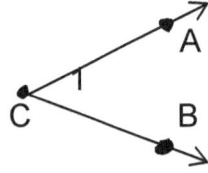 $\overrightarrow{CA}$ (read ray CA) and $\overrightarrow{CB}$ are the sides of the angle.
The angle can be called $\angle ABC$, $\angle BCA$, $\angle C$ or $\angle 1$.

Angles are classified according to their size as follows:

acute: between 0 and 90 degrees.
right: exactly 90 degrees.
obtuse: between 90 and 180 degrees.
straight: exactly 180 degrees

Angles can be classified in a number of ways. Some of those classifications are outlined here.

Adjacent angles have a common vertex and one common side by no interior points in common.

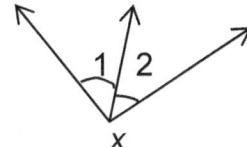

Complementary angles add up to 90 degrees.

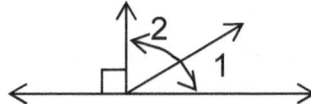

Supplementary angles add up to 180 degrees.

Vertical angles have sides that form two pairs of opposite rays.

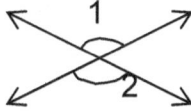

Corresponding angles are in the same corresponding position on two parallel lines cut by a transversal.

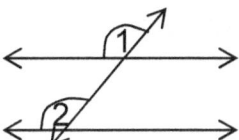

Parallel Lines Postulate: If two lines are parallel and are cut by a transversal, corresponding angles have the same measure.

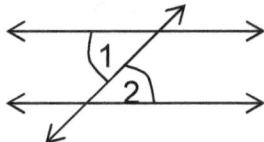

Alternate Interior Angles Theorem: If two parallel lines are cut by a transversal, the alternate interior angles are congruent.

Alternate exterior angles are diagonal angles on the outside of two lines cut by a transversal.

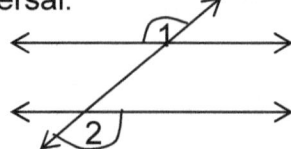

Lines and planes are classified as parallel, perpendicular, intersecting or skew.

A **triangle** is a polygon with three sides.
Triangles can be classified by the types of angles or the lengths of their sides.

Classifying by angles:
An **acute** triangle has exactly three *acute* angles.
A **right** triangle has one *right* angle.
An **obtuse** triangle has one *obtuse* angle.

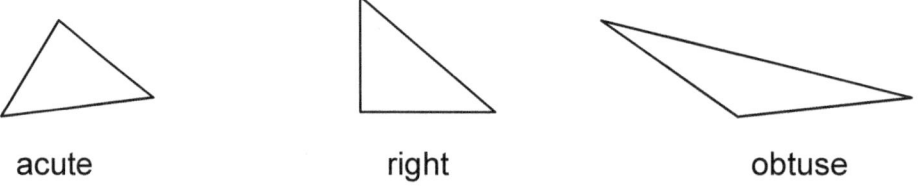

acute   right   obtuse

Classifying by sides:
All *three* sides of an **equilateral** triangle are the same length.
Two sides of an **isosceles** triangle are the same length.
None of the sides of a **scalene** triangle are the same length.

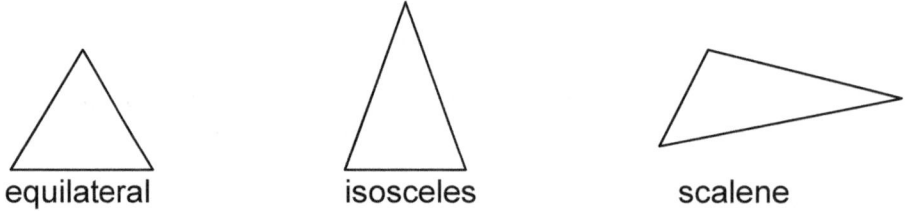

equilateral   isosceles   scalene

The sum of the measures of the angles of a **triangle** is 180°.

Example 1:
Can a triangle have two right angles?
No. A right angle measures 90°, therefore the sum of two right angles would be 180° and there could not be a third angle.

Example 2:
Can a right triangle have two obtuse angles?
No. Since an obtuse angle measures more than 90° the sum of two obtuse angles would be greater than 180°.

Example 3:
Can a right triangle be obtuse?
No. Once again, the sum of the angles would be more than 180°.

Example 4:
In a triangle, the measure of the second angle is three times the first. The third angle equals the sum of the measures of the first two angles. Find the number of degrees in each angle.

Let x = the number of degrees in the first angle
$3x$ = the number of degrees in the second angle
$x + 3x$ = the measure of the third angle

Since the sum of the measures of all three angles is 180°.

$$x + 3x + (x + 3x) = 180$$
$$8x = 180$$
$$x = 22.5$$
$$3x = 67.5$$
$$x + 3x = 90$$

Thus the angles measure 22.5°, 67.5°, and 90°. Additionally, the triangle is a right triangle.

Parallelism (SMR 2.1)

Skill b. **Know that variants of the Parallel Postulate produce non-Euclidean geometries (e.g. spherical, hyperbolic)**

Euclid wrote a set of 13 books around 330 B.C. called the Elements. He outlined ten axioms and then deduced 465 theorems. Euclidean geometry is based on the undefined concept of the point, line and plane.

The fifth of Euclid's axioms (referred to as the parallel postulate) was not as readily accepted as the other nine axioms. Many mathematicians throughout the years have attempted to prove that this axiom is not necessary because it could be proved by the other nine. Among the many who attempted to prove this was Carl Friedrich Gauss. His works led to the development of hyperbolic geometry. Elliptical, Spherical or Riemannian geometry was suggested by G.F. Berhard Riemann. He based his work on the theory of surfaces and used models as physical interpretations of the undefined terms that satisfy the axioms.

The chart below lists the fifth axiom (The Parallel Postulate) as it is given in each of the three geometries:

Euclidean Geometry	Spherical or Riemannian Geometry	Hyperbolic or Saddle Geometry
Through a point not on a line, there is no more than one line parallel to that line.	If *l* is any line and *P* is any point not on *l*, then there are no lines through *P* that are parallel to *l*.	If *l* is any line and *P* is any point not on *l*, then there exists at least 2 lines through *P* that are parallel to *l*.

Euclidean Geometry is the study of flat, 2-dimensional space. Elliptical or Spherical Geometry is the study of **curved surfaces**, such as a sphere and has direct connection to our experiences since we live on a curved surface, the Earth. In Elliptical Geometry, the sum of the angles of a triangle is greater than 180°. Hyperbolic Geometry is the study of saddle shaped space like a Pringle's Potato Chip and has application in various areas of science such as astronomy. Einstein's statement that space is curved and his theory of relativity are founded on hyperbolic geometry.

Plane Euclidean Geometry (SMR 2.2)

Skill a. **Prove theorems and solve problems involving similarity and congruence**

About Euclidean Geometry proofs:

In a **2 column proof**, the left side of the proof should be the given information, or statements that could be proved by deductive reasoning. The right column of the proof consists of the reasons used to determine that each statement to the left was verifiably true. The right side can identify given information, or state theorems, postulates, definitions or algebraic properties used to prove that particular line of the proof is true.

Assume the opposite of the conclusion. Keep your hypothesis given information the same. Proceed to develop the steps of the proof, looking for a statement that contradicts your original assumption or some other known fact. This contradiction indicates that the assumption you made at the beginning of the proof was incorrect; therefore, the original conclusion has to be true.

The following **algebraic postulates** are frequently used as reasons for statements in 2 column geometric properties:

Addition Property:

$\quad$ If $a = b$ and $c = d$, then $a + c = b + d$.

Subtraction Property:

$\quad$ If $a = b$ and $c = d$, then $a - c = b - d$.

Multiplication Property:

$\quad$ If $a = b$ and $c \neq 0$, then $ac = bc$.

Division Property:

$\quad$ If $a = b$ and $c \neq 0$, then $a/c = b/c$.

Reflexive Property:	$a = a$
Symmetric Property:	If $a = b$, then $b = a$.
Transitive Property:	If $a = b$ and $b = c$, then $a = c$.
Distributive Property:	$a(b + c) = ab + ac$
Substitution Property:	If $a = b$, then b may be substituted for a in any other expression (a may also be substituted for b).

Triangle Congruence:

Example: Congruent Triangles ($\cong$ means congruent)

$$\triangle ABC \cong \triangle DEF$$

The 2 triangles ABC and DEF are congruent if these 6 conditions are met:

1. $\angle A \cong \angle D$
2. $\angle B \cong \angle E$
3. $\angle C \cong \angle F$
4. $\overline{AB} \cong \overline{DE}$
5. $\overline{BC} \cong \overline{EF}$
6. $\overline{AC} \cong \overline{DF}$

The various congruent angles and segments "correspond" to each other.

Two triangles are congruent if each of the three angles and three sides of one triangle match up in a one-to-one fashion with congruent angles and sides of the second triangle. In order to see how the sides and angles match up, it is sometimes necessary to imagine rotating or reflecting one of the triangles so the two figures are oriented in the same position.

There are shortcuts to the above procedure for proving two triangles congruent.

Side-Side-Side (SSS) Congruence--If the three sides of one triangle match up in a one-to-one congruent fashion with the three sides of the other triangle, then the two triangles are congruent. With SSS it is not necessary to compare the angles; they will automatically be congruent.

Angle-Side-Angle (ASA) Congruence--If two angles of one triangle match up in a one-to-one congruent fashion with two angles in the other triangle and if the sides between the two angles are congruent, then the two triangles are congruent. With ASA the sides that are used for congruence must be located between the two angles used in the first part of the proof.

Side-Angle-Side (SAS) Congruence--If two sides of one triangle match up in a one-to-one congruent fashion with two sides in the other triangle and if the angles between the two sides are congruent, then the two triangles are congruent. With SAS the angles that are used for congruence must be located between the two sides used in the first part of the proof.

SAS Postulate
If two sides and the included angle of one triangle are congruent to two sides and the included angle of another triangle, then the two triangles are congruent.

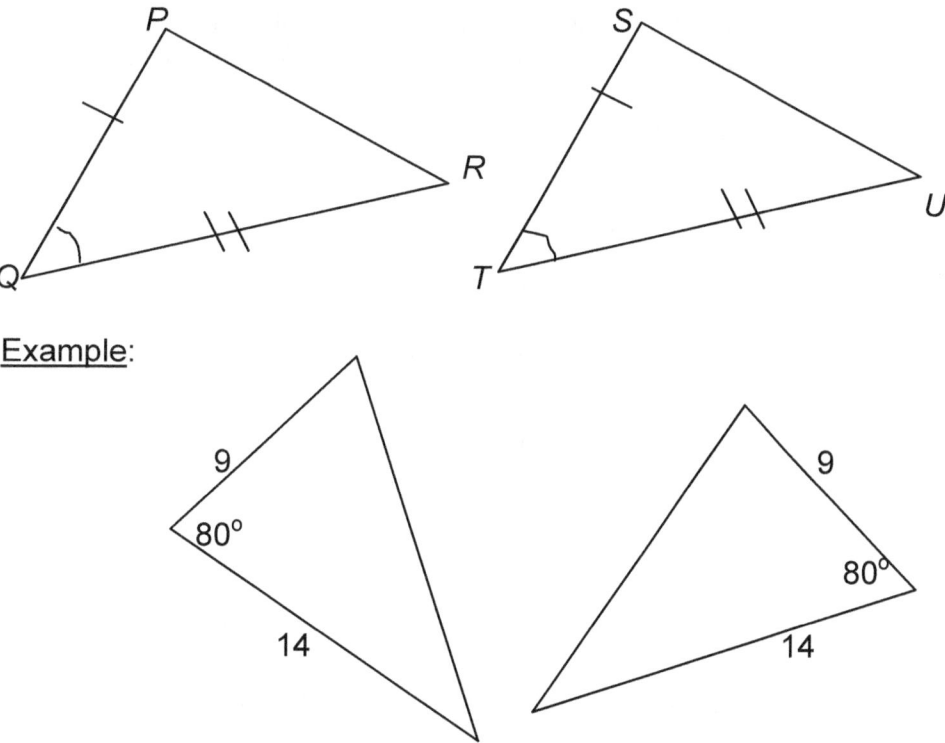

Example:

The two triangles are congruent by SAS.

In addition to SSS, ASA, and SAS, **Angle-Angle-Side (AAS)** is also a congruence shortcut.

AAS states that if two angles of one triangle match up in a one-to-one congruent fashion with two angles in the other triangle and if two sides that are not between the aforementioned sets of angles are also congruent, then the triangles are congruent. ASA and AAS are very similar, the only difference is where the congruent sides are located. If the sides are between the congruent sets of angles, use ASA. If the sides are not located between the congruent sets of angles, use AAS.

Hypotenuse-Leg (HL) is a congruence shortcut that can only be used with right triangles. If the hypotenuse and leg of one right triangle are congruent to the hypotenuse and leg of the other right triangle, then the two triangles are congruent.

Two triangles are overlapping if a portion of the interior region of one triangle is shared in common with all or a part of the interior region of the second triangle.

The most effective method for proving two overlapping triangles congruent is to draw the two triangles separated. Separate the two triangles and label all of the vertices using the labels from the original overlapping figures. Once the separation is complete, apply one of the congruence shortcuts: SSS, ASA, SAS, AAS, or HL.

Triangle Theorem Proofs:

Example:

Prove the SAS Theorem that says:

$$\angle A \cong \angle D, \overline{AB} \cong \overline{DE} \text{ and } \overline{AC} \cong \overline{DF}, \text{ then } \triangle ABC \cong \triangle DEF$$

Move △ABC such that point A coincides with point D, and line AB coincides with DE.

Point B will coincide with E, because AB ≅ DE.

Also, segment AC will coincide with DF, because $\angle A \cong \angle D$.

Point C will coincide with F, because AC ≅ DF.

Line BC will coincide with EF, because two lines cannot enclose a space.

Finally, side BC is congruent to side EF, because the lines and endpoints of each coincide.

Therefore, $\angle B \cong \angle E$, $\angle C \cong \angle F$, and △ABC ≅ △DEF

There is an implicit assumption that says that for any two lines L and L', it is always possible to "move" line L so that it coincides with L'.

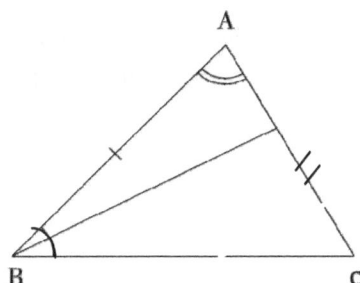
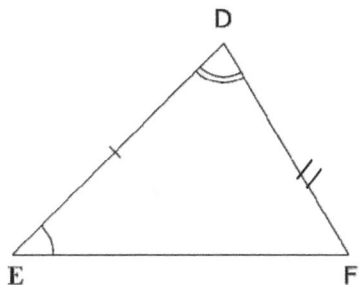

Two triangles can be proven congruent by comparing pairs of appropriate congruent corresponding parts.

SSS POSTULATE

If three sides of one triangle are congruent to three sides of another triangle, then the two triangles are congruent.

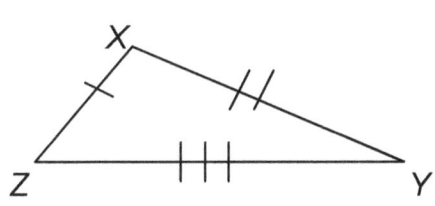
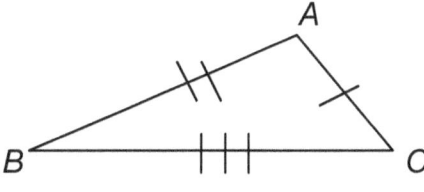

Since $AB \cong XY$, $BC \cong YZ$ and $AC \cong XZ$, then $\triangle ABC \cong \triangle XYZ$.

Example: Given isosceles triangle ABC with D the midpoint of base AC, prove the two triangles formed by AD are congruent.

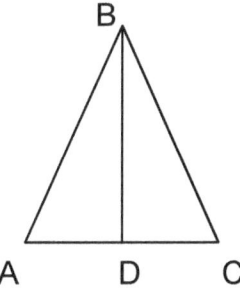

Proof:
1. Isosceles triangle ABC,
   D midpoint of base AC — Given
2. $AB \cong BC$ — An isosceles $\triangle$ has two congruent sides
3. $AD \cong DC$ — Midpoint divides a triangle into two equal parts
4. $BD \cong BD$ — Reflexive
5. $\triangle ABD \cong \triangle ACD$ — SSS

ASA POSTULATE

If two angles and the included side of one triangle are congruent to two angles and the included side of another triangle, the triangles are congruent.

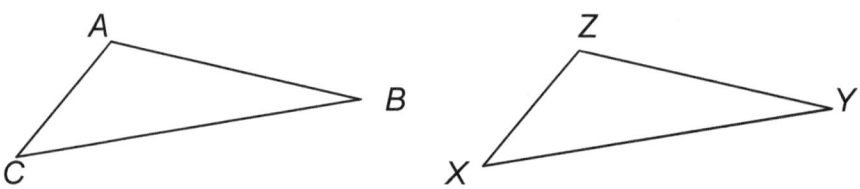

$\angle A \cong \angle X$, $\angle B \cong \angle Y$, $AB \cong XY$ then $\triangle ABC \cong \triangle XYZ$ by ASA

<u>Example 1</u>: Given two right triangles with one leg of each measuring 6 cm and the adjacent angle 37°, prove the triangles are congruent.

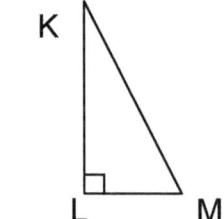

1. Right triangles *ABC* and *KLM*
   $AB = KL = 6$ cm
   $\angle A = \angle K = 37°$
	Given

2. $AB \cong KL$ $\angle A \cong \angle K$	Figures with the same measure are congruent
3. $\angle B \cong \angle L$	All right angles are congruent.
4. $\triangle ABC \cong \triangle KLM$	ASA

<u>Example 2</u>:
What method would you use to prove the triangles congruent?

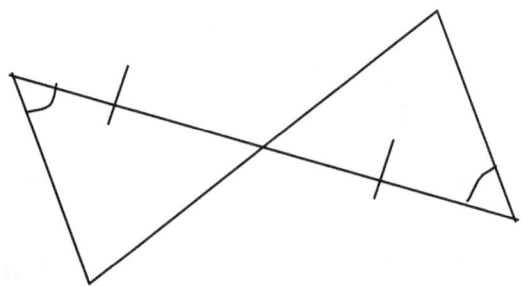

ASA because vertical angles are congruent.

AAS THEOREM

If two angles and a non-included side of one triangle are congruent to the corresponding parts of another triangle, then the triangles are congruent.

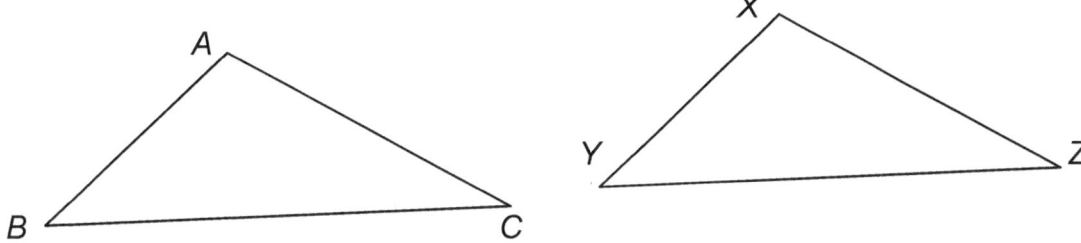

$\angle B \cong \angle Y$, $\angle C \cong \angle Z$, $AC \cong XZ$, then $\triangle ABC \cong \triangle XYZ$ by AAS.

We can derive this theorem because if two angles of the triangles are congruent, then the third angle must also be congruent. Therefore, we can use the ASA postulate.

HL THEOREM

If the hypotenuse and a leg of one right triangle are congruent to the corresponding parts of another right triangle, the triangles are congruent.

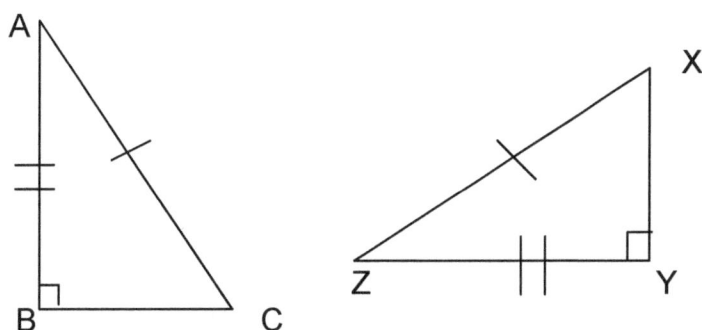

Since $\angle B$ and $\angle Y$ are right angles and $AC \cong XZ$ (hypotenuse of each triangle), $AB \cong YZ$ (corresponding leg of each triangle), then $\triangle ABC \cong \triangle XYZ$ by HL.

Example: What method would you use to prove the triangles congruent?

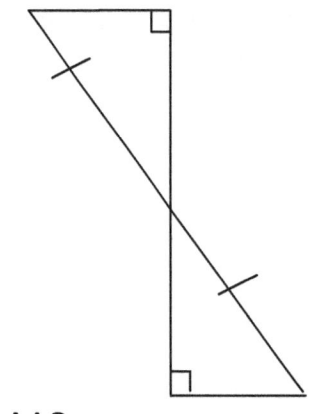

AAS

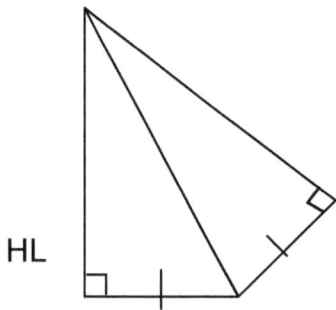

HL

Plane Euclidean Geometry (SMR 2.2)

Skill b. Understand, apply, and justify properties of triangles (e.g., the Exterior Angle Theorem, concurrence theorems, trigonometric ratios, Triangle Inequality, Law of Sines, Law of Cosines, the Pythagorean Theorem and its converse)

Trigonometric ratios: Exterior Angles
Two adjacent angles form a linear pair when they have a common side and their remaining sides form a straight angle. Angles in a linear pair are supplementary. An exterior angle of a triangle forms a linear pair with an angle of the triangle.

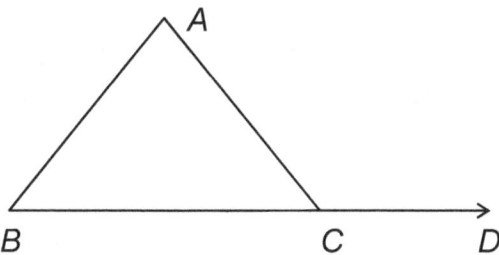

$\angle ACD$ is an exterior angle of triangle ABC, forming a linear pair with $\angle ACB$.

The measure of an exterior angle of a triangle is equal to the sum of the measures of the two non-adjacent interior angles.

Example:
In triangle ABC, the measure of $\angle A$ is twice the measure of $\angle B$. $\angle C$ is $30°$ more than their sum. Find the measure of the exterior angle formed at $\angle C$.

$$\begin{aligned}
\text{Let } x &= \text{the measure of } \angle B \\
2x &= \text{the measure of } \angle A \\
x + 2x + 30 &= \text{the measure of } \angle C \\
x + 2x + x + 2x + 30 &= 180 \\
6x + 30 &= 180 \\
6x &= 150 \\
x &= 25 \\
2x &= 50
\end{aligned}$$

It is not necessary to find the measure of the third angle, since the exterior angle equals the sum of the opposite interior angles. Thus the exterior angle at $\angle C$ measures $75°$.

Trigonometric ratios: Right Triangles

Given triangle ABC, the adjacent side and opposite side can be identified for each angle A and B.

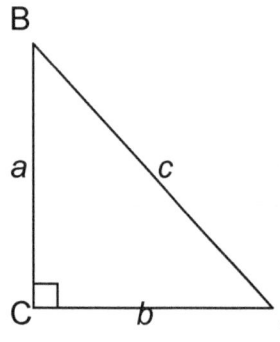

Looking at angle A, it can be determined that side *b* is adjacent to angle A and side *a* is opposite angle A.

If we now look at angle B, we see that side *a* is adjacent to angle B and side *b* is opposite angle B.

The longest side (opposite the 90 degree angle is always called the hypotenuse.

The basic trigonometric ratios are listed below:

Sine = opposite/hypotenuse   Cosine = adjacent/hypotenuse   Tangent = opposite/adjacent

Example:

1. Use triangle ABC to find the sin, cos and tan for angle A.

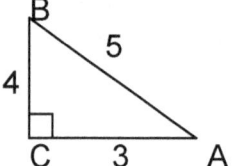

Sin A = 4/5
Cos A = 3/5
Tan A = 4/3

Use the basic trigonometric ratios of sine, cosine and tangent to solve for the missing sides of right triangles when given at least one of the acute angles.

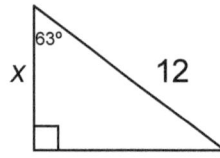

In the triangle ABC, an acute angle of 63 degrees and the length of the hypotenuse (12). The missing side is the one adjacent to the given angle.

The appropriate trigonometric ratio to use would be cosine since we are looking for the adjacent side and we have the length of the hypotenuse.

Cos*x* = adjacent/hypotenuse   1. Write formula.

$\cos 63 = \dfrac{x}{12}$ 2. Substitute known values.

$x = 5.448$ 3. Solve.

A **right triangle** is a triangle with one right angle. The side opposite the right angle is called the **hypotenuse**. The other two sides are the **legs**. An **altitude** is a line drawn from one vertex, perpendicular to the opposite side.

When an altitude is drawn to the hypotenuse of a right triangle, then the two triangles formed are similar to the original triangle and to each other.

Example:

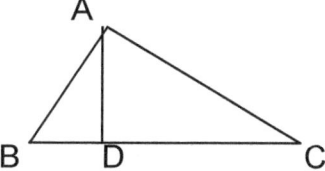

Given right triangle ABC with right angle at A, altitude AD drawn to hypotenuse BD at D.

△ABC ~ △ABD ~ △ACD The triangles formed are similar to each other and to the original right triangle.

If a, b and c are positive numbers such that $\dfrac{a}{b} = \dfrac{b}{c}$ then b is called the **geometric mean** between a and c.

Example:
Find the geometric mean between 6 and 30.

$$\dfrac{6}{x} = \dfrac{x}{30}$$
$$x^2 = 180$$
$$x = \sqrt{180} = \sqrt{36 \cdot 5} = 6\sqrt{5}$$

The geometric mean is significant when the altitude is drawn to the hypotenuse of a right triangle.

The length of the altitude is the geometric mean between each segment of the hypotenuse,
    and
Each leg is the geometric mean between the hypotenuse and the segment of the hypotenuse that is adjacent to the leg.

Example:

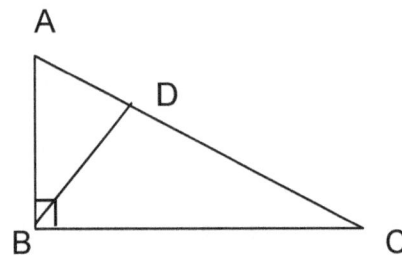

△ABC is a right △
∠ABC is a right ∠
AB = 6
AC = 12
Find AD, CD, BD, and BC

$\dfrac{12}{6} = \dfrac{6}{AD}$ $\dfrac{3}{BD} = \dfrac{BD}{9}$ $\dfrac{12}{BC} = \dfrac{BC}{9}$

12(AD) = 36 $(BD)^2 = 27$ $(BC)^2 = 108$

AD = 3
BD = $\sqrt{27}$ = $\sqrt{9 \cdot 3}$ = $3\sqrt{3}$
BC = $6\sqrt{3}$
CD = 12 - 3 = 9

The Pythagorean theorem states that the square of the length of the hypotenuse is equal to the sum of the squares of the lengths of the legs. Symbolically, this is stated as:

$$c^2 = a^2 + b^2$$

Given the right triangle below, find the missing side.

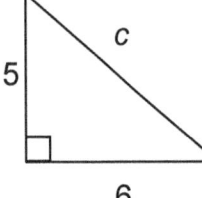

$c^2 = a^2 + b^2$ 1. write formula
$c^2 = 5^2 + 6^2$ 2. substitute known values
$c^2 = 61$ 3. take square root
$c = \sqrt{61}$ or 7.81 4. solve

FOUNDATION LEV. MATH.

The Converse of the Pythagorean Theorem states that if the square of one side of a triangle is equal to the sum of the squares of the other two sides, then the triangle is a right triangle.

Example:
Given $\triangle XYZ$, with sides measuring 12, 16 and 20 cm. Is this a right triangle?

$$c^2 = a^2 + b^2$$
$$20^2 \;?\; 12^2 + 16^2$$
$$400 \;?\; 144 + 256$$
$$400 = 400$$

Yes, the triangle is a right triangle.

This theorem can be expanded to determine if triangles are obtuse or acute.

If the square of the longest side of a triangle is greater than the sum of the squares of the other two sides, then the triangle is an obtuse triangle.
and
If the square of the longest side of a triangle is less than the sum of the squares of the other two sides, then the triangle is an acute triangle.

Example:
Given $\triangle LMN$ with sides measuring 7, 12, and 14 inches. Is the triangle right, acute, or obtuse?

$$14^2 \;?\; 7^2 + 12^2$$
$$196 \;?\; 49 + 144$$
$$196 > 193$$

Therefore, the triangle is obtuse.

Given the special right triangles below, we can find the lengths of other special right triangles.

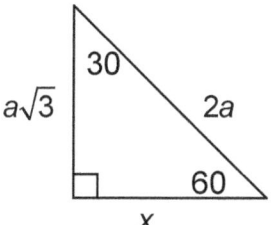
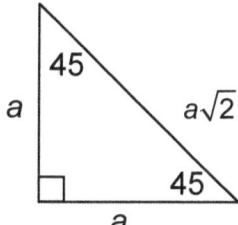

Example:

1. if $8 = a\sqrt{2}$ then $a = 8/\sqrt{2}$ or 5.657

2. if $7 = a$ then $c = a\sqrt{2} = 7\sqrt{2}$ or 9.899

3. if $2a = 10$ then $a = 5$ and $x = a\sqrt{3} = 5\sqrt{3}$ or 8.66

Plane Euclidean Geometry (SMR 2.2)

Skill c. Understand, apply, and justify properties of polygons and circles from an advanced standpoint (e.g., derive the area formulas for regular polygons and circles from the area of a triangle)

Polygons:

A **polygon** is a simple closed figure composed of line segments. In a **regular polygon** all sides are the same length and all angles are the same measure.

A **quadrilateral** is a polygon with four sides.
The sum of the measures of the angles of a convex quadrilateral is 360°.

A **trapezoid** is a quadrilateral with exactly <u>one</u> pair of parallel sides.

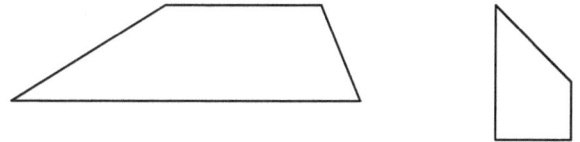

In an **isosceles trapezoid**, the non-parallel sides are congruent.

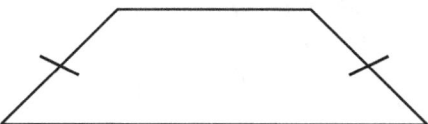

A **parallelogram** is a quadrilateral with <u>two</u> pairs of parallel sides.

A **rectangle** is a parallelogram with a right angle.

A **rhombus** is a parallelogram with all sides equal length.

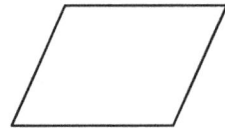

A **square** is a rectangle with all sides equal length.

Perimeter and area of polygons

The **perimeter** of any polygon is the sum of the lengths of the sides.

The **area** of a polygon is the number of square units covered by the figure or the space that a figure occupies.

FIGURE	AREA FORMULA	PERIMETER FORMULA
Rectangle	LW	$2(L+W)$
Triangle	$\frac{1}{2}bh$	$a+b+c$
Parallelogram	bh	sum of lengths of sides
Trapezoid	$\frac{1}{2}h(a+b)$	sum of lengths of sides

Example: A farmer has a piece of land shaped as shown below. He wishes to fence this land at an estimated cost of $25 per linear foot. What is the total cost of fencing this property to the nearest foot?

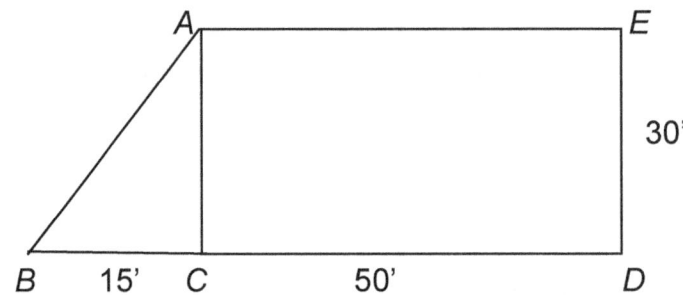

From the right triangle ABC, AC = 30 and BC = 15.

Since $(AB) = (AC)^2 + (BC)^2$
$(AB) = (30)^2 + (15)^2$

So $\sqrt{(AB)^2} = AB = \sqrt{1125} = 33.5410$ feet

To the nearest foot AB = 34 feet.
Perimeter of the piece of land is = $AB + BC + CD + DE + EA$

= 34 + 15 + 50 + 30 + 50 = 179 feet

Cost of fencing = $25 x 179 = $4,475.00

Example: Find the area of a parallelogram whose base is 6.5 cm and the height of the altitude to that base is 3.7 cm.

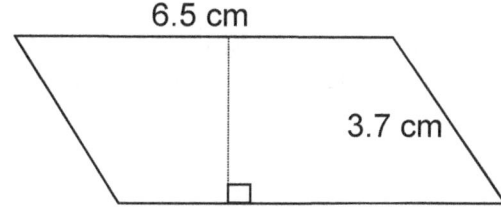

$A_{parallelogram}$ = bh
= (3.7 cm)(6.5 cm)
= 24.05 cm²

Example: Find the area of the triangle below.

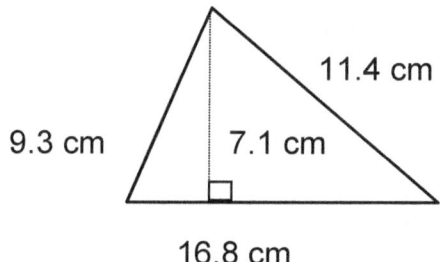

$A_{triangle}$ = ½ bh
= (0.5)(16.8 cm)(7.1 cm)
= 59.64 cm²

Example: Find the area of the trapezoid below.

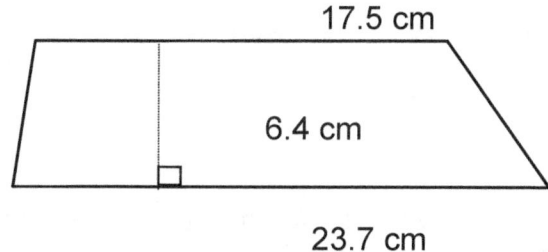

The area of a trapezoid equals one-half the sum of the bases times the altitude.

$$A_{trapezoid} = \tfrac{1}{2}h(b_1 + b_2)$$
$$= 0.5 \,(6.4 \text{ cm})\,(17.5 \text{ cm} + 23.7 \text{ cm})$$
$$= 131.84 \text{ cm}^2$$

The sum of the measures of the **interior angles** of a polygon can be determined using the following formula, where n represents the number of angles in the polygon.

$$\text{Sum of } \angle s = 180(n-2)$$

The measure of each angle of a regular polygon can be found by dividing the sum of the measures by the number of angles.

$$\text{Measure of } \angle = \frac{180(n-2)}{n}$$

Example: Find the measure of each angle of a regular octagon. Since an octagon has eight sides, each angle equals:

$$\frac{180(8-2)}{8} = \frac{180(6)}{8} = 135°$$

The sum of the measures of the **exterior angles** of a polygon, taken one angle at each vertex, equals 360°.

The measure of each exterior angle of a regular polygon can be determined using the following formula, where n represents the number of angles in the polygon.

Measure of exterior $\angle$ of regular polygon

$$= 180 - \frac{180(n-2)}{n} \quad \text{or, more simply} = \frac{360}{n}$$

Example: Find the measure of the interior and exterior angles of a regular pentagon.

Since a pentagon has five sides, each exterior angle measures:

$$\frac{360}{5} = 72°$$

Since each exterior angles is supplementary to its interior angle, the interior angle measures 180 - 72 or 108°.

A **parallelogram** exhibits these properties.

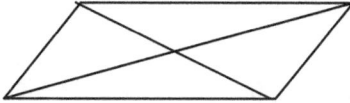

The diagonals bisect each other.
Each diagonal divides the parallelogram into two congruent triangles.
Both pairs of opposite sides are congruent.
Both pairs of opposite angles are congruent.
Two adjacent angles are supplementary.

Example 1:
Find the measures of the other three angles of a parallelogram if one angle measures 38°.

Since opposite angles are equal, there are two angles measuring 38°.

Since adjacent angles are supplementary, 180 - 38 = 142 so the other two angles measure 142° each.

$$\begin{array}{r} 38 \\ 38 \\ 142 \\ +\ 142 \\ \hline 360 \end{array}$$

Example 2:
The measures of two adjacent angles of a parallelogram are $3x + 40$ and $x + 70$.
Find the measures of each angle.

$$2(3x + 40) + 2(x + 70) = 360$$
$$6x + 80 + 2x + 140 = 360$$
$$8x + 220 = 360$$
$$8x = 140$$
$$x = 17.5$$
$$3x + 40 = 92.5$$
$$x + 70 = 87.5$$

Thus the angles measure 92.5°, 92.5°, 87.5°, and 87.5°.
Since a **rectangle** is a special type of parallelogram, it exhibits all the properties of a parallelogram. All the angles of a rectangle are right angles because of congruent opposite angles. Additionally, the diagonals of a rectangle are congruent.

A **rhombus** also has all the properties of a parallelogram. Additionally, its diagonals are perpendicular to each other and they bisect its angles.

A **square** has all the properties of a rectangle and a rhombus.

Example 1:

True or false?
All squares are rhombuses.	True
All parallelograms are rectangles.	False - some parallelograms are rectangles
All rectangles are parallelograms.	True
Some rhombuses are squares.	True
Some rectangles are trapezoids.	False - only one pair of parallel sides
All quadrilaterals are parallelograms.	False - some quadrilaterals are parallelograms
Some squares are rectangles.	False - all squares are rectangles
Some parallelograms are rhombuses.	True

Example 2:
In rhombus $ABCD$ side $AB = 3x - 7$ and side $CD = x + 15$. Find the length of each side.
Since all the sides are the same length, $3x - 7 = x + 15$
$$2x = 22$$
$$x = 11$$
Since $3(11) - 7 = 25$ and $11 + 15 = 25$, each side measures 25 units.

A trapezoid is a quadrilateral with exactly one pair of parallel sides. A trapezoid is different from a parallelogram because a parallelogram has two pairs of parallel sides.

The two parallel sides of a trapezoid are called the bases, and the two non-parallel sides are called the legs. If the two legs are the same length, then the trapezoid is called isosceles.

The segment connecting the two midpoints of the legs is called the median. The median has the following two properties.

The median is parallel to the two bases.

The length of the median is equal to one-half the sum of the length of the two bases.

Example: **trapezoid** is a quadrilateral with exactly <u>one</u> pair of parallel sides.

In an **isosceles trapezoid**, the non-parallel sides are congruent.

An isosceles trapezoid has the following properties:

The diagonals of an isosceles trapezoid are congruent.
The base angles of an isosceles trapezoid are congruent.

Example:

An isosceles trapezoid has a diagonal of 10 and a base angle measure of 30°. Find the measure of the other 3 angles.

Based on the properties of trapezoids, the measure of the other base angle is 30° and the measure of the other diagonal is 10.

The other two angles have a measure of:

$$360 = 30(2) + 2x$$
$$x = 150°$$ The other two angles measure 150° each.

Properties of Triangles:

The segment joining the midpoints of two sides of a triangle is called a **median**. All triangles have three medians. Each median has the following two properties.

A median is parallel to the third side of the triangle.
The length of a median is one-half the length of the third side of the triangle.

A median is a segment that connects a vertex to the midpoint of the side opposite from that vertex. Every triangle has exactly three medians.

An altitude is a segment that extends from one vertex and is perpendicular to the side opposite that vertex. In some cases, the side opposite from the vertex used will need to be extended in order for the altitude to form a perpendicular to the opposite side. The length of the altitude is used when referring to the height of the triangle.

If the three segments that bisect the three angles of a triangle are drawn, the segments will all intersect in a single point. This point is equidistant from all three sides of the triangle. Recall that the distance from a point to a side is measured along the perpendicular from the point to the side.

If two planes are parallel and a third plane intersects the first two, then the three planes will intersect in two lines, which are also parallel.

Given a line and a point that is not on the line but is in the same plane, then there is exactly one line through the point that is parallel to the given line and exactly one line through the point that is perpendicular to the given line.

If three or more segments intersect in a single point, the point is called a **point of concurrency**.

The following sets of special segments all intersect in points of concurrency.

1. Angle Bisectors
2. Medians
3. Altitudes
4. Perpendicular Bisectors

The points of concurrency can lie inside the triangle, outside the triangle, or on one of the sides of the triangle. The following table summarizes this information.

Possible Location(s) of the Points of Concurrency

	Inside the Triangle	Outside the Triangle	On the Triangle
Angle Bisectors	X		
Medians	X		
Altitudes	X	X	x
Perpendicular Bisectors	X	X	x

Circles:

The distance around a circle is the **circumference**. The ratio of the circumference to the diameter is represented by the Greek letter pi. $\pi \sim 3.14$.

The circumference of a circle is found by the formula $C = 2\pi r$ or $C = \pi d$ where r is the radius of the circle and d is the diameter.

The **area** of a circle is found by the formula $A = \pi r^2$.

Example: Find the circumference and area of a circle whose radius is 7 meters.

$C = 2\pi r$
$= 2(3.14)(7 \text{ m})$
$= 43.96 \text{ m}$

$A = \pi r^2$
$= 3.14(7 \text{ m})(7 \text{ m})$
$= 153.86 \text{ m}^2$

The equation of a circle with its center at (h, k) and a radius r units is:

$$(x - h)^2 + (y - k)^2 = r^2$$

Examples:

1. Given the equation $x^2 + y^2 = 9$, find the center and the radius of the circle. Then graph the equation.

First, writing the equation in standard circle form gives:

$$(x-0)^2 + (y-0)^2 = 3^2$$

therefore, the center is (0,0) and the radius is 3 units.

Sketch the circle:

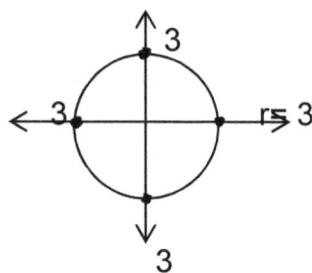

2. Given the equation $x^2 + y^2 - 3x + 8y - 20 = 0$, find the center and the radius. Then graph the circle.

First, write the equation in standard circle form by completing the square for both variables.

$x^2 + y^2 - 3x + 8y - 20 = 0$ 1. Complete the squares.

$(x^2 - 3x + 9/4) + (y^2 + 8y + 16) = 20 + 9/4 + 16$

$(x - 3/2)^2 + (y + 4)^2 = 153/4$

The center is $(3/2, ^-4)$ and the radius is $\dfrac{\sqrt{153}}{2}$ or $\dfrac{3\sqrt{17}}{2}$.

Graph the circle.

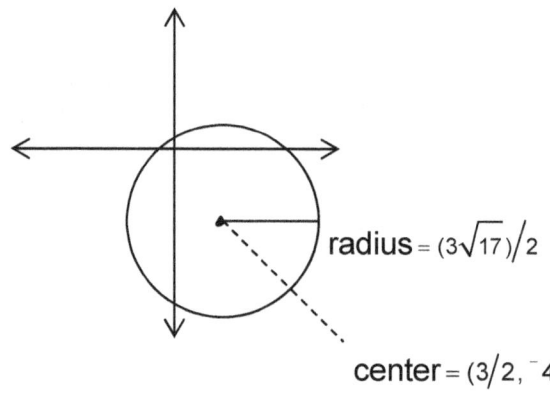

To **write the equation** given the center and the radius use the standard form of the equation of a circle:

$$(x-h)^2 + (y-k)^2 = r^2$$

Examples:
Given the center and radius, write the equation of the circle.

1. Center $(^-1, 4)$; radius 11

   $(x-h)^2 + (y-k)^2 = r^2$ 1. Write standard equation.

   $(x-(^-1))^2 + (y-(^-4))^2 = 11^2$ 2. Substitute.

   $(x+1)^2 + (y-4)^2 = 121$ 3. Simplify.

2. Center $(\sqrt{3}, ^-1/2)$; radius $= 5\sqrt{2}$

   $(x-h)^2 + (y-k)^2 = r^2$ 1. Write standard equation.

   $(x-\sqrt{3})^2 + (y-(^-1/2))^2 = (5\sqrt{2})^2$ 2. Substitute.

   $(x-\sqrt{3})^2 + (y+1/2)^2 = 50$ 3. Simplify.

If two circles have radii that are in a ratio of $a:b$, then the following ratios are also true for the circles.

The diameters are also in the ratio of $a:b$.
The circumferences are also in the ratio $a:b$.
The areas are in the ratio $a^2:b^2$, or the ratio of the areas is the square of the ratios of the radii.

A circle is inscribed in a triangle if the three sides of the triangle are each tangent to the circle. The center of an inscribed circle is called the incenter of the triangle. To find the incenter, draw the three angle bisectors of the triangle. The point of concurrency of the angle bisectors is the incenter or center of the inscribed circle. Each triangle has only one inscribed circle.

A circle is circumscribed about a triangle if the three vertices of the triangle are all located on the circle. The center of a circumscribed circle is called the circumcenter of the triangle. To find the circumcenter, draw the three perpendicular bisectors of the sides of the triangle. The point of concurrency of the perpendicular bisectors is the circumcenter or the center of the circumscribing circle. Each triangle has only one circumscribing circle.

A median is a segment that connects a vertex to the midpoint of the side opposite that vertex. Every triangle has three medians. The point of concurrency of the three medians is called the **centroid**.

The centroid divides each median into two segments whose lengths are always in the ratio of 1:2. The distance from the vertex to the centroid is always twice the distance from the centroid to the midpoint of the side opposite the vertex.

Circle major and minor arcs:

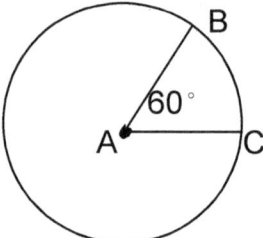

Central angle BAC = 60°
Minor arc BC = 60°
Major arc BDC = 360 − 60 = 300°

If you draw **two radii** in a circle, the angle they form with the center as the vertex is a central angle. The piece of the circle "inside" the angle is an arc. Just like a central angle, an arc can have any degree measure from 0 to 360. The measure of an arc is equal to the measure of the central angle that forms the arc. Since a diameter forms a semicircle and the measure of a straight angle like a diameter is 180°, the measure of a semicircle is also 180°.

Given two points on a circle, the two points form two different arcs. Except in the case of semicircles, one of the two arcs will always be greater than 180° and the other will be less than 180°. The arc less than 180° is a minor arc and the arc greater than 180° is a major arc.

Examples:
1.

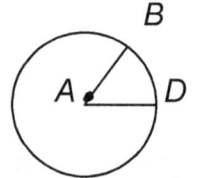

$m\angle BAD = 45°$
What is the measure of the major arc BD?

∠BAD = minor arc BD

The measure of the central angle 45° = minor arc BD is the same as the measure of the arc it forms.

360 − 45 = major arc BD

A major and minor arc always add to 360°.

315° = major arc BD

2.

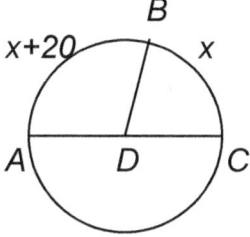

$\overline{AC}$ is a diameter of circle D. What is the measure of $\angle BDC$?

$m\angle ADB + m\angle BDC = 180°$

$x + 20 + x = 180$

$2x + 20 = 180$

$2x = 160$

$x = 80$

minor arc $BC = 80°$

$m\angle BDC = 80°$

A diameter forms a semicircle that has a measure of $180°$.

A central angle has the same measure as the arc it forms.

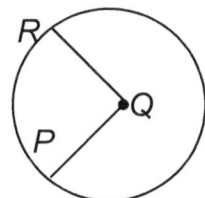

$$\frac{\angle PQR}{360°} = \frac{\text{length of arc } RP}{\text{circumference of } \angle Q} = \frac{\text{area of sector } PQR}{\text{area of } \angle Q}$$

While an arc has a measure associated to the degree measure of a central angle, it also has a length that is a fraction of the circumference of the circle.

For each central angle and its associated arc, there is a sector of the circle that resembles a pie piece. The area of such a sector is a fraction of the area of the circle.

The fractions used for the area of a sector and length of its associated arc are both equal to the ratio of the central angle to 360°.

Examples:

1.

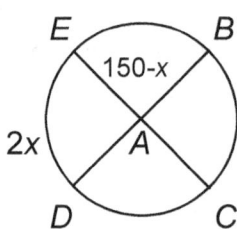

$2x + 150 - x = 180$

$x + 150 = 180$

$x = 30$

Arc $ED = 2(30) = 60°$

$\dfrac{60}{360} = \dfrac{\text{arc length } ED}{2\pi 4}$

$\dfrac{1}{6} = \dfrac{\text{arc length}}{8\pi}$

$\dfrac{8\pi}{6} = \text{arc length}$

arc length $ED = \dfrac{4\pi}{3}$ cm

⊙A has a radius of 4 cm. What is the length of arc ED?

Arc BC and arc DC make a semicircle.

The ratio 60° to 360° is equal to the ratio of arch length ED to the circumference of ⊙A.

Cross multiply and solve for the arc length.

2.

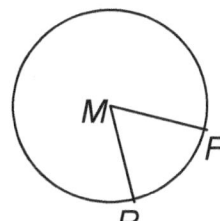

The radius of ⊙M is 3 cm. The length of arc PF is 2π cm. What is the area M of sector MPF?

Circumference of ⊙$M = 2\pi(3) = 6\pi$

Area of ⊙$M = \pi(3)^2 = 9\pi$

$\dfrac{\text{area of } MPF}{9\pi} = \dfrac{2\pi}{6\pi}$

$\dfrac{\text{area of } MPF}{9\pi} = \dfrac{1}{3}$

area of $MPF = \dfrac{9\pi}{3}$

area of $MPF = 3\pi$

Find the circumference and area of the circle.

The ratio of the sector area to the circle area is the same as the arc length to the circumference.

Solve for the area of the sector.

A **tangent line** intersects a circle in exactly one point. If a radius is drawn to that point, the radius will be perpendicular to the tangent.

A **chord** is a segment with endpoints on the circle. If a radius or diameter is perpendicular to a chord, the radius will cut the chord into two equal parts and vice-versa.

If **two chords** in the same circle have the same length, the two chords will have arcs that are the same length, and the two chords will be equidistant from the center of the circle. Distance from the center to a chord is measured by finding the length of a segment from the center perpendicular to the chord.

Examples:

1.

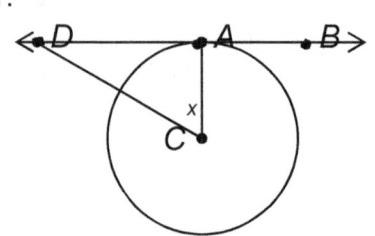

$\overrightarrow{DB}$ is tangent to $\angle C$ at A.
$m\angle ADC = 40°$ Find x.

$\overline{AC} \perp \overrightarrow{DB}$ A radius is $\perp$ to a tangent at the point of tangency.

$m\angle DAC = 90°$ Two segments that are $\perp$ form a 90° angle.

$40 + 90 + x = 180$ The sum of the angles of a triangle is 180°.

$x = 50°$ Solve for x.

2.

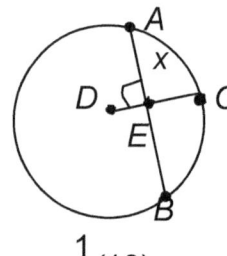

$\overline{CD}$ is a radius and $\overline{CD} \perp$ chord $\overline{AB}$.
$\overline{AB} = 10$. Find x.

$x = \dfrac{1}{2}(10)$

$x = 5$ If a radius is $\perp$ to a chord, the radius bisects the chord.

X=5

Angles with their vertices on the circle:

An inscribed angle is an angle whose vertex is on the circle. Such an angle could be formed by two chords, two diameters, two secants, or a secant and a tangent. An inscribed angle has one arc of the circle in its interior. The measure of the inscribed angle is one-half the measure of this intercepted arc. If two inscribed angles intercept the same arc, the two angles are congruent (i.e. their measures are equal). If an inscribed angle intercepts an entire semicircle, the angle is a right angle.

Angles with their vertices in a circle's interior:

When two chords intersect inside a circle, two sets of vertical angles are formed. Each set of vertical angles intercepts two arcs that are across from each other. The measure of an angle formed by two chords in a circle is equal to one-half the sum of the angle intercepted by the angle and the arc intercepted by its vertical angle.

Angles with their vertices in a circle's exterior:

If an angle has its vertex outside of the circle and each side of the circle intersects the circle, then the angle contains two different arcs. The measure of the angle is equal to one-half the difference of the two arcs.

Examples:

1.

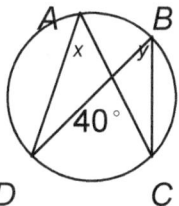

Find x and y.

$m\angle DAC = \frac{1}{2}(40) = 20°$

$\angle DAC$ and $\angle DBC$ are both inscribed angles, so each one has a measure equal to one-half the measure of arc DC.

$m\angle DBC = \frac{1}{2}(40) = 20°$

$x = 20°$ and $y = 20°$

Intersecting chords:

If two chords intersect inside a circle, each chord is divided into two smaller segments. The product of the lengths of the two segments formed from one chord equals the product of the lengths of the two segments formed from the other chord.

Intersecting tangent segments:

If two tangent segments intersect outside of a circle, the two segments have the same length.

Intersecting secant segments:

If two secant segments intersect outside a circle, a portion of each segment will lie inside the circle and a portion (called the exterior segment) will lie outside the circle. The product of the length of one secant segment and the length of its exterior segment equals the product of the length of the other secant segment and the length of its exterior segment.

Tangent segments intersecting secant segments:

If a tangent segment and a secant segment intersect outside a circle, the square of the length of the tangent segment equals the product of the length of the secant segment and its exterior segment.

Examples:

1.

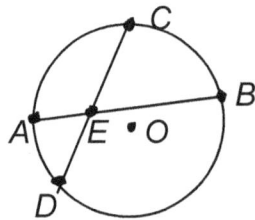

$\overline{AB}$ and $\overline{CD}$ are chords.
CE=10, ED=x, AE=5, EB=4

$(AE)(EB) = (CE)(ED)$

$5(4) = 10x$

$20 = 10x$

$x = 2$

Since the chords intersect in the circle, the products of the segment pieces are equal.

Solve for x.

2.

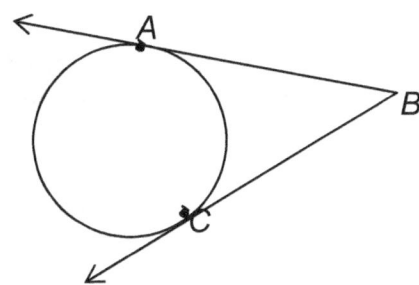

$\overline{AB}$ and $\overline{CD}$ are chords.
$\overline{AB} = x^2 + x - 2$
$\overline{CB} = 5 - 3x - x^2$
find the length of
$\overline{AB}$ and $\overline{BC}$

$\overline{AB} = x^2 + x - 2$
$\overline{BC} = x^2 - 3x + 5$ Given

$\overline{AB} = \overline{BC}$ Intersecting tangents are equal.

$x^2 + x - 2 = x^2 - 3x + 5$ Set the expression equal and solve.

$4x = 7$
$x = 1.75$ Substitute and solve.

$(1.75)^2 + 1.75 - 2 = \overline{AB}$
$\overline{AB} = \overline{BC} = 2.81$

Loci:
A locus is the set of all points that satisfy a given condition. The solution to a locus problem is both a figure showing the locus and a statement or equation that names the locus and defines its position.

Example:

What is the locus of points 6 cm from a fixed point (0,0) in a plane?

1. Draw figure.

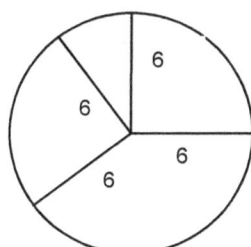

2. Write statement to name locus and define its position.

The locus is a circle with (0,0) as the center and a radius of 6 centimeters. The equation of this circle would be $x^2 + y^2 = 36$.

TEACHER CERTIFICATION STUDY GUIDE

Plane Euclidean Geometry (SMR 2.2)

Skill d. **Justify and perform the classical constructions (e.g., angle bisector, perpendicular bisector, replicating shapes, regular n-gons for n equal to 3, 4, 5, 6, and 8)**

Classical construction refers to the use of a ruler and compass for creating angles, hexagons, circles, pentagons, etc. Construction of a regular pentagon, for example, can be accomplished using only a compass and ruler: make a circle with your compass, use the ruler to draw a line through the center of the circle (diameter). Then using compass and ruler, draw a vertical perpendicular line to the diameter (a radii). Next, using the same 2 tools, find the midpoint between point B and the center, point C, of the circle and draw another line from the midpoint of $\overline{BC}$ to point D. Next bisect $\angle a$ in half to a point on $\overline{DC}$.

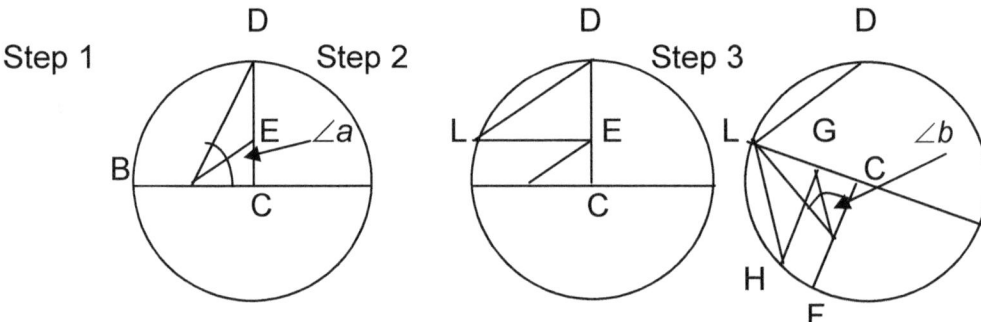

In Step 2, draw a line from point E to the edge of the circle that is parallel to $\overline{BC}$ and then connect points L and D with a line- this is the first side of your regular pentagon: $\overline{LD}$. To construct the 2nd side, simply draw a line from point L through the center, point C to the other side of the circle that we'll call point F. We're going to repeat the entire process of Steps 1 and 2 to find the 2nd side of our regular pentagon: from the midpoint of $\overline{FC}$, draw a line to point L, then bisect $\angle b$ to a point on $\overline{LC}$ which we'll call point G. Once again, draw a line that is parallel to $\overline{FC}$ from point G to the circle's edge, which we'll call point H. Connect point L and point H and you have created the 2nd side of the regular pentagon. Repeat these steps until all 5 sides have been drawn and you have just created a regular pentagon (all sides equal and all angles = 108° just by using a compass and ruler!!

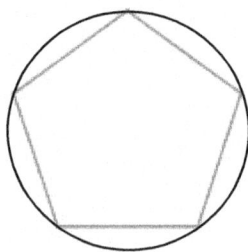

FOUNDATION LEV. MATH.

The Angle Bisector Theorem

For a triangle **ABC** let the angle bisector of angle **A** intersect side **BC** at a point **D**. The angle bisector theorem states that the ratio of the length of the line segment **BD** to the length of segment **DC** is equal to the ratio of the length of side **AB** to the length of side **AC**.

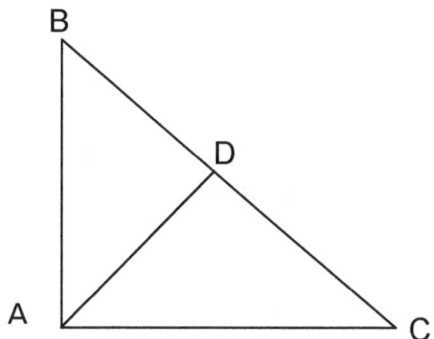

Classical Construction of an Angle Bisector

To **bisect a given angle** such as angle *FUZ*, follow these steps.

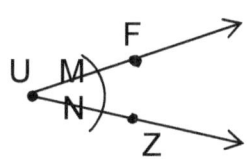

1. Swing an arc of any length with its center at point U. This arc will intersect rays *UF* and *UZ* at M and N.

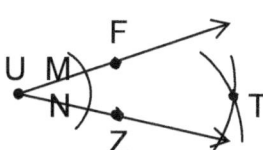

2. Open the compass to any length and swing one arc from point M and another arc of the same radius from point N. These arcs will intersect in the interior or angle *FUZ* at point T.

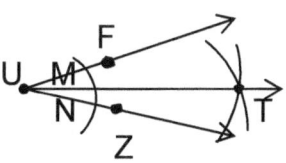

3. Connect U and T for the ray which bisects angle *FUZ*. Ray *UT* is the angle bisector of angle *FUZ*

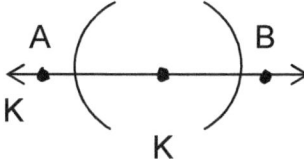

1. Swing an arc of any radius from point so that it intersects line l in two points, A and B.

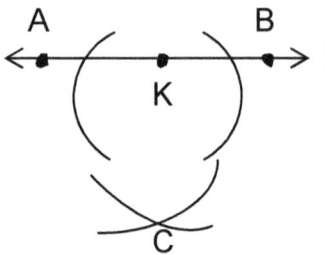

2. Open the compass to any length and swing one arc from B and another from A so that the two arcs intersect at point C.

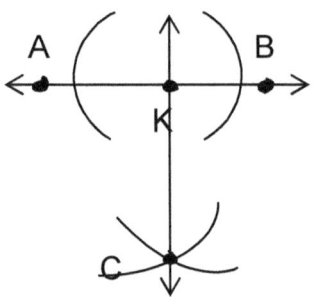

3. Connect K and C to form line KC that is perpendicular to line l.

For additional coordinate geometry proofs, go to
www.mathwarehouse.com/coordinate-geometry/

Plane Euclidean Geometry (SMR 2.2)

Skill e.   Use techniques in coordinate geometry to prove geometric theorems

By definition, a parallelogram has diagonals that bisect each other. Prove that quadrilateral $\square ABCD$ with vertices A(-3,0), B(-1,0), C(0,3) and D(2,3) is in fact a parallelogram using coordinate geometry:

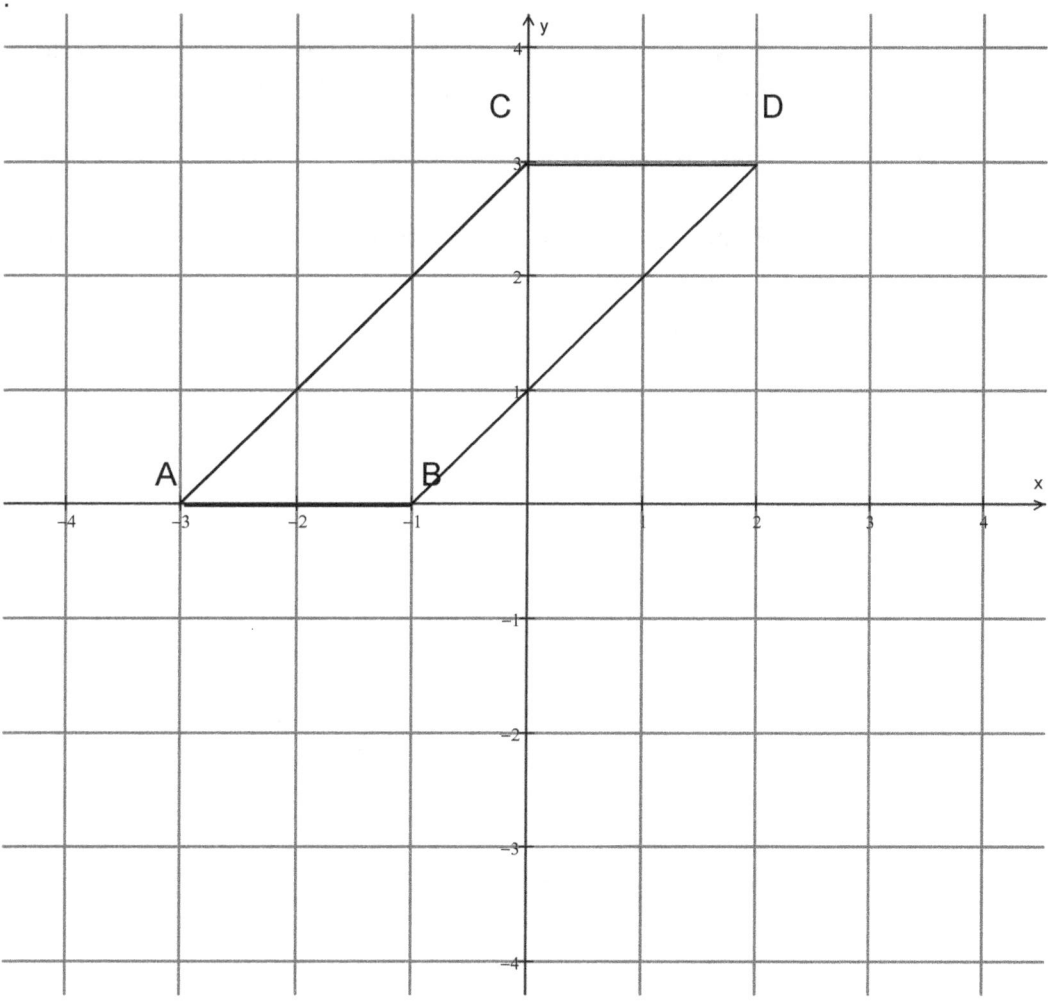

Using the midpoint formula, $(x,y) = \left(\dfrac{x_1 + x_2}{2}, \dfrac{y_1 + y_2}{2}\right)$, find the midpoints of $\overline{AD}$ and $\overline{BC}$.

The midpoint of $\overline{BC} = \left(\dfrac{-1+0}{2}, \dfrac{0+3}{2}\right) = \left(\dfrac{-1}{2}, \dfrac{3}{2}\right)$ and the midpoint of $\overline{AD} = \left(\dfrac{-3+2}{2}, \dfrac{0+3}{2}\right) = \left(\dfrac{-1}{2}, \dfrac{3}{2}\right)$ ∴ since the midpoints of the diagonals are the same, the polygon is a parallelogram.

Perpendicular Bisector Theorem: The perpendicular bisector is a line, segment, ray or plane that is perpendicular to a segment S at its midpoint such that it is the locus of all points that are equidistant from the endpoint of segment S.

Prove that $\overline{CD}$ is a perpendicular bisector to $\overline{AB}$ and therefore $\triangle ABC$:

$\triangle ABC$ is an isosceles and $\overline{CD}$ is the altitude to base $\overline{AB}$

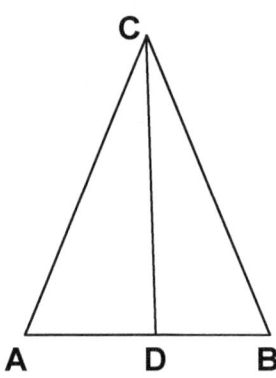

∠CDA = 90deg ($\overline{CD}$ is an altitude)

∠CDB = 90deg ($\overline{CD}$ is an altitude)

∠CDA = ∠CDB (both 90deg)

In the triangles △ADC, △BDC:

$\overline{AC} = \overline{BC}$ (△ABC isosceles)

$\overline{CD} = \overline{CD}$ (common)

∠CDA = ∠CDB (proved)

Given that triangles △ADC, △BDC are congruent (RHS).
∠DCA = ∠DCB (corresponding angles in congruent triangles)

Therefore $\overline{CD}$ bisects ∠ACB.

Three-Dimensional Geometry (SMR 2.3)

Skill a. Demonstrate an understanding of parallelism and perpendicularity of lines and planes in three dimensions

Parallelism and Perpendicularity:

The distance between two parallel lines, such as line AB and line CD as shown below is the line segment RS, the perpendicular between the two parallels.

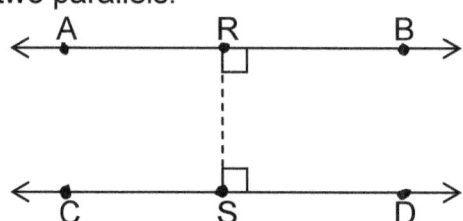

In order to accomplish the task of finding the distance from a given point to another given line the perpendicular line that intersects the point and line must be drawn and the equation of the other line written. From this information the point of intersection can be found. This point and the original point are used in the distance formula given below:

$$D = \sqrt{(x_2 - x_1)^2 + (y_2 - y_1)^2}$$

Example:
1. Given the point $(^-4, 3)$ and the line $y = 4x + 2$, find the distance from the point to the line.

   $y = 4x + 2$ 1. Find the slope of the given line by solving for y.

   $y = 4x + 2$ 2. The slope is $4/1$, the perpendicular line will have a slope of $^-1/4$.

   $y = \left(^-1/4\right)x + b$ 3. Use the new slope and the given point to find the equation of the perpendicular line.

   $3 = \left(^-1/4\right)\left(^-4\right) + b$ 4. Substitute $(^-4, 3)$ into the equation.

   $3 = 1 + b$ 5. Solve.
   $2 = b$ 6. Given the value for b, write the equation of the perpendicular line.

   $y = \left(^-1/4\right)x + 2$ 7. Write in standard form.

FOUNDATION LEV. MATH.

$x + 4y = 8$	8. Use both equations to solve by elimination to get the point of intersection.
$^-4x + y = 2$ $\underline{x + 4y = 8}$	9. Multiply the bottom row by 4.
$^-4x + y = 2$ $\underline{4x + 16y = 32}$ $17y = 34$ $y = 2$	10. Solve.
$y = 4x + 2$ $2 = 4x + 2$ $x = 0$	11. Substitute to find the x value. 12. Solve.

(0,2) is the point of intersection. Use this point on the original line and the original point to calculate the distance between them.

$D = \sqrt{(x_2 - x_1)^2 + (y_2 - y_1)^2}$ where points are (0,2) and (-4,3).

$D = \sqrt{(^-4 - 0)^2 + (3 - 2)^2}$ 1. Substitute.

$D = \sqrt{(16) + (1)}$ 2. Simplify.

$D = \sqrt{17}$

In geometry the point, line and plane are key concepts and can be discussed in relation to each other.

collinear points
are all on the same line

non-collinear points
are not on the same line

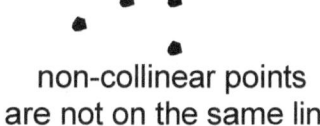

coplanar points
are on the same plane

non-coplanar points
are not on the same plane

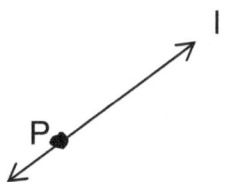

Point P is in line l
Point P is on line l
l contains P
l passes through P

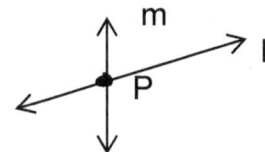 l and m intersect at P
P is the intersection of l and m

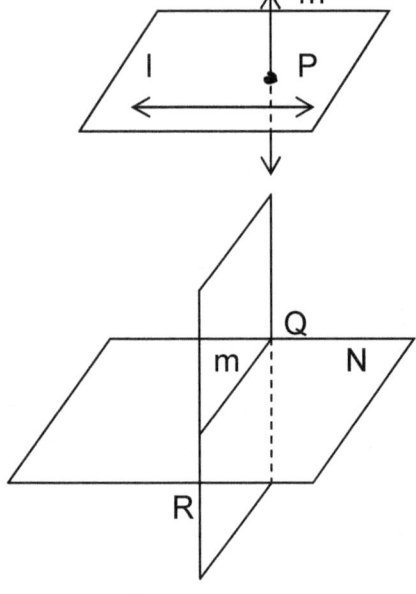

l and P are in N
N contains P and l
m intersects N at P
P is the intersection of m and N

M and N intersect at RQ
RQ is the intersection of M and N
PQ is in M and N
M and N contain PQ

Intersecting lines share a common point and intersecting planes share a common set of points or line.

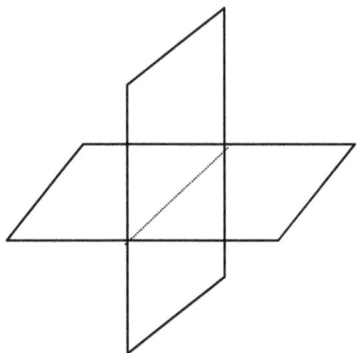

skew lines do not intersect and do not lie on the same plane.

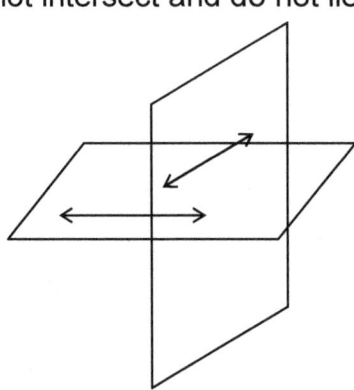

TEACHER CERTIFICATION STUDY GUIDE

Three-Dimensional Geometry (SMR 2.3)

Skill b. Understand, apply, and justify properties of three-dimensional objects from an advanced standpoint (e.g., derive the volume and surface area formulas for prisms, pyramids, cones, cylinders, and spheres)

Understand and apply properties of 3-D objects:

Use the formulas to find the volume and surface area.

FIGURE	VOLUME	TOTAL SURFACE AREA
Right Cylinder	$\pi r^2 h$	$2\pi rh + 2\pi r^2$
Right Cone	$\dfrac{\pi r^2 h}{3}$	$\pi r\sqrt{r^2 + h^2} + \pi r^2$
Sphere	$\dfrac{4}{3}\pi r^3$	$4\pi r^2$
Rectangular Solid	LWH	$2LW + 2WH + 2LH$

Note: $\sqrt{r^2 + h^2}$ is equal to the slant height of the cone.

Example:

1. Given the figure below, find the volume and surface area.

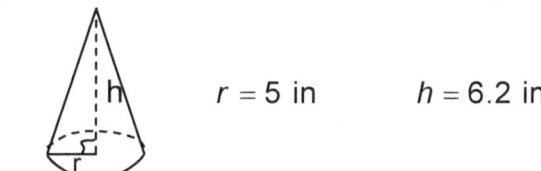

$r = 5$ in $h = 6.2$ in

Volume $= \dfrac{\pi r^2 h}{3}$ First write the formula.

$\dfrac{1}{3}\pi(5^2)(6.2)$ Then substitute.

162.31562 cubic inches   Finally solve the problem.

Surface area $= \pi r\sqrt{r^2 + h^2} + \pi r^2$ First write the formula.

$\pi 5\sqrt{5^2 + 6.2^2} + \pi 5^2$ Then substitute.
203.652 square inches   Compute.

Note: volume is always given in cubic units and area is always given in square units.

FOUNDATION LEV. MATH.

FIGURE	LATERAL AREA	TOTAL AREA	VOLUME
Right prism	sum of area of lateral faces (rectangles)	lateral area plus 2 times the area of base	area of base times height
regular pyramid	sum of area of lateral faces (triangles)	lateral area plus area of base	1/3 times the area of the base times the height

Find the total area of the given figure:

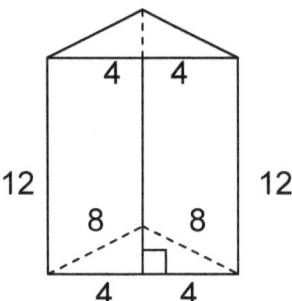

1. Since this is a triangular prism, first find the area of the bases.

2. Find the area of each rectangular lateral face.

3. Add the areas together.

$A = \frac{1}{2}bh$ $A = LW$ 1. write formula

$A = \frac{1}{2}(8)(6.928)$ $A = (8)(12)$

2. substitute known values

$A = 27.713$ sq. units $A = 96$ sq. units   3. compute

Total Area $= 2(27.713) + 3(96)$
$= 343.426$ sq. units

FIGURE	VOLUME	TOTAL SURFACE AREA	LATERAL AREA
Right Cylinder	$\pi r^2 h$	$2\pi rh + 2\pi r^2$	$2\pi rh$
Right Cone	$\dfrac{\pi r^2 h}{3}$	$\pi r \sqrt{r^2 + h^2} + \pi r^2$	$\pi r \sqrt{r^2 + h^2}$

Note: $\sqrt{r^2 + h^2}$ is equal to the slant height of the cone.

Example:
1. A water company is trying to decide whether to use traditional cylindrical paper cups or to offer conical paper cups since both cost the same. The traditional cups are 8 cm wide and 14 cm high. The conical cups are 12 cm wide and 19 cm high. The company will use the cup that holds the most water.

1. Draw and label a sketch of each.

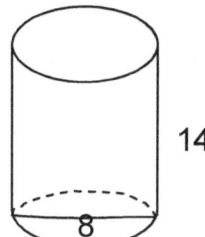 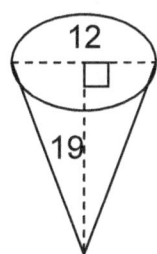

$V = \pi r^2 h$ $V = \dfrac{\pi r^2 h}{3}$ 1. write formula

$V = \pi(4)^2(14)$ $V = \dfrac{1}{3}\pi(6)^2(19)$ 2. substitute

$V = 703.717 \text{ cm}^3$ $V = 716.283 \text{ cm}^3$ 3. solve

The choice should be the conical cup since its volume is more.

FIGURE	VOLUME	TOTAL SURFACE AREA
Sphere	$\dfrac{4}{3}\pi r^2$	$4\pi r^2$

Example:

1. How much material is needed to make a basketball that has a diameter of 15 inches? How much air is needed to fill the basketball?

Draw and label a sketch:

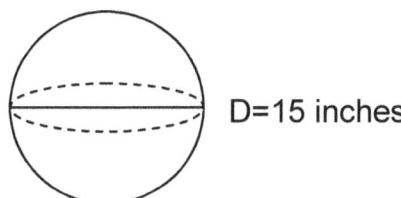 D=15 inches

Total surface area   Volume

$TSA = 4\pi r^2$ $V = \dfrac{4}{3}\pi r^2$ 1. write formula

$= 4\pi(7.5)^2$ $= \dfrac{4}{3}\pi(7.5)$ 2. substitute

$= 706.9 \text{ in}^3$ $= 1767.1 \text{ in}^3$ 3. Solve

Derive the volume and surface area formulas for prisms, pyramids, cones, cylinders, and spheres:

Derive the formula for the total surface area of a cone:

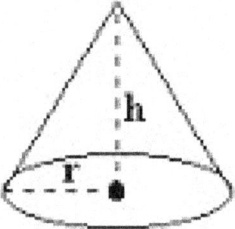

The formula is: $TSA_{cone} = \pi r^2 + \pi r s$

Given a right circular cone T (the base is a circle and $r \perp h$) with a base of radius r and a height of h, how do we calculate its total surface area using geometry? First notice the triangle formed by segments h, r and s.

S = side or slant height

$T_{cone} = T_{base\ area} + T_{base\ side\ area}$

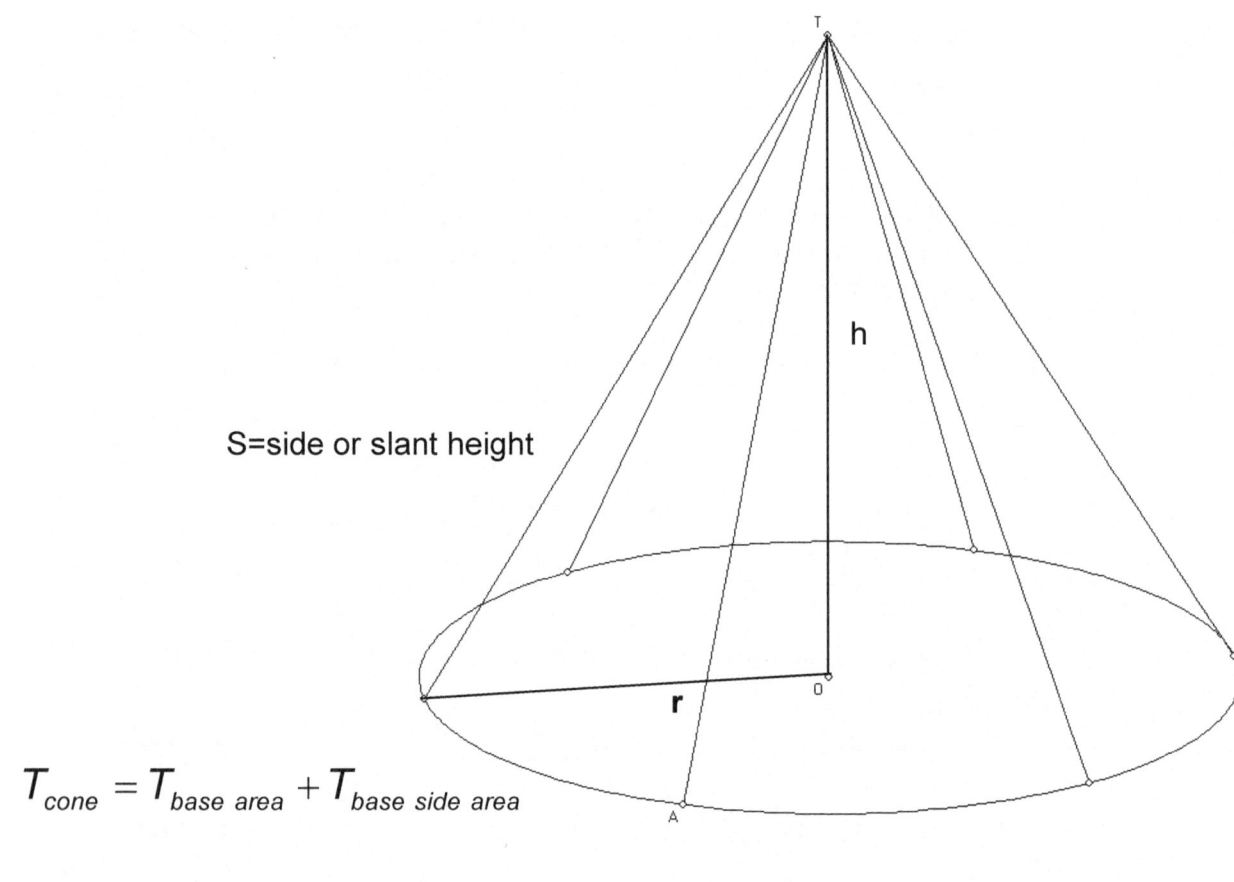

Cone

The base is easy as its area is πr^2. The side can be determined using the Pythagorean Theorem: $r^2 + h^2 = s^2$. Taking the square root of both sides: $s = \sqrt{r^2 + h^2}$. If we flatten or unroll the cone by cutting it (see below) into a circular disk it will be missing a piece; the circumference of the base of the cone and the circumference of our flattened cone (the circular disk missing a piece) are exactly the same length because the partial circular edge of the flattened cone defined the base of the cone before it was flattened or unrolled:

What the cone looks like flattened with a radius of s:

The area of the flattened cone= πs^2 but it doesn't account for the piece missing as a result of the flattening of the cone.

How do we take into account the missing piece? What is its area? We know the circumference of the base of the cone T from above is $2\pi r$ and the circumference of our flattened cone disk $2\pi s$ and we know that they are equal in size. We can use this information to create a ratio for cone T, the ratio $2\pi r / 2\pi s$ = r/s and apply it to the entire disk. If we multiply this ratio, r/p by the area of the full disk, we get $(r/s)\pi s^2 = \pi rs$.

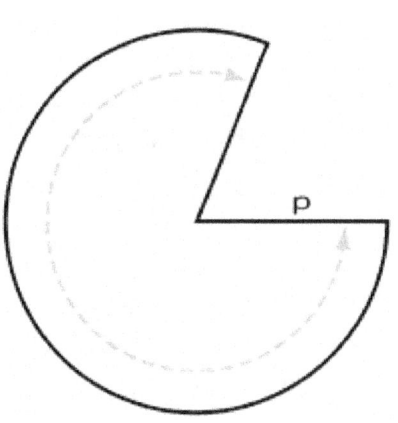

Add everything up $T_{cone} = T_{base\ area} + T_{base\ side\ area}$ and we get the following for the total area of cone T:

$T_{cone} = \pi r^2 + \pi rs$ is the formula for the total surface of a cone

$T_{cone} = \pi r(r + s)$ factor

$T_{cone} = \pi r\left(r + \sqrt{(r^2 + h^2)}\right)$ substitute for s and you can see the formula with the work we did with the Pythagorean Theorem.

We derived the formula for the total surface area of a cone expressed as: $\pi r^2 + \pi rs$ (where "s" is the slant height of the cone, "h" is the height of the cone and "r" is the radius of the cone's base).

Derive the formula for the volume of a cylinder:

A cylinder is a prism with a circular top and bottom (bases). The formula for the volume of a cylinder is $\pi r^2 h$, where "r" is the radius of the bottom or top circle of the cylinder and "h" is its height.

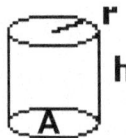

Given that the cylinder bases are circular, their area is πr^2; If you imagine cutting off the top and bottom base, you will be left with an open tube. Now imagine cutting the tube straight from the bottom to the top and flattening it out. What you are left with is a rectangle that has the same height as the cylinder and is as wide as the circumference of its top or bottom $2\pi r$. From here we can deduce that the area of the side is:

$A_{side} = (h)(2\pi r)$, and the total surface area of the cylinder is equal to $A_{side} + A_{top} + A_{bottom}$

The volume of the cylinder, which is a right solid, is the product of the top area times the height. Therefore, the cylinder's volume (V) = the area of the base (A) x height or length (h) of the cylinder: A= $\pi r^2 h$.

Transformational Geometry (SMR 2.4)

Skill a. **Demonstrate an understanding of the basic properties of isometries in two- and three dimensional space (e.g., rotation, translation, reflection)**

An **isometry** of the plane is a linear transformation, which preserves length.

A **transformation** is a change in the position, shape, or size of a geometric figure. **Transformational geometry** is the study of manipulating objects by flipping, twisting, turning and scaling.

Symmetry is exact similarity between two parts or halves, as if one were a mirror image of the other.

The transformation of an object is called its *image.* If the original object was labeled with letters, such as $ABCD$, the image may be labeled with the same letters followed by a prime symbol, $A'B'C'D'$.

A **translation** is a transformation that "slides" an object a fixed distance in a given direction. The original object and its translation have the same shape and size, and they face in the same direction.

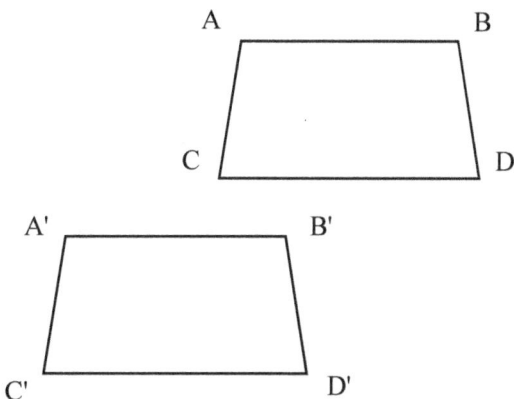

An example of a translation in architecture would be stadium seating. The seats are the same size and the same shape and face in the same direction.

A **rotation** is a transformation that turns a figure about a fixed point called the center of rotation. An object and its rotation are the same shape and size, but the figures may be turned in different directions. Rotations can occur in either a clockwise or a counterclockwise direction.

Rotation:

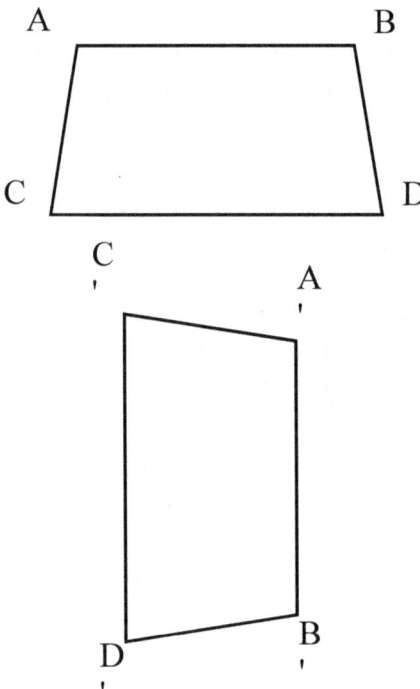

An object and its **reflection** have the same shape and size, but the figures face in opposite directions.

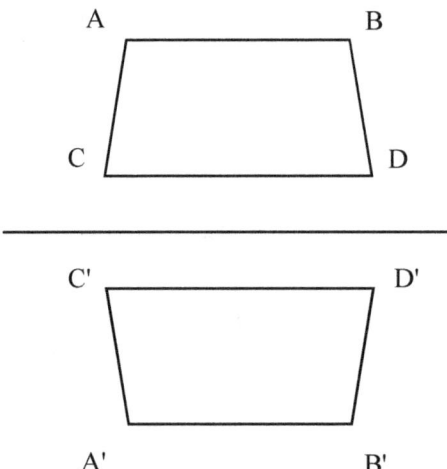

The line (where a mirror may be placed) is called the **line of reflection**. The distance from a point to the line of reflection is the same as the distance from the point's image to the line of reflection.

A **glide reflection** is a combination of a reflection and a translation.

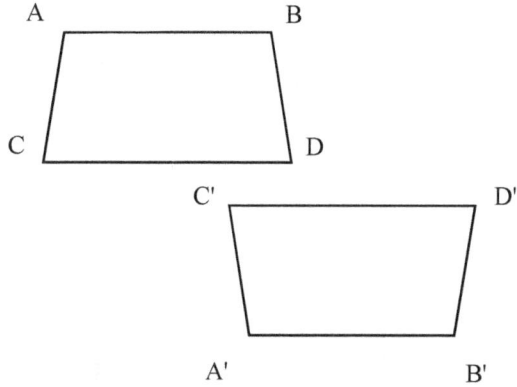

A figure on a coordinate plane can be translated by changing the ordered pairs.

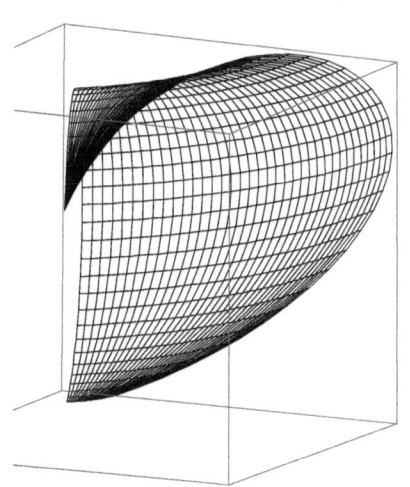
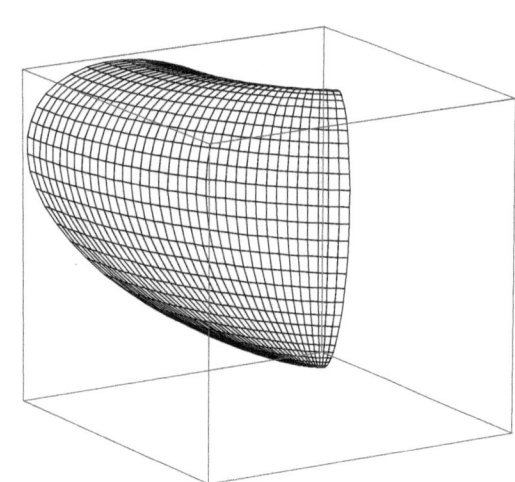

Above is an example of the rotation of a 3-dimensional object. A 3D coordinate system consists of x, y and z axes that cross each other at the origin and just like in a 2D graph, the position of an object is measured along each axis. 3D objects can be rotated, reflected, translated and dilated just like 2-dimensional objects. To translate a 3-D point, you can change each dimension separately:

$x' = x + a1$

$y' = y + a1$

$z' = z + a1$

TEACHER CERTIFICATION STUDY GUIDE

Below is a representation of a cube on the xyz axes.

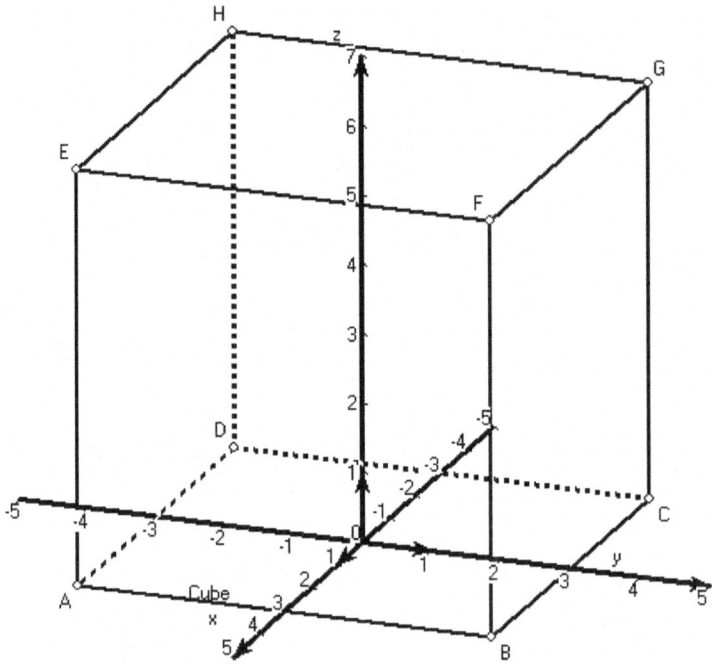

For more information on 3D manipulations, visit
http://demonstrations.wolfram.com/Understanding3DTranslations/

Transformational Geometry (SMR 2.4)

Skill b. **Understand and prove the basic properties of dilations (e.g., similarity transformations or change of scale)**

Translations and dilations can be transformed using matrices. The points on a coordinate plane can be represented by matrices as follow:

$\begin{bmatrix} x \\ y \end{bmatrix}$ which represents the coordinate pair (x,y).

Matrices are used to calculate transformations, which are functions that map the points of a preimage onto its image. The transformation is an isometry if the image and preimage are congruent.

One type of isometry is translation, when a shape is moved from one place to another without changing its shape, size or orientation. By using matrix addition and a translation matrix, you can find the coordinates of the translated shape.

Definition of similarity transformation: The transformation t of a plane onto itself is a similarity with a ratio r, if there is a real number r (non-zero) so that for any 2 points A and B where $A' = f(A), B' = (f)B, d(A',B') = |r|d(A,B)$. The number r is called the ratio of the similarity.

Polygons can be represented by placing the column matrices of the coordinates of the vertices into a matrix, which is called a vertex matrix.

$\triangle BCD$ with vertices $B(4,3), C(4,0), D(0,3)$ can be represented by the vertex matrix:

$\triangle BCD = \begin{bmatrix} 4 & 4 & 0 \\ 3 & 0 & 3 \end{bmatrix}$ ← x-coordinates
← y-coordinates

Example: ▵B'C'D' is the result of a translation of ▵BCD, using the coordinates given above $B(4,3), C(4,0), D(0,3)$: Find the coordinates if ▵BCD is translated 4 units to the left (-4 units on x) and one unit up(plus 1 unit on y):

$$\begin{bmatrix} 4 & 4 & 0 \\ 3 & 0 & 3 \end{bmatrix}$$ by *adding* to this matrix the translation matrix:

$$\begin{bmatrix} -4 & -4 & -4 \\ 1 & 1 & 1 \end{bmatrix} = \begin{bmatrix} 0 & 0 & -4 \\ 4 & 1 & 4 \end{bmatrix}$$ ← new translated x, y coordinates

▵BCD	▵B'C'D'
(4,3)	(0,4)
(4,0)	(0,1)
(0,3)	(-4,4)

Translation of ▵BCD 4 units left and 1 unit up resulting in ▵B'C'D' Note that the triangles are still the same size and shape and are. therefore congruent.

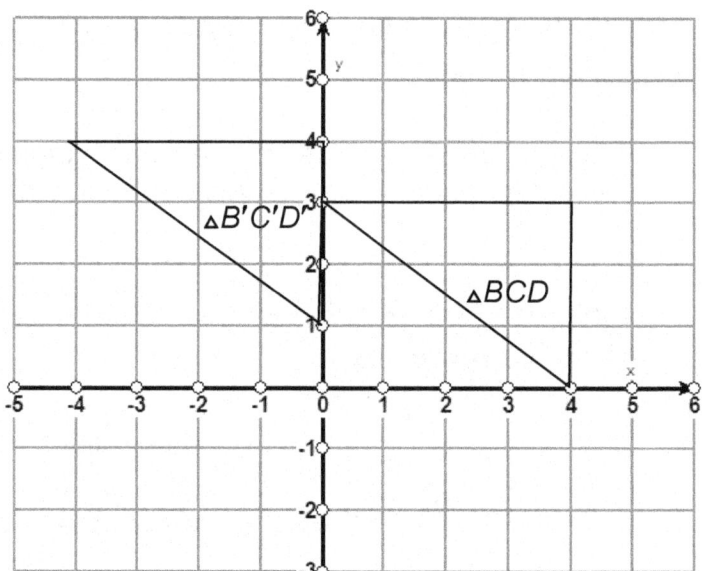

Example:
Rectangle RECT has the vertices of R (2,3) E (5,2), C(4,-2) T(1,-1). Find it's translation if it if move 2 units up and 4 units left.

Vertex Matrix   Translation   Vertex Matrix
  of RECT   Matrix   R'E'C'T'

$$\begin{bmatrix} 2 & 5 & 4 & 1 \\ 3 & 2 & -2 & -1 \end{bmatrix} + \begin{bmatrix} -4 & -4 & -4 & -4 \\ 2 & 2 & 2 & 2 \end{bmatrix} = \begin{bmatrix} -2 & 1 & 0 & -3 \\ 5 & 4 & 0 & 1 \end{bmatrix}$$

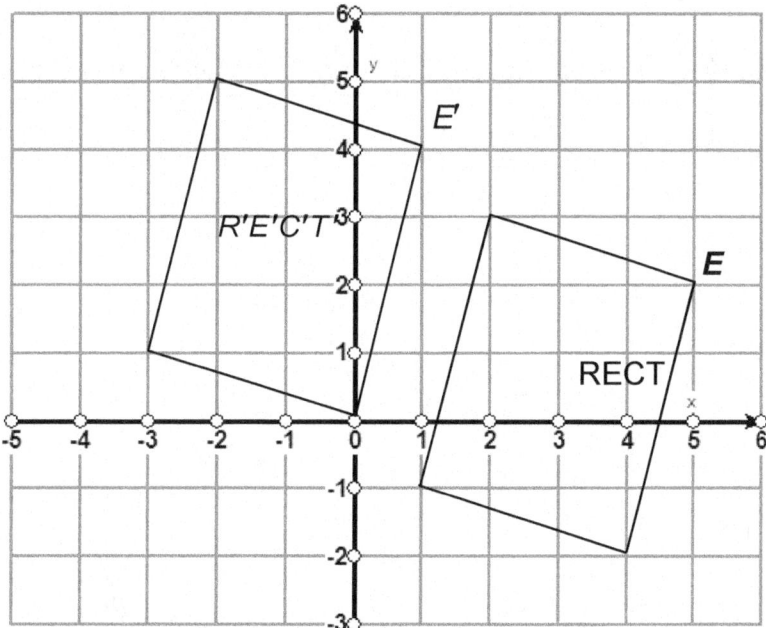

Look at vertex E and E', E' is clearly 2 units above E and 4 units to the left of E. The translation of RECT is easy to see. The original image and the preimage are also the same size and shape- they are congruent.

Definition of dilation: A dilation with center C and ratio r, denoted $H_{c,r}$, is a transformation of a plane where $H_{c,r}(C) = C$ and if P is distince from C, then $P' = H_{c,r}(P)$ so that C, P, P' are collinear and $d(C, P') = |r| d(C, P)$.
Dilation is a transformation that "shrinks" or "makes it bigger."

Example:

△EFG has vertices $E(-1,0), F(-3,5), G(2,3)$. Dilate △EFG so that it's dilation is $\frac{1}{2}$ △EFG. The perimeter of the dilated triangle will be $\frac{1}{2}$ the size of the original lengths. Multiply the vertex matrix of △EFG by the scale factor of $\frac{1}{2}$ to find the new triangle △E'F'G':

$$\frac{1}{2}\begin{bmatrix} -1 & -3 & 2 \\ 0 & 5 & 3 \end{bmatrix} = \begin{bmatrix} -\frac{1}{2} & -\frac{3}{2} & 1 \\ 0 & \frac{5}{2} & \frac{3}{2} \end{bmatrix}$$

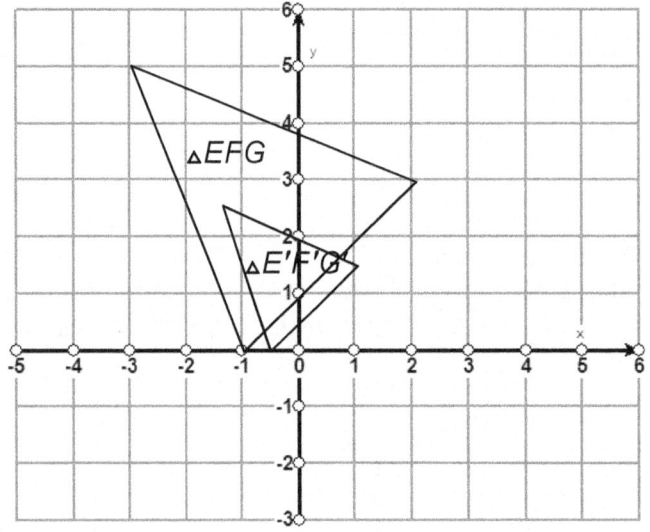

△EFG	△E'F'G'
(-1,0)	$(-\frac{1}{2}, 0)$
(-3,5)	$(-\frac{3}{2}, \frac{5}{2})$
(2,3)	$(1, \frac{3}{2})$

Notice that the triangles **are not** congruent as the image has sides that are half the length of the original triangle.

Using dilation to transform a diagram.

Starting with a triangle whose center of dilation is point P,

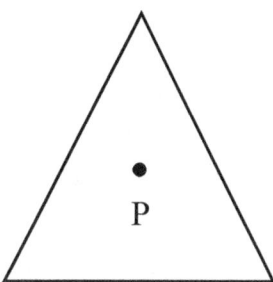

we dilate the lengths of the sides by the same factor to create a new triangle.

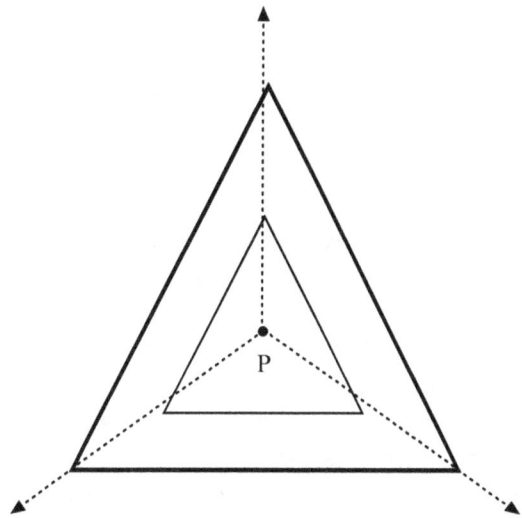

Two figures that have the **same shape** are **similar**. Two polygons are similar if corresponding angles are congruent and corresponding sides are in proportion. Corresponding parts of **similar** polygons are proportional. This should not be confused with congruence, which means that all angles and sides are the same measurement.

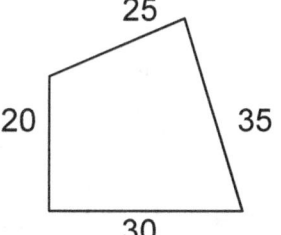 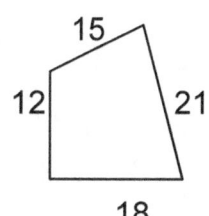

NUMBER THEORY (SMR 3.0)

Natural Numbers (SMR 3.1)

Skill a. **Apply the Fundamental Theorem of Arithmetic (e.g., find the greatest common factor and the least common multiple, show that every fraction is equivalent to a unique fraction where the numerator and denominator are relatively prime, prove that the square root of any number, not a perfect square number, is irrational)**

The Fundamental Theorem of Arithmetic:

Every integer greater than 1 can be written uniquely in the form:

$$p_1^{e_1} \, p_2^{e_2} \cdots p_k^{e_k}.$$

The p_i are distinct primes and the e_i are positive integers.

GCF is the abbreviation for the **greatest common factor**. The GCF is the largest number that is a factor of all the numbers given in a problem. The GCF can be no larger than the smallest number given in the problem. If no other number is a common factor, then the GCF will be the number 1. To find the GCF, list all possible factors of the smallest number given (include the number itself). Starting with the largest factor (which is the number itself), determine if it is also a factor of all the other given numbers. If so, that is the GCF. If that factor doesn't work, try the same method on the next smaller factor. Continue until a common factor is found. That is the GCF. Note: There can be other common factors besides the GCF.

Example: Find the GCF of 12, 20, and 36.

The smallest number in the problem is 12. The factors of 12 are 1,2,3,4,6 and 12. 12 is the largest factor, but it does not divide evenly into 20. Neither does 6, but 4 will divide into both 20 and 36 evenly.
Therefore, 4 is the GCF.

Example: Find the GCF of 14 and 15.

Factors of 14 are 1,2,7 and 14. 14 is the largest factor, but it does not divide evenly into 15. Neither does 7 or 2. Therefore, the only factor common to both 14 and 15 is the number 1, the GCF.

FOUNDATION LEV. MATH.

LCM is the abbreviation for **least common multiple**. The least common multiple of a group of numbers is the smallest number that all of the given numbers will divide into. The least common multiple will always be the largest of the given numbers or a multiple of the largest number.

Example: Find the LCM of 20, 30 and 40.

The largest number given is 40, but 30 will not divide evenly into 40. The next multiple of 40 is 80 (2 x 40), but 30 will not divide evenly into 80 either. The next multiple of 40 is 120. 120 is divisible by both 20 and 30, so 120 is the LCM (least common multiple).

Example: Find the LCM of 96, 16 and 24.

The largest number is 96. 96 is divisible by both 16 and 24, so 96 is the LCM.

Natural Numbers (SMR 3.1)

Skill b. Use the Principle of Mathematical Induction to prove results in number theory

The Principle of Mathematical Induction

Let p(n) denote the statement involving the integer variable n.

If p(1) is true and, for each integer $k \geq 1$, p(k+1) is true whenever p(k) is true then p(n) is true for all $n \geq 1$.

Algebraic properties of natural numbers:

	Addition	multiplication
Closure:	$a + b$ is a natural number	$a \times b$ is a natural number
Associative:	$a + (b + c) = (a + b) + c$	$a \times (b \times c) = (a \times b) \times c$
Commutative:	$a + b = b + a$	$a \times b = b \times a$
Identity:	$a + 0 = a$	$a \times 1 = a$
Distributive:		$a \times (b + c) = (a \times b) + (a \times c)$
No zero dividers:		if $ab = 0$, then either $a = 0$ or $b = 0$ (or both)

Proof by induction implies that a statement is true for all numbers if the following two statements are true:

1. The statement is true for $n = 1$.
2. If the statement is true for $n = k$, then it is also true for $n = k+1$.

The four basic components of induction proofs are: (1) the statement to be proved, (2) the beginning step ("let $n = 1$"), (3) the assumption step ("let $n = k$ and assume the statement is true for k, and (4) the induction step ("let $n = k+1$").

Example: Prove that the sum of all numbers from 1 to n is equal to $\frac{(n)(n+1)}{2}$.

Let $n = 1$.   Beginning step.
Then the sum of 1 to 1 is 1.

And $\frac{(n)(n+1)}{2} = 1$.

Thus, the statement is true for $n = 1$.   Statement is true in a particular instance.

Assumption

Let $n = k + 1$
    $k = n - 1$

Then $[1 + 2 +\ldots + k] + (k+1)$ Substitute the assumption.

$= \frac{(k)(k+1)}{2} + (k+1)$

$= \frac{(k)(k+1)}{2} + \frac{2(k+1)}{2}$ Common denominator.

$= \frac{(k)(k+1) + 2(k+1)}{2}$ Add fractions.

$= \frac{(k+2)(k+1)}{2}$ Simplify.

$= \frac{((k+1)+1)(k+1)}{2}$ Write in terms of $k+1$.

Thus we can conclude that the original statement is true for $n = k+1$ if it is assumed to be true for $n = k$.

TEACHER CERTIFICATION STUDY GUIDE

Natural Numbers (SMR 3.1)

Skill c.   **Prove and use basic properties of natural numbers (e.g., properties of divisibility)**

The most basic properties of the natural numbers are called the Peano Axioms, and are defined (being axioms they need not be derived) as follows:

- There exists a natural number 0.
- Every natural number "a" has a natural number successor, denoted by $S(a)$.
- There is no natural number whose successor is 0.
- Distinct natural numbers have distinct successors: if $a \neq b$, then $S(a) \neq S(b)$.
- If a property is possessed by 0 and also by the successor of every natural number that possesses it, then it is possessed by all natural numbers. (This postulate ensures that the proof technique of mathematic induction is valid.)

It should be noted that the "0" in the above definition need not correspond to what we normally consider to be the number zero. "0" simply means some object that when combined with an appropriate successor function, satisfies the Peano axioms. All systems that satisfy these axioms are isomorphic, the name "0" is used here for the first element, which is the only element that is not a successor. For example, the natural numbers starting with one also satisfy the axioms.

Divisibility Tests

a. A number is divisible by 2 if that number is an even number (which means it ends in 0,2,4,6 or 8).

1,354 ends in 4, so it is divisible by 2. 240,685 end in a 5, so it is not divisible by 2.

b. A number is divisible by 3 if the sum of its digits is evenly divisible by 3.

The sum of the digits of 964 is 9+6+4 = 19. Since 19 is not divisible by 3, neither is 964. The digits of 86,514 is 8+6+5+1+4 = 24. Since 24 is divisible by 3, 86,514 is also divisible by 3.

c. A number is divisible by 4 if the number in its last 2 digits is evenly divisible by 4.

FOUNDATION LEV. MATH.

The number 113,336 ends with the number 36 in the last 2 columns. Since 36 is divisible by 4, then 113,336 is also divisible by 4.

The number 135,627 ends with the number 27 in the last 2 columns. Since 27 is not evenly divisible by 4, then 135,627 is also not divisible by 4.

d. A number is divisible by 5 if the number ends in either a 5 or a 0.

225 ends with a 5 so it is divisible by 5. The number 470 is also divisible by 5 because its last digit is a 0. 2,358 is not divisible by 5 because its last digit is an 8, not a 5 or a 0.

e. A number is divisible by 6 if the number is even and the sum of its digits is evenly divisible by 3 or 6.

4,950 is an even number and its digits add to 18. (4+9+5+0 = 18) Since the number is even and the sum of its digits is 18 (which is divisible by 3 and/or 6), then 4950 is divisible by 6. 326 is an even number, but its digits add up to 11. Since 11 is not divisible by 3 or 6, then 326 is not divisible by 6. 698,135 is not an even number, so it cannot possibly be divided evenly by 6.

f. A number is divisible by 8 if the number in its last 3 digits is evenly divisible by 8.

The number 113,336 ends with the 3-digit number 336 in the last 3 columns. Since 336 is divisible by 8, then 113,336 is also divisible by 8. The number 465,627 ends with the number 627 in the last 3 columns. Since 627 is not evenly divisible by 8, then 465,627 is also not divisible by 8.

g. A number is divisible by 9 if the sum of its digits is evenly divisible by 9.

The sum of the digits of 874 is 8+7+4 = 19. Since 19 is not divisible by 9, neither is 874. The digits of 116,514 is 1+1+6+5+1+4 = 18. Since 18 is divisible by 9, 116,514 is also divisible by 9.

h. A number is divisible by 10 if the number ends in the digit 0.

305 ends with a 5 so it is not divisible by 10. The number 2,030,270 is divisible by 10 because its last digit is a 0. 42,978 is not divisible by 10 because its last digit is an 8, not a 0.

i. Why these rules work.

All even numbers are divisible by 2 by definition. A 2-digit number (with T as the tens digit and U as the ones digit) has as its sum of the digits, T + U. Suppose this sum of T + U is divisible by 3. Then it equals 3 times some constant, K. So, T + U = 3K. Solving this for U, U = 3K - T. The original 2 digit number would be represented by 10T + U. Substituting 3K - T in place of U, this 2-digit number becomes 10T + U = 10T + (3K - T) = 9T + 3K. This 2-digit number is clearly divisible by 3, since each term is divisible by 3. Therefore, if the sum of the digits of a number is divisible by 3, then the number itself is also divisible by 3. Since 4 divides evenly into 100, 200, or 300, 4 will divide evenly into any amount of hundreds. The only part of a number that determines if 4 will divide into it evenly is the number in the last 2 columns. Numbers divisible by 5 ends in 5 or 0. This is clear if you look at the answers to the multiplication table for 5. Answers to the multiplication table for 6 are all even numbers. Since 6 factors into 2 times 3, the divisibility rules for 2 and 3 must both work. Any number of thousands is divisible by 8. Only the last 3 columns of the number determine whether or not it is divisible by 8. A 2 digit number (with T as the tens digit and U as the ones digit) has as its sum of the digits, T + U. Suppose this sum of T + U is divisible by 9. Then it equals 9 times some constant, K. So, T + U = 9K. Solving this for U, U = 9K - T.

The original 2-digit number would be represented by 10T + U. Substituting 9K - T in place of U, this 2-digit number becomes 10T + U = 10T + (9K - T) = 9T + 9K. This 2-digit number is clearly divisible by 9, since each term is divisible by 9. Therefore, if the sum of the digits of a number is divisible by 9, then the number itself is also divisible by 9. Numbers divisible by 10 must be multiples of 10 that all end in a zero.

Natural Numbers (SMR 3.1)

Skill d.   Know and apply the Euclidean Algorithm

The Euclidean Algorithm

By recursive use of the division algorithm, we may find the GCD of two positive integers a and b without factoring either, and the x and y in Theorem 2.1 (and so, a specific solution in Corollary 2.4). For example, for a = 329 and b = 182, we compute

$$329 = 1 \cdot 182 + 147,$$
$$182 = 1 \cdot 147 + 35,$$
$$147 = 4 \cdot 35 + 7,$$
$$35 = 5 \cdot 7,$$

and stop when there is no remainder. The last dividend is the GCD, so in our example, GCD (329,182) = 7. Now, working through the above equations backwards,

$$7 = 147 - 4 \cdot 35 = 147 - 4 \cdot (182 - 1 \cdot 147)$$
$$= 5 \cdot 147 - 4 \cdot 182 = 5 \cdot (329 - 182) - 4 \cdot 182$$
$$= 5 \cdot 329 - 9 \cdot 182.$$

The proof that the square root of any prime number is irrational uses prime decomposition. Suppose that sqrt(n) is rational. For some a and b:

$n = a^2/b^2$

Now write a and b as products of prime factors, canceling any common factors.

$n = p_1^2 \times p_2^2 \times \cdots / q_1^2 \times q_2^2 \times \cdots$

where p1, p2, ..., q1, q2, ... are primes and $p_j \neq q_k$ for all j, k.

n is an integer. Therefore the denominator $q_1^2 \times q_2^2 \times \ldots$ is equal to unity.

Therefore, if sqrt(n) is rational, n is a product of squares of integers, and not a prime. The square root of any non-square number is irrational. Thus, the square root of any integer is either an integer, or irrational.

To determine if two fractions are equivalent, multiply the denominator and numerator of one fraction so that the denominators of the two fractions are equal.

For example, 1/2 = 3/6 because if you multiply the numerator and denominator of 1/2 by 3, you get:

$$\frac{1 \times 3}{2 \times 3} = \frac{3}{6}$$

It can be shown that a fraction $\frac{a}{b}$ is irreducible if, and only if, a and b are relatively prime, or equivalently, if a and b have a greatest common divisor of 1.

PROBABILITY AND STATISTICS (SMR Domain 4)

Probability (SMR 4.1)

Skill a. **Prove and apply basic principles of permutations and combinations**

Permutations and Combinations:

The difference between permutations and combinations is that in permutations all possible ways of writing an arrangement of objects are given while in a combination a given arrangement of objects is listed only once.

Given the set {1, 2, 3, 4}, list the arrangements of two numbers that can be written as a combination and as a permutation.

Combination	Permutation
12, 13, 14, 23, 24, 34	12, 21, 13, 31, 14, 41,
	23, 32, 24, 42, 34, 43,
six ways	twelve ways

Using the formulas given below the same results can be found.

$$_nP_r = \frac{n!}{(n-r)!}$$

The notation $_nP_r$ is read "the number of permutations of n objects taken r at a time."

$$_4P_2 = \frac{4!}{(4-2)!}$$

Substitute known values.

$$_4P_2 = 12$$

Solve.

$$_nC_r = \frac{n!}{(n-r)r!}$$

The number of combination when r objects are selected from n objects.

$$_4C_2 = \frac{4!}{(4-2)!2!}$$

Substitute known values.

$$_4C_2 = 6$$

Solve.

FOUNDATION LEV. MATH.

Probability (SMR 4.1)

Skill b. Illustrate finite probability using a variety of examples and models (e.g., the fundamental counting principles)

Finite Probability and the Fundamental Counting Principals:

The Addition Principle of Counting states:

If A and B are events, $n(A \text{ or } B) = n(A) + n(B) - n(A \cap B)$.

Example:

In how many ways can you select a black card or a Jack from an ordinary deck of playing cards?

Let B denote the set of black cards and let J denote the set of Jacks. Then, $n(B) = 26, n(J) = 4, n(B \cap J) = 2$ and

$$n(B \text{ or } J) = n(B) + n(J) - n(B \cap A)$$
$$= 26 + 4 - 2$$
$$= 28.$$

The Addition Principle of Counting for Mutually Exclusive Events states:

If A and B are mutually exclusive events, $n(A \text{ or } B) = n(A) + n(B)$.

Example:

A travel agency offers 40 possible trips: 14 to Asia, 16 to Europe and 10 to South America. In how many ways can you select a trip to Asia or Europe through this agency?

Let A denote trips to Asia and let E denote trips to Europe. Then, $A \cap E = \emptyset$ and

$$n(A \text{ or } E) = 14 + 16 = 30.$$

Therefore, the number of ways you can select a trip to Asia or Europe is 30.

FOUNDATION LEV. MATH.

The Multiplication Principle of Counting for Dependent Events states:

Let A be a set of outcomes of Stage 1 and B a set of outcomes of Stage 2. Then the number of ways $n(A\,and\,B)$, that A and B can occur in a two-stage experiment is given b

$$n(A\,and\,B) = n(A)n(B|A),$$

where $n(B|A)$ denotes the number of ways B can occur given that A has already occurred.

Example:

How many ways from an ordinary deck of 52 cards can two Jacks be drawn in succession if the first card is drawn but not replaced in the deck and then the second card is drawn?

This is a two-stage experiment for which we wish to compute $n(A\,and\,B)$, where A is the set of outcomes for which a Jack is obtained on the first draw and B is the set of outcomes for which a Jack is obtained on the second draw.

If the first card drawn is a Jack, then there are only three remaining Jacks left to choose from on the second draw. Thus, drawing two cards without replacement means the events A and B are dependent.

$$n(A\,and\,B) = n(A)n(B|A) = 4 \cdot 3 = 12$$

The Multiplication Principle of Counting for Independent Events states:

Let A be a set of outcomes of Stage 1 and B a set of outcomes of Stage 2. If A and B are independent events then the number of ways $n(A\,and\,B)$, that A and B can occur in a two-stage experiment is given by:

$$n(A\,and\,B) = n(A)n(B).$$

Example:

How many six-letter code "words" can be formed if repetition of letters is not allowed?

Since these are code words, a word does not have to look like a word; for example, abcdef could be a code word. Since we must choose a first letter *and* a second letter *and* a third letter *and* a fourth letter *and* a fifth letter *and* a sixth letter, this experiment has six stages.

Since repetition is not allowed there are 26 choices for the first letter; 25 for the second; 24 for the third; 23 for the fourth; 22 for the fifth; and 21 for the sixth. Therefore, we have:

$$n(\text{six-letter code words without repetition of letters})$$
$$= 26 \cdot 25 \cdot 24 \cdot 23 \cdot 22 \cdot 21$$
$$= 165,765,600$$

TEACHER CERTIFICATION STUDY GUIDE

Probability (SMR 4.1)

Skill c.   **Use and explain the concept of conditional probability**

Conditional Probability:
Dependent events occur when the probability of the second event depends on the outcome of the first event. For example, consider the two events (A) it is sunny on Saturday and (B) you go to the beach. If you intend to go to the beach on Saturday, rain or shine, then A and B may be independent.

If however, you plan to go to the beach only if it is sunny, then A and B may be dependent. In this situation, the probability of event B will change depending on the outcome of event A.

Suppose you have a pair of dice, one red and one green. If you roll a three on the red die and then roll a four on the green die, we can see that these events do not depend on the other. The total probability of the two independent events can be found by multiplying the separate probabilities.

$$P(A \text{ and } B) = P(A) \times P(B)$$
$$= 1/6 \times 1/6$$
$$= 1/36$$

Many times, events are not independent. Suppose a jar contains 12 red marbles and 8 blue marbles. If you randomly pick a red marble, replace it and then randomly pick again, the probability of picking a red marble the second time remains the same. However, if you pick a red marble, and then pick again without replacing the first red marble, the second pick becomes dependent upon the first pick (conditional probability).

$$P(\text{Red and Red}) \text{ with replacement} = P(\text{Red}) \times P(\text{Red})$$
$$= 12/20 \times 12/20$$
$$= 9/25$$

$$P(\text{Red and Red}) \text{ without replacement} = P(\text{Red}) \times P(\text{Red})$$
$$= 12/20 \times 11/19$$
$$= 33/95$$

FOUNDATION LEV. MATH.

Probability (SMR 4.1)

Skill d.   **Interpret the probability of an outcome**

Odds are defined as the ratio of the number of favorable outcomes to the number of unfavorable outcomes. The sum of the favorable outcomes and the unfavorable outcomes should always equal the total possible outcomes.

For example, given a bag of 12 red and 7 green marbles compute the odds of randomly selecting a red marble.

Odds of red = $\dfrac{12}{19}$ Odds of not getting red = $\dfrac{7}{19}$

In the case of flipping a coin, it is equally likely that a head or a tail will be tossed. The odds of tossing a head are 1:1. This is called even odds.

A **Bernoulli trial** is an experiment whose outcome is random and can be either of two possible outcomes, called "success" or "failure." Tossing a coin would be an example of a Bernoulli trial. We make the outcomes into a random variable by assigning the number 0 to one outcome and the number 1 to the other outcome. Traditionally, the "1" outcome is considered the "success" and the "0" outcome is considered the "failure." The probability of success is represented by p, with the probability of failure being $1-p$, or q.

Bernoulli trials can be applied to any real-life situation in which there are just two possible outcomes. For example, concerning the birth of a child, the only two possible outcomes for the sex of the child are male or female.

FOUNDATION LEV. MATH.

TEACHER CERTIFICATION STUDY GUIDE

Probability (SMR 4.1)

Skill e. **Use normal, binomial, and exponential distributions to solve and interpret probability problems**

A **normal distribution** is the distribution associated with most sets of real-world data. It is frequently called a **bell curve**. A normal distribution has a **random variable** X with mean μ and variance σ^2.

Example:

Albert's Bagel Shop's morning customer load follows a normal distribution, with **mean** (average) 50 and **standard deviation** 10. The standard deviation is the measure of the variation in the distribution. Determine the probability that the number of customers tomorrow will be less than 42.

First convert the raw score to a **z-score**. A z-score is a measure of the distance in standard deviations of a sample from the mean.

The z-score = $\dfrac{X_i - \bar{X}}{s} = \dfrac{42 - 50}{10} = \dfrac{-8}{10} = -.8$

Next, use a table to find the probability corresponding to the z-score. The table gives us .2881. Since our raw score is negative, we subtract the table value from .5.

$$.5 - .2881 = .2119$$

We can conclude that $P(x < 42) = .2119$. This means that there is about a 21% chance that there will be fewer than 42 customers tomorrow morning.

Example:

The scores on Mr. Rogers' statistics exam follow a normal distribution with mean 85 and standard deviation 5. A student is wondering what the probability is that she will score between a 90 and a 95 on her exam.

We wish to compute $P(90 < x < 95)$.

Compute the z-scores for each raw score.

$$\dfrac{90 - 85}{5} = \dfrac{5}{5} = 1 \text{ and } \dfrac{95 - 85}{5} = \dfrac{10}{5} = 2.$$

Now we want $P(1 < z < 2)$.

Since we are looking for an occurrence between two values, we subtract:

$P(1 < z < 2) = P(z < 2) - P(z < 1)$.

We use a table to get :

$P(1 < z < 2) = .9772 - .8413 = .1359$. (Remember that since the z-scores are positive, we add .5 to each probability.)

We can then conclude that there is a 13.6% chance that the student will score between a 90 and a 95 on her exam.

The **binomial distribution** is a sequence of probabilities with each probability corresponding to the likelihood of a particular event occurring. It is called a binomial distribution because each trial has precisely two possible outcomes. An **event** is defined as a sequence of Bernoulli trials that has within it a specific number of successes. The order of success is not important.

Note: There are two parameters to consider in a binomial distribution:

1. p = the probability of a success
2. n = the number of Bernoulli trials (i.e., the length of the sequence).

Example:

Toss a coin two times. Each toss is a Bernoulli trial as discussed above. Consider heads to be success. One event is one sequence of two coin tosses. Order does not matter.

There are two possibilities for each coin toss. Therefore, there are four (2·2) possible subevents: 00, 01, 10, 11 (where 0 = tail and 1 = head).

According to the multiplication rule, each subevent has a probability of $\frac{1}{4}\left(\frac{1}{2} \cdot \frac{1}{2}\right)$.

One subevent has zero heads, so the event of zero heads in two tosses is $p(h=0) = \frac{1}{4}$.

Two subevents have one head, so the event of one head in two tosses $p(h=1) = \frac{2}{4}$.

One subevent has two heads, so the event of two heads in two tosses $p(h=2) = \frac{1}{4}$.

So the binomial distribution for two tosses of a fair coin is:

$$p(h=0) = \frac{1}{4}, p(h=1) = \frac{2}{4}, p(h=2) = \frac{1}{4}.$$

Statistics (SMR 4.2)

Skill a. **Compute and interpret the mean, median, and mode of both discrete and continuous distributions**

Mean, median and mode:

These are three measures of central tendency. The **mean** is the average of the data items. The **median** is found by putting the data items in order from smallest to largest and selecting the item in the middle (or the average of the two items in the middle). The **mode** is the most frequently occurring item.

Example:

Find the mean, median, mode and range of the test score listed below:

85	77	65
92	90	54
88	85	70
75	80	69
85	88	60
72	74	95

Mean (X) = sum of all scores ÷ number of scores
 = 78

Median = put numbers in order from smallest to largest. Pick middle number.

54, 60, 65, 69, 70, 72, 74, 75, 77, 80, 85, 85, 85, 88, 88, 90, 92, 95
                                    -- --
                              both in middle

Therefore, median is average of two numbers in the middle or 78.5

Mode = most frequent number
  = 85

Range = largest number minus the smallest number
  = 95 − 54
  = 41

Statistics (SMR 4.2)

Skill b. **Compute and interpret quartiles, range, variance, and standard deviation of both discrete and continuous distributions**

Range, Quartiles, Variance and Standard Deviation:

Range is a measure of variability. It is found by subtracting the smallest value from the largest value.

Percentiles divide data into 100 equal parts. A person whose score falls in the 65th percentile has outperformed 65 percent of all those who took the test. This does not mean that the score was 65 percent out of 100 nor does it mean that 65 percent of the questions answered were correct. It means that the grade was higher than 65 percent of all those who took the test.

Stanine "standard nine" scores combine the understandability of percentages with the properties of the normal curve of probability. Stanines divide the bell curve into nine sections, the largest of which stretches from the 40th to the 60th percentile and is the "Fifth Stanine" (the average of taking into account error possibilities).

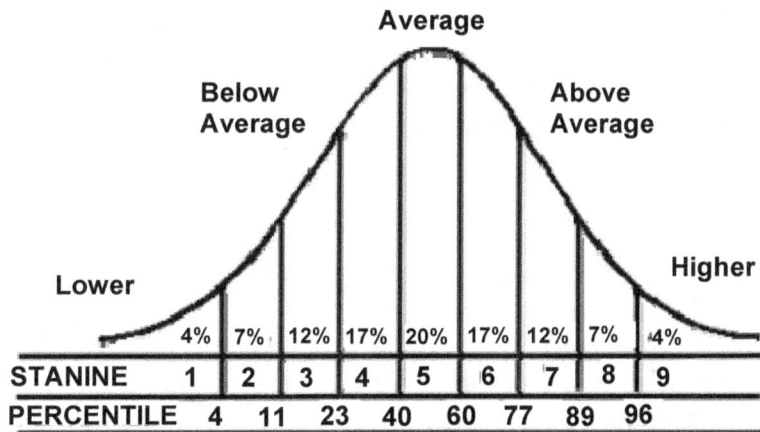

Quartiles divide the data into 4 parts. First find the median of the data set (Q2), then find the median of the upper (Q3) and lower (Q1) halves of the data set. There is some confusion in determining the upper and lower quartile and statisticians don't agree on which method to use. Tukey's method for finding the quartile values is to find the median of the data set, then find the median of the upper and lower halves of the data set. If there are an odd number of values in the data set, include the median value in both halves when finding the quartile values. For example, if we have the data set:

$$\{1, 4, 9, 16, 25, 36, 49, 64, 81\}$$

First find the median value, which is 25. Since there are an odd number of values in the data set (9), we include the median in both halves. To find the quartile values, we must find the medians of:

$$\{1, 4, 9, 16, 25\} \text{ and } \{25, 36, 49, 64, 81\}$$

Since each of these subsets has an odd number of elements (5), we use the middle value. Thus the lower quartile value is 9 and the upper quartile value is 49.

If the test you are taking allows the use of the TI-83, know that it uses a method described by Moore and McCabe (sometimes referred to as "M-and-M") to find quartile values. Their method is similar to Tukey's, but you *don't* include the median in either half when finding the quartile values. Using M-and-M on the data set above:

$$\{1, 4, 9, 16, 25, 36, 49, 64, 81\}$$

First find that the median value is 25. This time we'll exclude the median from each half. To find the quartile values, we must find the medians of:

$$\{1, 4, 9, 16\} \text{ and } \{36, 49, 64, 81\}$$

Since each of these data sets has an even number of elements (4), we average the middle two values. Thus the lower quartile value is $(4+9)/2 = 6.5$ and the upper quartile value is $(49+64)/2 = 56.5$.

With each of the above methods, the quartile values are always either one of the data points, or exactly half way between two data points.

An understanding of the definitions is important in determining the validity and uses of statistical data. All definitions and applications in this section apply to ungrouped data.

Data item: each piece of data is represented by the letter X.

Mean: the average of all data represented by the symbol $\overline{X}$.

Range: difference between the highest and lowest value of data items.

Sum of the Squares: sum of the squares of the differences between each item and the mean.

$$Sx^2 = (X - \overline{X})^2$$

Variance: the sum of the squares quantity divided by the number of items.

(the lower case Greek letter sigma (σ) squared represents variance). $\quad \dfrac{Sx^2}{N} = \sigma^2$

The larger the value of the variance the larger the spread

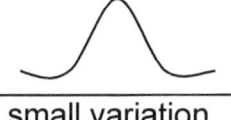
small variation

larger variation

Standard Deviation: the square root of the variance. The lower case Greek letter sigma (σ) is used to represent standard deviation. $\quad \sigma = \sqrt{\sigma^2}$

Most statistical calculators have standard deviation keys on them and should be used when asked to calculate statistical functions. It is important to become familiar with the calculator and the location of the keys needed.

Example:

Given the ungrouped data below, calculate the mean, range, standard deviation and the variance.

```
15    22    28    25    34    38
18    25    30    33    19    23
```

Mean (X) = 25.8333333
Range: $38 - 15 = 23$
standard deviation $(\sigma) = 6.699137$
Variance $(\sigma^2) = 48.87879$

Statistics (SMR 4.2)

Skill c. **Select and evaluate sampling methods appropriate to a task (e.g., random, systematic, cluster, convenience sampling) and display the results**

Methods of Sampling:

Random sampling supplies every combination of items from the frame, or stratum, as a known probability of occurring. A large body of statistical theory quantifies the risk and thus enables an appropriate sample size to be chosen.

Systematic sampling selects items in the frame according to the kth sample. The first item is chosen to be the rth, where r is a random integer in the range $1,...,k-1$.

There are three stages to **Cluster or Area sampling**: the target population is divided into many regional clusters (groups); a few clusters are randomly selected for study; a few subjects are randomly chosen from within a cluster.

Convenience sampling is the method of choosing items arbitrarily and in an unstructured manner from the frame.

Statistics (SMR 4.2)

Skill d. **Know the method of least squares and apply it to linear regression and correlation**

Method of Least Squares, Linear Correlation and Regression:

The **method of least squares** assumes that the best-fit curve of a given type is the curve that has the minimal sum of the deviations squared (least square error) from a given set of data.

Suppose that the data points are $(x_1, y_1), (x_2, y_2), ..., (x_n, y_n)$ where x is the independent variable and y is the dependent variable. The fitting curve $f(x)$ has the deviation (error) d from each data point, i.e., $d_1 = y_1 - f(x_1), d_2 = y_2 - f(x_2), ..., d_n = y_n - f(x_n)$ According to the method of least squares, the best fitting curve has the property that:

$$\Pi = d_1^2 + d_2^2 + ... + d_n^2 = \sum_{i=1}^{n} d_i^2 = \sum_{i=1}^{n} [y_i - f(x_i)]^2 = \text{a minimum}$$

Linear regression is a method of estimating the conditional expected value of one variable y given the values of some other variable or variables x. The variable of interest, y, is conventionally called the "response variable". The terms "endogenous variable" and "output variable" are also used.

$$y = \alpha + \beta x$$

Correlation is a measure of association between two variables. It varies from -1 to 1, with 0 being a random relationship, 1 being a perfect positive linear relationship, and -1 being a perfect negative linear relationship.

The **correlation coefficient** (r) is used to describe the strength of the association between the variables and the direction of the association:

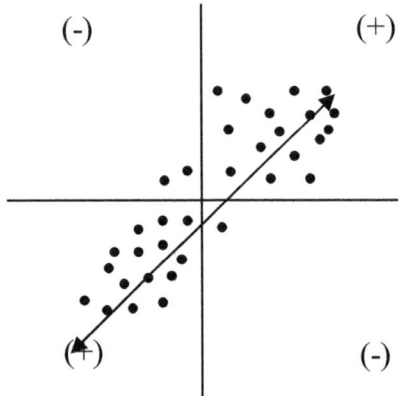

Horizontal and vertical lines are drawn through the point of averages which is the point on the averages of the x and y values. This divides the scatter plot into four quadrants. If a point is in the lower left quadrant, the product of two negatives is positive; in the upper right, the product of two positives is positive.

The positive quadrants are depicted with the positive sign (+). In the two remaining quadrants (upper left and lower right), the product of a negative and a positive is negative. The negative quadrants are depicted with the negative sign (-). If r is positive, then there are more points in the positive quadrants and if r is negative, then there are more points in the two negative quadrants.

Regression is a form of statistical analysis used to predict a dependent variable (y) from values of an independent variable (x). A regression equation is derived from a known set of data.

The simplest regression analysis models the relationship between two variables using the following equation: $y = a + bx$, where y is the dependent variable and x is the independent variable. This simple equation denotes a linear relationship between x and y. This form would be appropriate if, when you plotted a graph of x and y, you tended to see the points roughly form along a straight line.

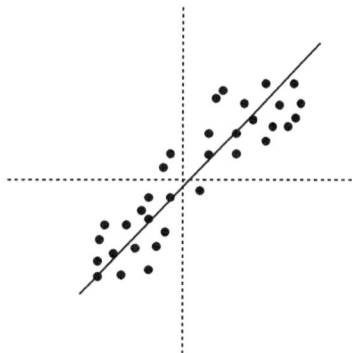

The line can then be used to make predictions.

If all of the data points fell on the line, there would be a perfect correlation ($r = 1.0$) between the x and y data points. These cases represent the best scenarios for prediction. A positive or negative r value represents how y varies with x. When r is positive, y increases as x increases. When r is negative, y decreases as x increases.

Statistics (SMR 4.2)

Skill e.   Know and apply the chi-square test

Chi-square tests:

Chi-square tests test a null hypothesis. A Chi-square is calculated by finding the difference between each observed and theoretical frequency, squaring them, dividing each by the theoretical frequency, and taking the sum of the results:

$$x^2 = \sum_{i=1}^{6} \frac{(O_i - E_i)^2}{E_i}$$

The **chi-square test** is a method of determining the odds for or against a given deviation from expected statistical distribution.

Example:

We want to determine if the odds of flipping a coin heads-up is the same as tails-up; is the coin flipped fairly? We collect data by flipping the coin 200 times. The coin landed heads-up 92 times and tails-up 108 times.

To perform a chi-square test we first must establish a null hypothesis. In this example, the null hypothesis states that the coin should be equally likely to land head-up or tails-up, every time. The null hypothesis allows us to state expected frequencies. For 200 tosses we would expect 100 heads and 100 tails.

Next, prepare a table:

	Heads	Tails	Total
Observed	92	108	200
Expected	100	100	200
Total	192	208	400

The observed values are the data gathered. The expected values are the frequencies expected, based on the null hypothesis.

We calculate chi-squared:

$$\text{Chi-squared} = \frac{(\text{observed}-\text{expected})^2}{(\text{expected})}$$

We have two classes to consider in this example, heads and tails.

$$\text{Chi-squared} = \frac{(100-92)^2}{100} + \frac{(100-108)^2}{100}$$
$$= \frac{(8)^2}{100} + \frac{(-8)^2}{100}$$
$$= 0.64 + 0.64$$
$$= 1.28$$

We then consult a table of critical values of the chi-squared distribution. Here is a portion of such a table:

df/prob.	0.99	0.95	0.90	0.80	0.70	0.50	0.30	0.20	0.10	0.05
1	0.00013	0.0039	0.016	0.64	0.15	0.46	1.07	1.64	2.71	3.84
2	0.02	0.10	0.21	0.45	0.71	1.39	2.41	3.22	4.60	5.99
3	0.12	0.35	0.58	1.99	1.42	2.37	3.66	4.64	6.25	7.82
4	0.3	0.71	1.06	1.65	2.20	3.36	4.88	5.99	7.78	9.49
5	0.55	1.14	1.61	2.34	3.00	4.35	6.06	7.29	9.24	11.07

We determine the degrees of freedom (df) by subtracting one from the number of classes. In this example we have two classes (heads and tails), so df is 1. Our chi-squared value is 1.28. In the table our value lies between 1.07 (a probability of .30) and 1.64 (a probability of .20). Interpolation gives us an estimated probability of 0.26. This value means that there is a 74% chance that the coin is biased. Because the chi-squared value we obtained is greater than 0.05 (0.26 to be exact), we accept the null hypothesis as true and conclude that the coin is fair.

CONSTRUCTED-RESPONSE EXAMPLES

Exercise 1: Interpreting Slope as a Rate of Change
Connection: Social Sciences/Geography

Real-life Application: Slope is often used to describe a constant or average rate of change. These problems usually involve units of measure such as miles per hour or dollars per year.

Problem:

The town of Verdant Slopes has been experiencing a boom in population growth. By the year 2000, the population had grown to 45,000, and by 2005, the population had reached 60,000.

Communicating about Algebra:

a. Using the formula for slope as a model, find the average rate of change in population growth, expressing your answer in people per year.

Extension:

b. Using the average rate of change determined in a., predict the population of Verdant Slopes in the year 2010.

Solution:

a. *Let t represent the time and p represent population growth. The two observances are represented by (t_1, p_1) and (t_2, p_2).*

1st observance = (t_1, p_1) = (2000, 45000)
2nd observance = (t_2, p_2) = (2005, 60000)

Use the formula for slope to find the average rate of change.

Rate of change = $\dfrac{p_2 - p_1}{t_2 - t_1}$

Substitute values.

$= \dfrac{60000 - 45000}{2005 - 2000}$

Simplify.

$$= \frac{15000}{5} = 3000 \, people/year$$

The average rate of change in population growth for Verdant Slopes between the years 2000 and 2005 was 3000 people/year.

b.
$$3000 \, people/year \times 5 \, years = 15000 \, people$$
$$60000 \, people + 15000 \, people = 75000 \, people$$

At a continuing average rate of growth of 3000 people/year, the population of Verdant Slopes could be expected to reach 75,000 by the year 2010.

Exercise 2:

(a) Find the midpoint between (5, 2) and (-13, 4).

Using the Midpoint Formula:

$$\left(\frac{x_1+x_2}{2}, \frac{y_1+y_2}{2}\right) = \left(\frac{5+(-13)}{2}, \frac{2+4}{2}\right) = \left(\frac{-8}{2}, \frac{6}{2}\right) = (-4, 3)$$

(b) Find the value of x_1 so that (-3, 5) is the midpoint between (x_1, 6) and (-2, 4)

Using the Midpoint Formula:

$$(-3, 5) = \left(\frac{x_1+x_2}{2}, \frac{y_1+y_2}{2}\right)$$

$$= \left(\frac{x_1+(-2)}{2}, \frac{6+4}{2}\right)$$

$$= \left(\frac{x_1-2}{2}, \frac{10}{2}\right)$$

$$= \left(\frac{x_1-2}{2}, 5\right)$$

Separate out the x value to determine x_1.

$$-3 = \frac{x_1 - 2}{2}$$
$$-6 = x_1 - 2$$
$$-4 = x_1$$

c) **Is $y = 3x - 6$ a bisector of the line segment with endpoints at (2, 4) and (8, -1)?**

Find the midpoint of the line segment and then see if the midpoint is a point on the given line. Using the Midpoint Formula:

$$P = \left(\frac{2+8}{2}, \frac{4+(-1)}{2}\right) = \left(\frac{10}{2}, \frac{4-1}{2}\right) = \left(5, \frac{3}{2}\right) = (5, 1.5)$$

Check to see if this point is on the line:

$$y = 3x - 6$$
$$y = 3(5) - 6 = 15 - 6 = 9$$

In order for this line to be a bisector, y must equal 1.5. However, since $y = 9$, the answer to the question is "No, this is not a bisector."

Exercise 3:

a) **One line passes through the points (-4, -6) and (4, 6); another line passes through the points (-5, -4) and (3, 8). Are these lines parallel, perpendicular or neither?**

Find the slopes.

$$m = \frac{y_2 - y_1}{x_2 - x_1}$$

$$m_1 = \frac{6 - (-6)}{4 - (-4)} = \frac{6 + 6}{4 + 4} = \frac{12}{8} = \frac{3}{2}$$

$$m_2 = \frac{8 - (-4)}{3 - (-5)} = \frac{8 + 4}{3 + 5} = \frac{12}{8} = \frac{3}{2}$$

Since the slopes are the same, the lines are parallel.

b) One line passes through the points (1, -3) and (0, -6); another line passes through the points (4, 1) and (-2, 3). Are these lines parallel, perpendicular or neither?

Find the slopes.

$$m = \frac{y_2 - y_1}{x_2 - x_1}$$

$$m_1 = \frac{-6 - (-3)}{0 - 1} = \frac{-6 + 3}{-1} = \frac{-3}{-1} = 3$$

$$m_2 = \frac{3 - 1}{-2 - 4} = \frac{2}{-6} = -\frac{1}{3}$$

The slopes are negative reciprocals, so the lines are perpendicular.

c) One line passes through the points (-2, 4) and (2, 5); another line passes through the points (-1, 0) and (5, 4). Are these lines parallel, perpendicular or neither?

Find the slopes.

$$m = \frac{y_2 - y_1}{x_2 - x_1}$$

$$m_1 = \frac{5 - 4}{2 - (-2)} = \frac{1}{2 + 2} = \frac{1}{4}$$

$$m_2 = \frac{4 - 0}{5 - (-1)} = \frac{4}{5 + 1} = \frac{4}{6} = \frac{2}{3}$$

Since the slopes are not the same, the lines are not parallel. Since they are not negative reciprocals, they are not perpendicular, either. Therefore, the answer is "neither."

Exercise 4:

For 2000 through 2005, the consumption of a certain product sweetened with sugar, as a percent, $f(t)$ of the total consumption of the product, can be modeled by:

$$f(t) = 75 + 37.25(0.615)^t$$

Where $t = 2$ represents 2000.

(a) Find a model for the consumption of the product sweetened with non-sugar sweeteners as a percent, $g(t)$ of the total consumption of the product.

Since 100% represents the total consumption of the product, the model can be found by subtracting the model for sugar-sweetened product from 100:

$$g(t) = 100 - (75 + 37.25(0.615)^t$$
$$= 100 - 75 - 37.25(0.615)^t$$
$$= 25 - 37.25(0.615)^t$$

(b) Sketch the graphs of f and g. Does the consumption of one type of product seem to be stabilizing compared to the other product? Explain.

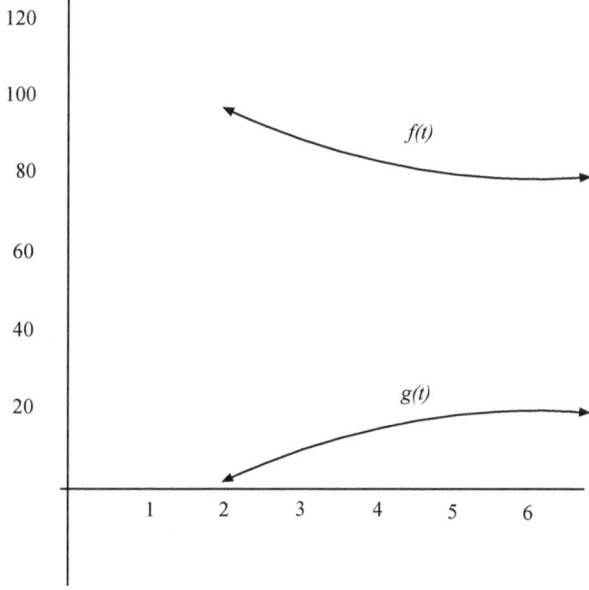

Yes, the consumption of the product sweetened with sugar (represented by $f(t)$) is decreasing less and less each year.

(c) Sketch the graph of $f(x) = 2^x$. Does it have an x-intercept? What does this tell you about the number of solutions of the equation $2^x = 0$? Explain.

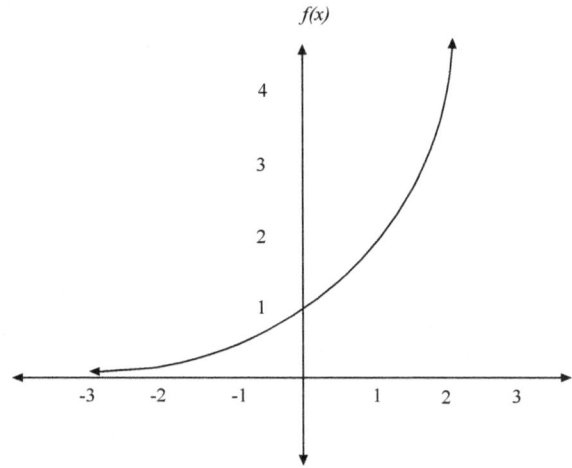

No, there is no solution. The solutions of $2^x = 0$ are the x-intercepts of $y = 2^x$.

Answer Key to Practice Problems

Page 40

Question #1 $x^2 - 10x + 25$

Question #2 $25x^2 - 10x - 48$

Question #3 $x^2 - 9x - 36$

Page 41

Question #1 $(6x - 5y)(36x^2 + 30xy + 25y^2)$

Question #2 $4(a - 2b)(a^2 + 2ab + 4b^2)$

Question #3 $5x^2(2x^9 + 3y)(4x^{18} - 6x^9 y + 9y^2)$

Page 61

Question #1   a, b, d, f are functions, d is a function, y = 3 is a function! c is not!

Question #2   Domain = $^-\infty, \infty$ Range = $^-5, \infty$

Page 62

Question #1   Domain = $^-\infty, \infty$ Range = $^-6, \infty$

Question #2   Domain = 1,4,7,6   Range = -2

Question #3   Domain = $x \neq 2, ^-2$

Question #4   Domain = $^-\infty, \infty$ Range = -4, 4
                Domain = $^-\infty, \infty$ Range = $2, \infty$

Question #5   Domain = $^-\infty, \infty$ Range = 5

Question #6   (3,9), (-4,16), (6,3), (1,9), (1,3)

Page 65

Question #1   slope = -5/7; y intercept = -10

FOUNDATION LEV. MATH.

Question #2   slope = $\frac{x}{2}$; y intercept = -7

Question #3   don't exist (x=3 is the final equation)

Question #4   slope = $\frac{-2}{5}x$; y intercept = 3

Page 76

Question #1 $x = 7, x = ^{-}5$

Question #2 $x = \frac{13}{8}$

Page 79

Question #1 $6a^4\sqrt{2a}$

Question #2 $7i\sqrt{2}$

Question #3 $-2x^2$

Question #4 $6x^4y^3 \sqrt[4]{3x^2y^3}$

Page 80

Question #1 $5\sqrt{6}$

Question #2 $^{-}5\sqrt{3} + 6\sqrt{5} = \sqrt{15} - 30$

Question #3 $^{-}3\sqrt{2} - 9\sqrt{3} - 3\sqrt{6} - 12$

Page 81

Question #1 $17\sqrt{6}$

Question #2 $84x^4y^8\sqrt{2}$

Question #3 $\dfrac{5a^4\sqrt{35b}}{8b}$

Question #4 $-5\left(3+\sqrt{3}+2\sqrt{5}\right)$

Page 83

Question #1 *x=17*

p. 88

Question #1

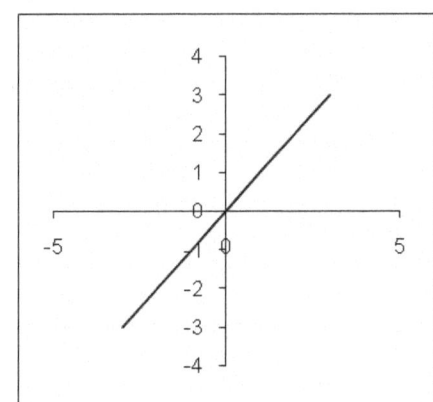

Question #2

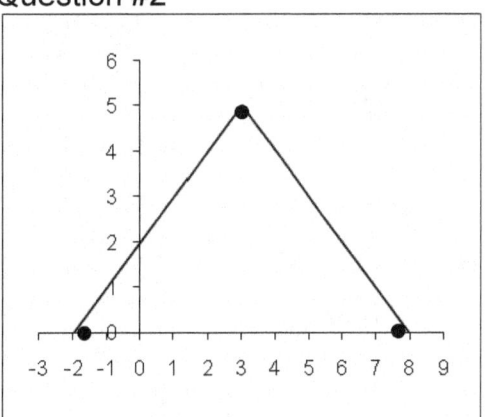

Question #3

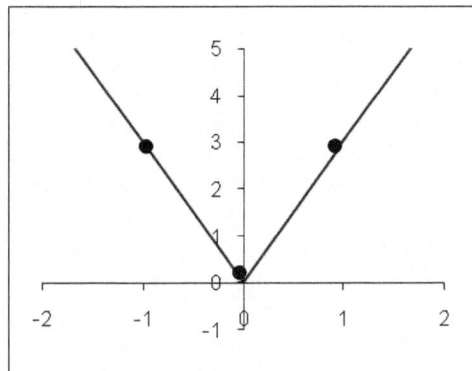

Question #4

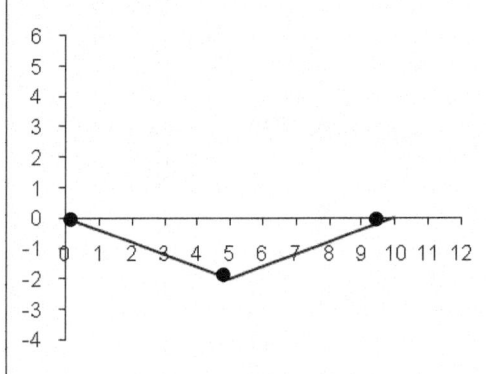

Page 91

    Question #1 $x = 9$

    Question #2 $x = 3$ or $x = 6$

    Question #3 $x = 1$

Page 103

    Question #1 $\begin{pmatrix} x \\ y \end{pmatrix} = \begin{pmatrix} 3 \\ 1 \end{pmatrix}$

    Question #2 $\begin{pmatrix} x \\ y \\ z \end{pmatrix} = \begin{pmatrix} 4 \\ 4 \\ 1 \end{pmatrix}$

Page 103

    Question #1 $\begin{pmatrix} -4 & 0 & -2 \\ 2 & 4 & -8 \end{pmatrix}$

    Question #2 $\begin{pmatrix} 9 \\ 34 \\ 32 \end{pmatrix}$

    Question #3 $\begin{pmatrix} -12 & 16 \\ -4 & -2 \\ 0 & 6 \end{pmatrix}$

TEACHER CERTIFICATION STUDY GUIDE

ESSENTIAL TIPS FOR EVERY MATH TEACHER

Pedagogical principles and teaching methods are important for all teachers. They are particularly critical, though, for math teaching since math teachers not only face the difficulty of communicating the subject matter to students but also that of surmounting an all-pervasive cultural fear of mathematics. Math teachers need to take particular care to foster learning in a non-threatening environment that is at the same time genuinely stimulating and challenging.

The National Council of Teachers of Mathematics (NCTM) (http://www.nctm.org/) Principles and Standards emphasizes the teacher's obligation to support all students not only in developing basic mathematics knowledge and skills but also in their ability to understand and reason mathematically to solve problems relevant to today's world. The use of technology in the classroom is strongly advocated.

Resources for middle school teachers are available on the NCTM website at http://www.nctm.org/resources/middle.aspx.

The Mathematics Pathway (http://msteacher.org/math.aspx) on the National Science Digital Library (NSDL) Middle School Portal provides a very comprehensive and rich treasure trove of helpful material linking to various resources on the web including articles as well as interactive instructional modules on various topics.

The Drexel University Math Forum website provides the opportunity to interact with mentors and other math educators online. Some of the material on this website requires paid subscription but there are openly available archives as well. An overview of what the site provides is available at http://mathforum.org/about.forum.html. You may find the "Teacher2Teacher" service particularly useful; you can ask questions or browse the archives for a wealth of nitty-gritty everyday teaching information, suggestions and links to teaching tools.

This website for sixth grade contains animated lessons, discussions of strategies and a glossary of terms using few words and plenty of illustrations.
http://students.resa.net/stoutcomputerclass/1math.htm

Other instructional and professional development resources:
http://archives.math.utk.edu/k12.html
http://www.learnalberta.ca/Launch.aspx?content=/content/mesg/html/math6web/math6shell.html
http://mmap.wested.org/webmath/

Pedagogical Principles

Maintain a supportive, non-threatening environment
Many students unfortunately perceive mathematics as a threat. This becomes a particular critical issue at the middle school level where they learn algebra for the first time and are required to think in new ways. Since fear "freezes" the brain and makes thinking really difficult, a student's belief that he is no good at math becomes a self-fulfilling prophecy. A teacher's primary task in this situation is to foster a learning environment where every student feels that he or she can learn to think mathematically. Here are some ways to go about this:

Accept all comments and questions: Acknowledge all questions and comments that students make. If what the student says is inaccurate or irrelevant to the topic in hand, point that out gently but also show your understanding of the thought process that led to the comment. This will encourage students to speak up in class and enhance their learning.

Set aside time for group work: Assign activities to groups of students comprised of mixed ability levels. It is often easier for students to put forward their own thoughts as part of a friendly group discussion than when they are sitting alone at their desks with a worksheet. The more proficient students can help the less able ones and at the same time clarify their own thinking. You will essentially be using the advanced students in the class as a resource in a manner that also contributes to their own development. The struggling students will feel supported by their peers and not isolated from them.

Encourage classroom discussion of math topics: For instance, let the whole class share different ways in which they approach a certain problem. It will give you insight into your students' ways of thinking and make it easier to help them. It will allow even those who just listen to understand and correct errors in their thinking without being put on the spot.

Engage and challenge students
Maintaining a non-threatening environment should not mean dumbing down the math content in the classroom. The right level of challenge and relevance to their daily lives can help to keep students interested and learning. Here are some ideas:

Show connections to the real world: Use real life examples of math problems in your teaching. Some suggestions are given in the next section. Explain the importance of math literacy in society and the pitfalls of not being mathematically aware. An excellent reference is "The 10 Things All Future Mathematicians and Scientists Must Know" by Edward Zaccaro. The title of the book is misleading since it deals with things that every educated person, not just mathematicians and scientists, should know.

Use technology: Make use of calculators and computers including various online, interactive resources in your teaching. The natural affinity today's children have for these devices will definitely help them to engage more deeply in their math learning.

Demonstrate "messy" math: Children often have the mistaken belief that every math problem can be solved by following a particular set of rules; they either know the rules or they don't. In real life, however, math problems can be approached in different ways and often one has to negotiate several blind alleys before getting to the real solution. Children instinctively realize this while doing puzzles or playing games. They just don't associate this kind of thinking with classroom math. The most important insight any math teacher can convey to students is the realization that even if they don't know how to do a problem at first, they can think about it and figure it out as long as they are willing to stay with the problem and make mistakes in the process. An obvious way to do this, of course, is to introduce mathematical puzzles and games in the classroom. The best way, however, is for teachers themselves to take risks occasionally with unfamiliar problems and demonstrate to the class how one can work one's way out of a clueless state.

Show the reasoning behind rules: Even when it is not a required part of the curriculum, explain, whenever possible, how a mathematical rule is derived or how it is connected to other rules. For instance, in explaining the rule for finding the area of a trapezoid, show how one can get to it by thinking of the trapezoid as two triangles. This will reinforce the students' sense of mathematics as something that can be logically arrived at and not something for which they have to remember innumerable rules. Another way to reinforce this idea is to do the same problem using different approaches.

Be willing to take occasional side trips: Be flexible at times and go off topic in order to explore more deeply any questions or comments from the students. Grab a teaching opportunity even if it is irrelevant to the topic under discussion.

Help every student gain a firm grasp of fundamentals
While discussion, reasoning and divergent thinking is to be encouraged, it can only be done on a firm scaffolding of basic math knowledge. A firm grasp of math principles, for most people, does require rote exercises and doing more and more of the same problems. Just as practicing scales is essential for musical creativity, math creativity can only be built on a foundation strengthened by drilling and repetition. Many educators see independent reasoning and traditional rule-based drilling as opposing approaches. An effective teacher, however, must maintain a balance between the two and ensure that students have the basic tools they need to think independently.

Make sure all students actually know basic math rules and concepts: Test students regularly for basic math knowledge and provide reinforcement with additional practice wherever necessary.

Keep reviewing old material: Don't underestimate your students' ability to forget what they haven't seen in a while. Link new topics whenever possible with things your students have learned before and take the opportunity to review previous learning. Most math textbooks nowadays have a spiral review section created with this end in mind.

Keep mental math muscles strong: The calculator, without question, is a very valuable learning tool. Many students, unfortunately, use it as a crutch to the point that they lose the natural feel for numbers and ability to estimate that people develop through mental calculations. As a result, they are often unable to tell when they punch a wrong button and get a very unreasonable answer. Take your students through frequent mental calculation exercises; you can easily integrate it into class discussions. Teach them useful strategies for making mental estimates.

Specific Teaching Methods

Some commonly used teaching techniques and tools are described below along with links to further information. The links provided in the first part of this chapter also provide a wealth of instructional ideas and material.

A very useful resource is the book "Family Math: The Middle School Years" from the Lawrence Hall of Science, University of California at Berkeley. Although this book was developed for use by families, teachers in school can choose from the many simple activities and games used to reinforce two significant middle school skills, algebraic reasoning and number sense. A further advantage is that all the activities are based on NCTM standards and each activity lists the specific math concepts that are covered.

Here are some tools you can use to make your teaching more effective:

Classroom openers
To start off your class with stimulated, interested and focused students, provide a short opening activity every day. You can make use of thought-provoking questions, puzzles or tricks. Also use relevant puzzles or tricks to illustrate specific topics at any point in your class. The following website provides some ideas:
http://mathforum.org/k12/k12puzzles/

Real life examples

Connect math to other aspects of your students' lives by using examples and data from the real world whenever possible. It will not only keep them engaged, it will also help answer the perennial question "Why do we have to learn math?" Online resources to get you started:

1. Using weather concepts to teach math:
   http://www.nssl.noaa.gov/edu/ideas/

2. Election math in the classroom:
   http://mathforum.org/t2t/faq/election.html

3. Math worksheets related to the Iditarod, an annual Alaskan sled dog race:
   http://www.educationworld.com/a_lesson/lesson/lesson302.shtml

4. Personal finance examples:
   http://www.publicdebt.treas.gov/mar/marmoneymath.htm

5. Graphing with real data:
   http://www.middleweb.com/Graphing.html

Manipulatives

Manipulatives can help all students learn; particularly those oriented more towards visual and kinesthetic learning. Here are some ideas for the use of manipulatives in the classroom:

1. Use tiles, pattern blocks or geoboards to demonstrate geometry concepts such as shapes, area and perimeter. In the example shown below, 12 tiles are used to form different rectangles.

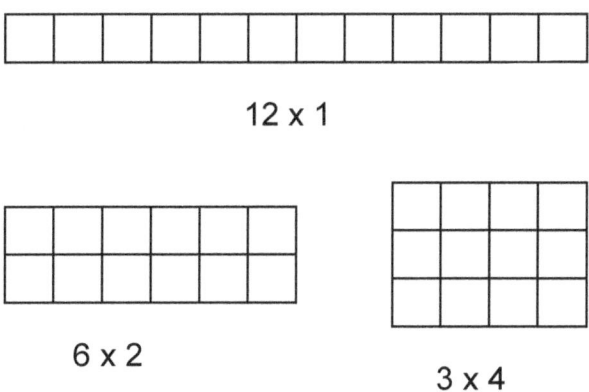

2. Stacks of blocks representing numbers are useful for teaching basic statistics concepts such as mean, median and mode. Rearranging the blocks to make each stack the same height would demonstrate the mean or average value of the data set. The example below shows a data set represented by stacks of blocks. Rearranging the blocks to make the height of each stack equal to three shows that this is the mean value.

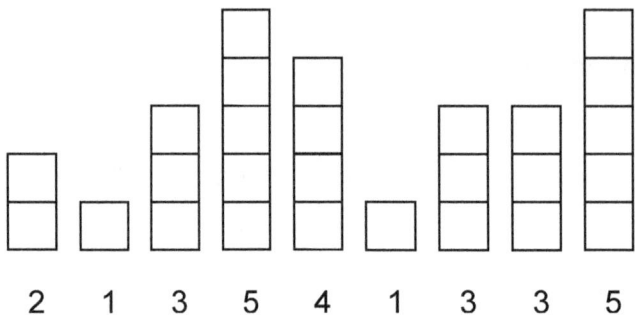

 2   1   3   5   4   1   3   3   5

3. Tiles, blocks, or other countable manipulatives such as beans can also be used to demonstrate numbers in different bases. Each stack will represent a place with the number of blocks in the stack showing the place value.

4. Playing cards can be used for a discussion of probability.

5. Addition and subtraction of integers, positive and negative, is a major obstacle for many middle school students. Two sets of tiles, marked with pluses and minuses respectively, can be used to demonstrate these concepts visually with each "plus" tile canceling a "minus" tile.

|+|+|+|+| |-|-|-|-|-| +4-5=-1

|-|-|-| |-|-|-|-| -3-4=-7

6. Percentages may be visualized using two parallel number lines, one showing the actual numbers, the other showing the percentages.

A practical demonstration of percent changes can be made by photocopying a figure using different copier magnifications.

7. Algeblocks are blocks designed specifically for the teaching of algebra with manipulatives:
http://www.etacuisenaire.com/algeblocks/algeblocks.jsp

Software

Many of the online references in this section link to software for learning. A good site that provides easy to use virtual manipulatives as well as accompanying worksheets in some cases is the following:
http://boston.k12.ma.us/teach/technology/select/index.html

Spreadsheets can be very effective math learning tools. Here are some ideas for using spreadsheets in the classroom:
http://www.angelfire.com/wi2/spreadsheet/necc.html

Word problem strategies

Word problems, a challenge for many students even in elementary school, become more complicated and sometimes intimidating in the middle grades. Here are some ideas students can use to tackle them:

1. Identify significant words and numbers in the problem. Highlight or underline them. If necessary, write them in the form of a table.

2. Draw diagrams to clarify the problem. Put down the main items or events and numbers on the diagram and show the relationships between them.

3. Rewrite the problem using fewer and simpler words. One way is to have a standard format for this as shown in the example below.
Problem: Calculate the cost of 3 pencils given that 5 pencils cost 25 cents.

Rewrite as:

Cost of 5 pencils = 25 cents
Cost of 1 pencil = 25/5 = 5 cents
Cost of 3 pencils = 5 X 3 = 15 cents

4. If you have no idea how to approach the problem, try the guess and check approach at first. That will give you a sense of the kind of problem you are dealing with.

5. Create similar word problems of your own.

Equation rule

Solving algebraic equations is a challenge for many learners particularly when they think they need to remember many different rules. Emphasize the fact that they only need to keep only one rule in mind whether they are adding, subtracting, multiplying or dividing numbers or variables:

"Do the same thing to both sides"

A balance or teeter-totter metaphor can help to clarify their understanding of equations. You can also use manipulatives to demonstrate.

Mental math practice

Give students regular practice in doing mental math. The following website offers many mental calculation tips and strategies:
http://mathforum.org/k12/mathtips/mathtips.html

Because frequent calculator use tends to deprive students of a sense of numbers, they will often approach a sequence of multiplications and divisions the hard way. For instance, asked to calculate 770 x 36/ 55, they will first multiply 770 and 36 and then do a long division with the 55. They fail to recognize that both 770 and 55 can be divided by 11 and then by 5 to considerably simplify the problem. Give students plenty of practice in multiplying and dividing a sequence of integers and fractions so they are comfortable with canceling top and bottom terms.

Math language

There is an explosion of new math words as students enter the middle grades and start learning algebra and geometry.

This website provides an animated, colorfully illustrated dictionary of math terms:
http://www.amathsdictionaryforkids.com/

The following site is not colorful and animated but contains brief and clear definitions and many more advanced math terms:
http://www.amathsdictionaryforkids.com/

FOUNDATION LEV. MATH.

WEB LINKS

ALGEBRA
Algebra in bite-size pieces with quiz at the end
http://library.thinkquest.org/20991/alg/index.html
Algebra II: http://library.thinkquest.org/20991/alg2/index.html

Different levels plus quiz
http://www.math.com/homeworkhelp/Algebra.html

Clicking on the number leads to solution
http://www.math.armstrong.edu/MathTutorial/index.html

Algebraic Structures
Symbols and sets of numbers:
http://www.wtamu.edu/academic/anns/mps/math/mathlab/beg_algebra/beg_alg_tut2_sets.htm

Integers: http://amby.com/educate/math/integer.html
Card game to add and subtract integers: http://www.education-world.com/a_tsl/archives/03-1/lesson001.shtml
Multiplying integers: http://www.aaastudy.com/mul65_x2.htm

Rational/irrational numbers: http://regentsprep.org/regents/math/math-topic.cfm?TopicCode=rational

Several complex number exercise pages:
http://math.about.com/od/complexnumbers/Complex_Numbers.htm

Polynomial Equations and Inequalities
Systems of equations lessons and practice:
http://regentsprep.org/regents/math/math-topic.cfm?TopicCode=syslin
More practice:
http://www.sparknotes.com/math/algebra1/systemsofequations/problems3.rhtml
Word problems system of equations:
http://regentsprep.org/REgents/math/ALGEBRA/AE3/PracWord.htm
Inequalities: http://regentsprep.org/regents/Math/solvin/PSolvIn.htm
Inequality tutorial, examples, problems
http://www.wtamu.edu/academic/anns/mps/math/mathlab/beg_algebra/beg_alg_tut18_ineq.htm
Graphing linear inequalities tutorial
http://www.wtamu.edu/academic/anns/mps/math/mathlab/beg_algebra/beg_alg_tut24_ineq.htm
Quadratic equations tutorial, examples, problems
http://www.wtamu.edu/academic/anns/mps/math/mathlab/col_algebra/col_alg_tut17_quad.htm

Practice factoring: http://regentsprep.org/Regents/math/math-topic.cfm?TopicCode=factor
Synthetic division tutorial:
http://www.wtamu.edu/academic/anns/mps/math/mathlab/col_algebra/col_alg_tut37_syndiv.htm
Synthetic division Examples and problems: http://www.tpub.com/math1/10h.htm

Functions
Function, domain, range intro and practice
http://www.mathwarehouse.com/algebra/relation/math-function.php
Equations with rational expressions tutorial
http://www.wtamu.edu/academic/anns/mps/math/mathlab/col_algebra/col_alg_tut15_rateq.htm
Practice with rational expressions
http://education.yahoo.com/homework_help/math_help/problem_list?id=minialg1_gt_7_1
Practice simplifying radicals
http://www.bhs87.org/math/practice/radicals/radicalpractice.htm
Radical equations – lesson and practice
http://regentsprep.org/REgents/mathb/mathb-topic.cfm?TopicCode=7D3
Logarithmic functions tutorial
http://www.wtamu.edu/academic/anns/mps/math/mathlab/col_algebra/col_alg_tut43_logfun.htm

Linear Algebra
Practice operations with matrices
http://www.castleton.edu/Math/finite/operation_practice.htm
Matrices, introduction and practice
http://www.math.csusb.edu/math110/src/matrices/basics.html
Vector practice tip: http://www.phy.mtu.edu/~suits/PH2100/vecdot.html

GEOMETRY
Geometry
http://library.thinkquest.org/20991/geo/index.html
http://www.math.com/students/homeworkhelp.html#geometry
http://regentsprep.org/Regents/math/geometry/math-GEOMETRY.htm

Parallelism
Parallel lines practice
http://www.algebralab.org/lessons/lesson.aspx?file=Geometry_AnglesParallelLinesTransversals.xml

Plane Euclidean Geometry
Geometry facts and practice http://www.aaaknow.com/geo.htm
Triangles intro and practice
http://www.staff.vu.edu.au/mcaonline/units/geometry/triangles.html
Polygons exterior and interior angles practice
http://regentsprep.org/Regents/Math/math-topic.cfm?TopicCode=poly
Angles in circles practice
http://regentsprep.org/Regents/math/geometry/GP15/PcirclesN2.htm
Congruence of triangles – lessons, practice
http://regentsprep.org/Regents/math/geometry/GP4/indexGP4.htm
Pythagorean theorem and converse
http://regentsprep.org/Regents/math/geometry/GP13/indexGP13.htm
Circle equation practice
http://www.regentsprep.org/Regents/math/algtrig/ATC1/circlepractice.htm
Interactive parabola http://www.mathwarehouse.com/geometry/parabola/
Ellipse practice problems http://www.mathwarehouse.com/ellipse/equation-of-ellipse.php#equationOfEllipse

Three-Dimensional Geometry
3D figures intro and examples
http://www.mathleague.com/help/geometry/3space.htm

Transformational Geometry
Interactive transformational geometry practice on coordinate plane
http://www.shodor.org/interactivate/activities/Transmographer/
Similar triangles practice
http://regentsprep.org/Regents/math/similar/PracSim.htm

http://www.algebralab.org/practice/practice.aspx?file=Geometry_UsingSimilarTriangles.xml

NUMBER THEORY
Natural Numbers
http://online.math.uh.edu/MiddleSchool/Vocabulary/NumberTheoryVocab.pdf
GCF and LCM practice
http://teachers.henrico.k12.va.us/math/ms/C1Files/01NumberSense/1_5/6035prac.htm

PROBABILITY AND STATISTICS

Probability

Probability intro and practice
http://www.mathgoodies.com/lessons/vol6/intro_probability.html
Permutation and combination practice
http://www.regentsprep.org/Regents/math/algtrig/ATS5/PCPrac.htm
Conditional probability problems
http://homepages.ius.edu/MEHRINGE/T102/Supplements/HandoutConditionalProbability.htm

Statistics

Statistics lessons and interactive practice
http://www.aaaknow.com/sta.htm
Range, mean, median, mode exercises
http://www.mathgoodies.com/lessons/vol8/practice_vol8.html
http://regentsprep.org/regents/Math/mean/Pmeasure.htm

Sample Test

1. Given W = whole numbers
   N = natural numbers
   Z = integers
   R = rational numbers
   I = irrational numbers

   Which of the following is not true?
   (SMR 1.1)(Easy Rigor.)

   A. $R \subset I$

   B. $W \subset Z$

   C. $Z \subset R$

   D. $N \subset W$

2. Which of the following is an irrational number?
   (SMR 1.1) (Easy Rigor)

   A. .362626262...

   B. $4^{\frac{1}{3}}$

   C. $\sqrt{5}$

   D. $-\sqrt{16}$

3. Express .0000456 in scientific notation.
   (SMR 1.1)(Easy Rigor)

   A. $4.56 x 10^{-4}$

   B. $45.6 x 10^{-6}$

   C. $4.56 x 10^{-6}$

   D. $4.56 x 10^{-5}$

4. Which denotes an imaginary number?
   (SMR 1.1)(Easy Rigor)

   A. 4.1212121212...

   B. $-\sqrt{16}$

   C. $\sqrt{127}$

   D. $\sqrt{-100}$

5. Choose the correct statement:
   (SMR 1.1) (Easy Rigor)

   A. Rational and irrational numbers are both proper subsets of the real numbers.

   B. The set of whole numbers is a proper subset of the set of natural numbers.

   C. The set of integers is a proper subset of the set of irrational numbers.

   D. The set of real numbers is a proper subset of the natural, whole, integers, rational, and irrational numbers.

6. Which statement is an example of the identity axiom of addition? (SMR 1.1)(Easy Rigor)

   A. $3 + -3 = 0$

   B. $3x = 3x + 0$

   C. $3 \cdot \frac{1}{3} = 1$

   D. $3 + 2x = 2x + 3$

7. Change $.\overline{63}$ into a fraction in simplest form. (SMR 1.1)(Easy Rigor)

   A. $63/100$

   B. $7/11$

   C. $6\ 3/10$

   D. $2/3$

8. Which is not true? (Easy Rigor)(SMR 1.1)

   A. All irrational numbers are real numbers

   B. All integers are rational

   C. zero is a natural number

   D. All whole numbers are integers

9. Which axiom is incorrectly applied? (SMR 1.1)(Average Rigor)

   $3x + 4 = 7$

   Step a $3x + 4 - 4 = 7 - 4$
   additive equality

   step b $3x + 4 - 4 = 3$
   commutative axiom of addition

   Step c. $3x + 0 = 3$
   additive inverse

   Step d. $3x = 3$
   additive identity

   A. step a

   B. step b

   C. step c

   D. step d

10. Which of the following sets is closed under division? (SMR 1.1)(Easy Rigor)

    A. integers

    B. rational numbers

    C. natural numbers

    D. whole numbers

11. How many real numbers lie between −1 and +1? (SMR 1.1)(Easy Rigor)

   A. 0

   B. 1

   C. 17

   D. an infinite number

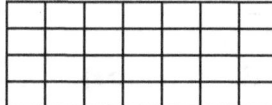

12. The above diagram would be most appropriate for illustrating which of the following? (SMR 1.1)(Easy Rigor)

   A. $7 \times 4 + 3$

   B. $31 \div 8$

   C. 28×3

   D. $31 - 3$

13. $24 - 3 \times 7 + 2 =$ (SMR 1.1) (Easy Rigor)

   A. 5

   B. 149

   C. −3

   D. 189

14. Which of the following does not correctly relate an inverse operation? (SMR 1.1) (Average Rigor)

   A. $-b = a + -b$

   B. $a \times b = b \div a$

   C. $\sqrt{a^2} = a$

   D. $a \times \frac{1}{a} = 1$

15. Given that x, y, and z are prime numbers, which of the following is true? (SMR 1.1) (Easy Rigor)

   A. x + y is always prime

   B. xyz is always prime

   C. xy is sometimes prime

   D. x + y is sometimes prime

16. Given that n is a positive even integer, 5n + 4 will always be divisible by: (SMR 1.1) (Easy Rigor)

   A. 4

   B. 5

   C. 5n

   D. 2

17. $(3.8 \times 10^{17}) \times (.5 \times 10^{-12})$
    (SMR 1.1) (Easy Rigor)

    A. 19×10^5

    B. 1.9×10^5

    C. 1.9×10^6

    D. 1.9×10^7

18. Evaluate $16\left(4^{\frac{1}{2}}\right)$

    (SMR 1.1) (Rigorous)

    A. $4^{\frac{5}{2}}$

    B. $\left(\sqrt{4}\right)^5$

    C. 32

    D. $64^{\frac{3}{4}}$

19. Simplify: $\sqrt{27} + \sqrt{75}$
    (SMR 1.1)(Easy Rigor)

    A. $8\sqrt{3}$

    B. 34

    C. $34\sqrt{3}$

    D. $15\sqrt{3}$

20. 2^{-3} is equivalent to
    (SMR 1.1)(Easy Rigor)

    A. 0.8

    B. −0.8

    C. 125

    D. .125

21. Simplify: $\dfrac{3.5(10^{-10})}{.7(10^4)}$

    (SMR 1.1)(Easy Rigor)

    A. 0.5×10^6

    B. 5.0×10^{-6}

    C. 5.0×10^{-14}

    D. 0.5×10^{-14}

22. Choose the set in which the members are <u>not</u> equivalent.
    (SMR 1.1)(Easy Rigor)

    A. 1/2, 0.5, 50%

    B. 10/5, 2.0, 200%

    C. 3/8, 0.385, 38.5%

    D. 7/10, 0.7, 70%

FOUNDATION LEV. MATH.

23. Find the GCF of $2^2 \cdot 3^2 \cdot 5$ and $2^2 \cdot 3$.
(SMR 1.2)(Average Rigor)

A. $2^5 \cdot 3^3 \cdot 5 \cdot 7$

B. $2 \cdot 3 \cdot 5 \cdot 7$

C. $2^2 \cdot 3$

D. $2^3 \cdot 3^2 \cdot 5 \cdot 7$

24. Given even numbers x and y, which could be the LCM of x and y?
(SMR 1.2)(Average Rigor)

A. $\frac{xy}{2}$

B. 2xy

C. 4xy

D. xy

25. A sofa sells for $520. If the retailer makes a 30% profit, what was the wholesale price? (SMR 1.2)(Rigorous)

A. $400

B. $676

C. $490

D. $364

26. Solve for x: $\frac{4}{x} = \frac{8}{3}$
(SMR 1.2) (Easy Rigor)

A. 0.66666...

B. 0.6

C. 15

D. 1.5

27. Simplify $\frac{a}{(\sqrt[3]{ax})^2}$
(SMR1.2)(Easy Rigor)

A. $\frac{a}{(ax)^3}$ 4

B. $\frac{\sqrt{ax}}{x^2}$

C. $\frac{\sqrt[3]{ax}}{x}$

D. $\frac{a\sqrt{ax}}{x}$

28. $7t - 4 \cdot 2t + 3t \cdot 4 \div 2 =$
(SMR 1.2) (Average Rigor)

A. 5t

B. 0

C. 31t

D. 18t

29. Solve for x: $3x + 5 \geq 8 + 7x$
    (SMR 1.2) (Rigorous)

    A. $x \geq -\frac{3}{4}$

    B. $x \leq -\frac{3}{4}$

    C. $x \geq \frac{3}{4}$

    D. $x \leq \frac{3}{4}$

30. Solve for x: $|2x +3| > 4$
    (SMR 1.2) Rigorous)

    A. $-\frac{7}{2} > x > \frac{1}{2}$

    B. $-\frac{1}{2} > x > \frac{7}{2}$

    C. $x < \frac{7}{2}$ or $x < -\frac{1}{2}$

    D. $x < -\frac{7}{2}$ or $x > \frac{1}{2}$

31. Solve the system of equations: $3x + 2y = 12$
    $12x + 8y = 15$
    (SMR 1.2) (Rigorous)

    A. all real numbers

    B. $x = 4, y = 4$

    C. $x = 2, y = -1$

    D. $\varnothing$

32. Solve the system of equations: $x = 3y + 7$
    $7x + 5y = 23$
    (SMR 1.2) (Rigorous)

    A. $(-1, 4)$

    B. $(4, -1)$

    C. $(\frac{-29}{7}, \frac{-26}{7})$

    D. $(10, 1)$

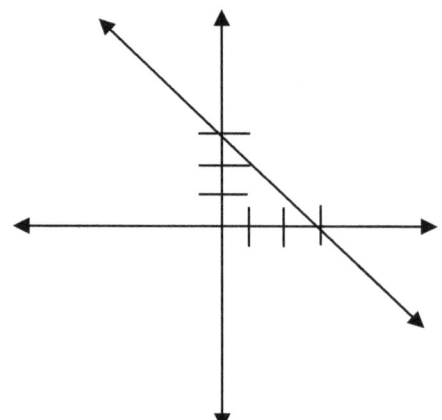

33. Which equation is represented by the above graph?
    (SMR 1.2) (Average Rigor)

    A. $x - y = 3$

    B. $x - y = -3$

    C. $x + y = 3$

    D. $x + y = -3$

34. Graph the solution:
   $|x| + 7 < 13$
   (SMR 1.2)(Rigorous)

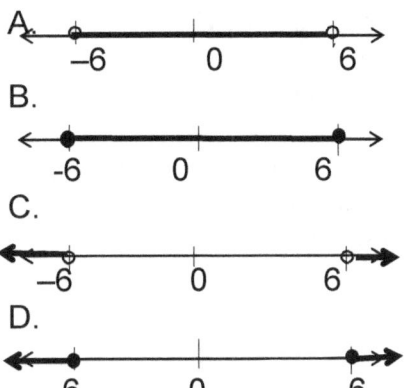

35. Three less than four times a number is five times the sum of that number and 6. Which equation could be used to solve this problem?
   (SMR 1.2)(Average rigor)

   A. $3 - 4n = 5(n + 6)$

   B. $3 - 4n + 5n = 6$

   C. $4n - 3 = 5n + 6$

   D. $4n - 3 = 5(n + 6)$

36. A boat travels 30 miles upstream in three hours. It makes the return trip in one and a half hours. What is the speed of the boat in still water?
   (SMR 1.2) (Rigorous)

   A. 10 mph

   B. 15 mph

   C. 20 mph

   D. 30 mph

37. Which of the following is a factor of $k^3 - m^3$?
   (SMR 1.2)(Rigorous)

   A. $k^2 + m^2$

   B. $k + m$

   C. $k^2 - m^2$

   D. $k - m$

38. Solve for x:
   $3x^2 - 2 + 4(x^2 - 3) = 0$
   (SMR1.2)(Rigorous)

   A. $\{-\sqrt{2}, \sqrt{2}\}$

   B. $\{2, -2\}$

   C. $\{0, \sqrt{3}, -\sqrt{3}\}$

   D. $\{7, -7\}$

39. The discriminant of a quadratic equation is evaluated and determined to be –3. The equation has
   (SMR 1.2)(Rigorous)

   A. one real root

   B. one complex root

   C. two roots, both real

   D. two roots, both complex

40. If y varies inversely as x and x is 4 when y is 6, what is the constant of variation? (SMR 1.2) (Rigorous)

   A. 2

   B. 12

   C. 3/2

   D. 24

41. If y varies directly as x and x is 2 when y is 6, what is x when y is 18? (SMR 1.2)(Rigorous)

   A. 3

   B. 6

   C. 26

   D. 36

42. The denominator of a fraction is 4 more than twice the numerator. If the numerator is doubled, and the denominator is increased by 4, the new fraction is equal to 3/4. Find the original number. (SMR 1.2)(Average Rigor)

   A. 12

   B. 8

   C. $\frac{3}{7}$

   D. 4

43. Solve the system of equations: (SMR 1.2) (Rigorous)

   3x + 2y = 18
   3x + 3y = 24

   A. (6,3)

   B. (2,6)

   C. (3, 4)

   D. (3,6)

44. Which of the following is incorrect?
(SMR 1.2)(Average Rigor)

A. $(x^2y^3)^2 = x^4y^6$

B. $m^2(2n)^3 = 8m^2n^3$

C. $\dfrac{(m^3n^4)}{(m^2n^2)} = mn^2$

D. $(x+y^2)^2 = x^2 + y^4$

45. Solve the system of equations for x, y and z.
(SMR 1.2) (Rigorous)

$3x + 2y - z = 0$
$2x + 5y = 8z$
$x + 3y + 2z = 7$

A. $(-1, 2, 1)$

B. $(1, 2, -1)$

C. $(-3, 4, -1)$

D. $(0, 1, 2)$

46. Simplify: $\dfrac{10}{1+3i}$
(SMR 1.2) (Rigorous)

A. $-1.25(1-3i)$

B. $1.25(1+3i)$

C. $1+3i$

D. $1-3i$

47. Which graph represents the solution set for $x^2 - 5x > -6$?
(SMR 1.2)(Rigorous)

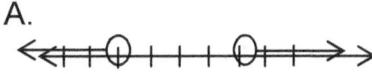

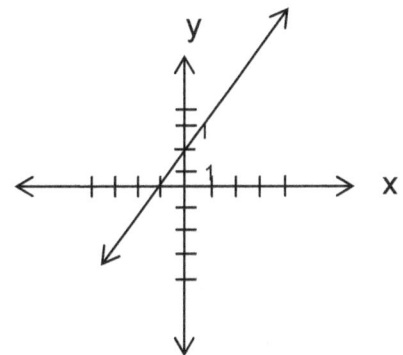

48. What is the equation of the above graph?
(SMR 1.2)(Average Rigor)

A. $2x + y = 2$

B. $2x - y = -2$

C. $2x - y = 2$

D. $2x + y = -2$

49. Which of the following is a factor of $6 + 48m^3$
 (SMR 1.2)(Rigorous)

   A.   (1 + 2m)

   B.   (1 – 8m)

   C.   (1 + m – 2m)

   D.   (1 – m + 2m)

50. Which graph (grid is 1) represents the equation of $y = x^2 + 3x$?
 (SMR 1.2)(Rigorous)

A)   B)

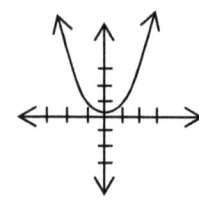   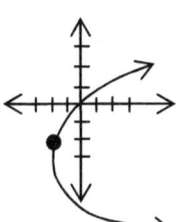

C)   D)

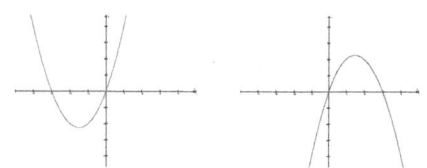

51. What is the slope of the equation 2y = 4 x + 3?
 (SMR 1.3)(Average Rigor)

   A. 2

   B. 3

   C. 1/2

   D. 4

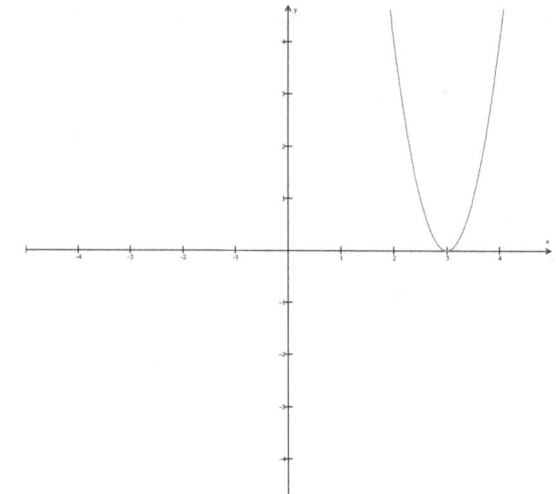

52. Which equation is graphed above? (grid is 1)
 (SMR 1.3) (Rigorous)

   A. y = 4 (x + 3)²

   B. y = 4 (x – 3)²

   C. y = 3 (x – 4)²

   D. y = 3 (x + 4)²

53. $f(x) = 3x - 2;\ f^{-1}(x) =$
 (SMR 1.3)(Rigorous)

   A. $3x + 2$

   B. $x/6$

   C. $2x - 3$

   D. $(x+2)/3$

54. Simplify: $\sqrt{75} + \sqrt{147} - \sqrt{48}$ (SMR 1.3)(Rigorous)

   A. 174
   B. $12\sqrt{3}$
   C. $8\sqrt{3}$
   D. 74

55. Which set illustrates a function? (SMR 1.3)(Easy Rigor)

   A. { (0,1) (0,2) (0,3) (0,4) }
   B. { (3,9) (–3,9) (4,16) (–4,16)}
   C. { (1,2) (2,3) (3,4) (1,4) }
   D. { (2,4) (3,6) (4,8) (4,16) }

56. Give the domain for the function over the set of real numbers: (SMR 1.3) (Average Rigor)

$$y = \frac{3x+2}{2x^2-3}$$

   A. all real numbers
   B. all real numbers, $x \neq 0$
   C. all real numbers, $x \neq -2$ or 3
   D. all real numbers, $x \neq \pm\frac{\sqrt{6}}{2}$

57. Factor completely: $8(x - y) + a(y - x)$ (SMR 1.3) (Rigorous)

   A. $(8 + a)(y - x)$
   B. $(8 - a)(y - x)$
   C. $(a - 8)(y - x)$
   D. $(a - 8)(y + x)$

58. Find the value of the determinant of this matrix: (SMR 1.3)(Average Rigor)

$$\begin{bmatrix} 4 & 5 \\ 6 & 2 \end{bmatrix}$$

   A. 22
   B. -10
   C. -22
   D. -16

59. Solve for x:
$\log_6(x-5) + \log_6 x = 2$
(SMR 1.3)(Rigorous)

A. x = -3, 8

B. x = -1, 10

C. x = 3, -9

D. x = -4, 9

60. Solve $\log_x 125 = 3$
(SMR 1.3) (Average Rigor)

A. 4

B. 5

C. 6

D. 3

61. What would be the total cost of a suit for $295.99 and a pair of shoes for $69.95 including 6.5% sales tax?
(SMR 1.3) (Average Rigor)

A. $389.73

B. $398.37

C. $237.86

D. $315.23

62. State the domain of the function $f(x) = \dfrac{3x-6}{x^2 - 25}$
(SMR1.3)(Rigorous)

A. $x \neq 2$

B. $x \neq 5, -5$

C. $x \neq 2, -2$

D. $x \neq 5$

63. Change $y = \log_4 32$ into exponential form.
(SMR 1.3)(Average Rigor)

A. $32 = 4^y$

B. $y = b^x$

C. $32 = y^4$

D. $32y^4 = 0$

64. If three cups of concentrate are needed to make 2 gallons of fruit punch, how many cups are needed to make 5 gallons?
(SMR 1.3)(Average Rigor)

A. 6 cups

B. 7 cups

C. 7.5 cups

D. 10 cups

65. Mr. Brown feeds his cat premium cat food, which costs $40 per month. Approximately how much will it cost to feed her for one year? (SMR 1.3) (Average Rigor)

A. $500

B. $400

C. $80

D. $4800

66. Find the value of the determinant of this matrix: (SMR 1.3)(Rigorous)

$$\begin{bmatrix} 4 & 3 & 2 \\ 5 & 7 & 8 \\ 9 & 1 & 6 \end{bmatrix}$$

A. 309

B. 123

C. 213

D. 146

67. Find the center of a circle with a diameter whose endpoints are (4,5) and (-4, -6). (Average Rigor) (SMR 2.1)

A. (-2, ½)

B. (0, -1/2)

C. (-1, 0)

D. (0, 1)

68. Two non-coplanar lines that do not intersect are labeled (SMR 2.1)(Average Rigor)

A. parallel lines

B. perpendicular lines

C. skew lines

D. alternate exterior lines

69. Find the angles of a parallelogram if one angle is 44 degrees. (SMR 2.1) (Rigorous)

A. 130, 130, 90

B. 44, 136, 136

C. 42, 140, 140

D. 40, 132, 138

70. Given $\overleftrightarrow{1} \parallel \overleftrightarrow{2}$ prove
$\angle b \cong \angle e$
(SMR 2.1)(Average Rigor)

1) $\angle b \cong \angle d$ 1) vertical angle theorem

2) $\angle d \cong \angle e$ 2) alternate interior angle theorem

3) $\angle b \cong \angle e$ 3) corresponding angles postulate

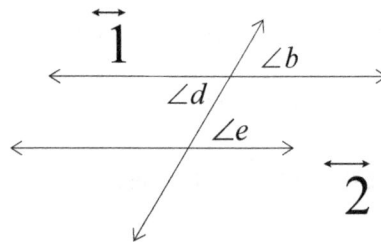

Which step is incorrectly justified?

A. step 1

B. step 2

C. step 3

D. no error

71. Given $\overline{XY} \cong \overline{ZY}$ and $\angle AYX \cong \angle AYZ$. Prove $\triangle AYZ \cong \triangle AYX$.

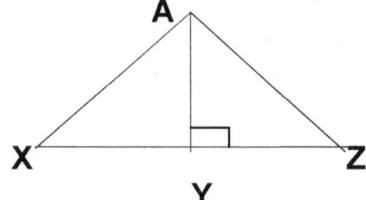

1) $\overline{XY} \cong \overline{ZY}$

2) $\angle AYX \cong \angle AYZ$

3) $\overline{AY} \cong \overline{AY}$

4) $\triangle AYZ \cong \triangle AYX$

Which property justifies step 3?
(SMR 2.1)(Easy Rigor)

A. reflexive

B. symmetric

C. transitive

D. identity

72. Define $\angle A$.
    (SMR 2.1) (Average Rigor)

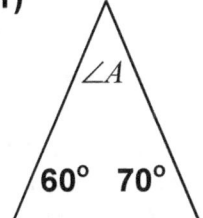

A. 30 degrees

B. 40 degrees

C. 50 degrees

D. 45 degrees

73. What is the supplementary angle to 75 degrees?
    (SMR 2.1) (Average Rigor)

A. 15 degrees

B. 105 degrees

C. 95 degrees

D. 290 degrees

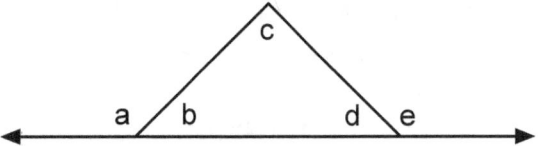

74. Which of the following statements is true about the number of degrees in each angle?
    (SMR 2.1) (Average Rigor)

A. a + b + c = 180°

B. a = e

C. b + c = e

D. c + d = e

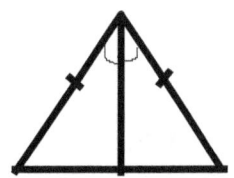

75. What method could be used to prove the above triangles congruent?
    (SMR2.1) (Average Rigor)

A. SSS

B. SAS

C. AAS

D. SSA

76. Find the distance between (3, 7) and (–3, 4).
   (SMR 2.1) (Rigorous)

   A. 9

   B. 45

   C. $3\sqrt{5}$

   D. $5\sqrt{3}$

77. Find the midpoint of (2,5) and (7,–4).
   (SMR 2.1)(Rigorous)

   A. (9,–1)

   B. (5, 9)

   C. (9/2, –1/2)

   D. (9/2, 1/2)

78. Given segment AC with B as its midpoint find the coordinates of C if A = (5,7) and B = (3, 6.5)>
   (SMR 2.1)(Rigorous)

   A. (4, 6.5)

   B. (1, 6)

   C. (2, 0.5)

   D. (16, 1)

79.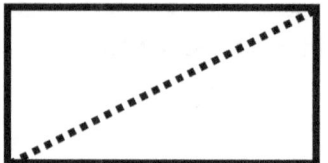

   The above diagram is most likely used in deriving a formula for which of the following.
   (SMR 2.1)(Average Rigor)

   A. the area of a rectangle

   B. the area of a triangle

   C. the perimeter of a triangle

   D. the surface area of a prism

80.

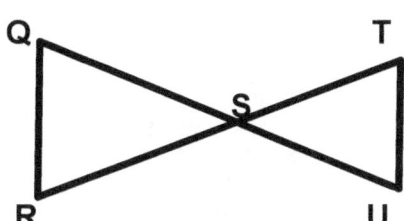

Given $\overline{QS} \cong \overline{TS}$ and $\overline{RS} \cong \overline{US}$, prove $\triangle QRS \cong \triangle TUS$. (SMR 2.1) (Average Rigor)

1) $\overline{QS} \cong \overline{TS}$ 1) Given
2) $\overline{RS} \cong \overline{US}$ 2) Given
3) $\angle TSU \cong \angle QSR$ 3) ?
4) $\triangle TSU \cong \triangle QSR$ 4) SAS

Give the reason that justifies step 3.

A. Congruent parts of congruent triangles are congruent

B. Reflexive axiom of equality

C. Alternate interior angle Theorem

D. Vertical angle theorem

81. In similar polygons, if the perimeters are in a ratio of x:y, the sides are in a ratio of: (SMR 2.1) (Rigorous)

A. $x : y$

B. $x^2 : y^2$

C. $2x : y$

D. $\dfrac{x}{2} : y$

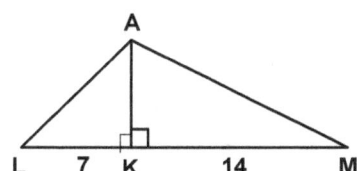

82. Given altitude AK in the right triangle ALM with measurements as indicated, determine the length of AK. (SMR 2.1)(Rigorous)

A. 98

B. $7\sqrt{2}$

C. $\sqrt{21}$

D. $7\sqrt{3}$

83. Which of the following can be defined? (SMR 2.1)(Easy rigor)

   A. point

   B. ray

   C. line

   D. plane

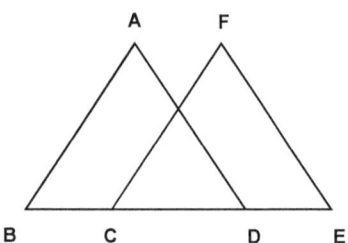

84. Which theorem could be used to prove △ABD ≅ △FEC, given $\overline{BC} \cong \overline{DE}$, ∠C ≅ ∠D, and $\overline{AD} \cong \overline{CF}$? (SMR 2.2)(Average Rigor)

   A. ASA

   B. SAS

   C. SAA

   D. SSS

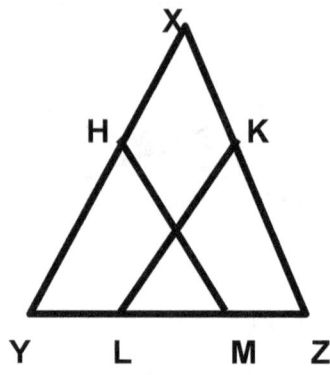

85. Prove △HYM ≅ △KZL, given $\overline{XZ} \cong \overline{XY}$, ∠L ≅ ∠M and $\overline{YL} \cong \overline{MZ}$

   1) $\overline{XZ} \cong \overline{XY}$ 1) Given
   2) ∠Y ≅ ∠Z   2) ?
   3) ∠L ≅ ∠M   3) Given
   4) $\overline{YL} \cong \overline{MZ}$ 4) Given
   5) $\overline{LM} \cong \overline{LM}$ 5) ?
   6) $\overline{YM} \cong \overline{LZ}$ 6) Add
   7) △HYM ≅ △KZL   7) ASA

   Which could be used to justify steps 2 and 5? (SMR 2.2) (Rigorous)

   A. CPCTC, Identity

   B. Isosceles Triangle Theorem, Identity

   C. SAS, Reflexive

   D. Isosceles Triangle Theorem, Reflexive

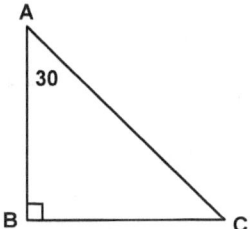

86. If $\overline{AC}$ = 12, determine $\overline{BC}$.
    (SMR 2.2)(Average Rigor)

    A. 6

    B. 4

    C. $6\sqrt{3}$

    D. $3\sqrt{6}$

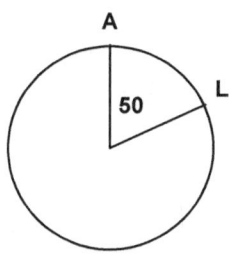

87. What is the measure of major arc AL?
    (SMR 2.2)(Average Rigor)

    A. 50°

    B. 25°

    C. 100°

    D. 310°

88. Given similar polygons with corresponding sides 6 and 8, what is the area of the smaller if the area of the larger is 64?
    (SMR 2.2)(Average Rigor)

    A. 48

    B. 36

    C. 144

    D. 78

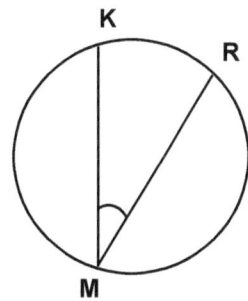

89. If arc KR = 70° what is the measure of ∠M?
    (SMR 2.2)(Average Rigor)

    A. 290°

    B. 35°

    C. 140°

    D. 110°

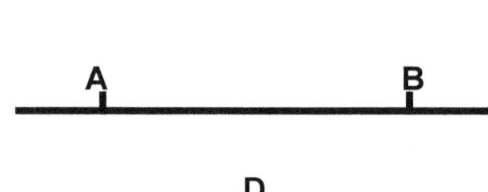

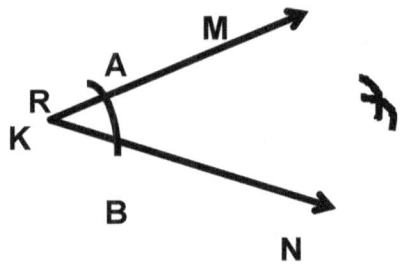

90. The above construction can be completed to make… (SMR 2.2)(Average Rigor)

A. an angle bisector

B. parallel lines

C. a perpendicular bisector

D. skew lines

91. A line from R to K will form.. (SMR 2.2)(Average Rigor)

A. an altitude of ∠ RMN

B. a perpendicular bisector of $\overline{MN}$

C. a bisector of ∠ MRN

D. a vertical angle

92. Find the missing side: (Average Rigor)(SMR 2.2)

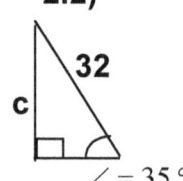

∠ = 35°

A. 11.65

B. 19.5

C. 23

D. 27.13

93. 4 square yards is equivalent to… (SMR 2.2)(Average Rigor)

A. 12 square feet

B. 48 square feet

C. 36 square feet

D. 108 square feet

94. If a circle has an area of 25 cm², what is its circumference to the nearest tenth of a centimeter? (SMR 2.2)(Average Rigor)

A. 78.5 cm

B. 17.7 cm

C. 8.9 cm

D. 15.7 cm

95. Find the area of the figure low.(SMR 2.2)Rigorous)

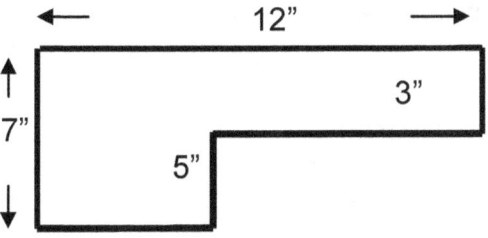

A. 56 in²

B. 27 in²

C. 71 in²

D. 170 in²

96. Find the area of the shaded region given square ABCD with side AB=10m and circle E. (SMR 2.2)(Rigorous)

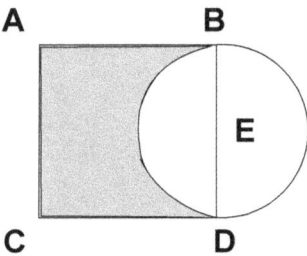

A. 178.5 m²

B. 139.25 m²

C. 71 m²

D. 60.75 m²

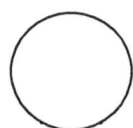

97. Given the regular hexagon in the circle above, determine the degree of the hexagon's central angle. (SMR 2.2) (Rigorous)

    A. 30°

    B. 60°

    C. 120°

    D. 90°

98. Given similar polygons with corresponding sides of lengths 9 and 15, find the perimeter of the smaller polygon if the perimeter of the larger polygon is 150 units. (SMR 2.2)(Rigorous)

    A. 54

    B. 135

    C. 90

    D. 126

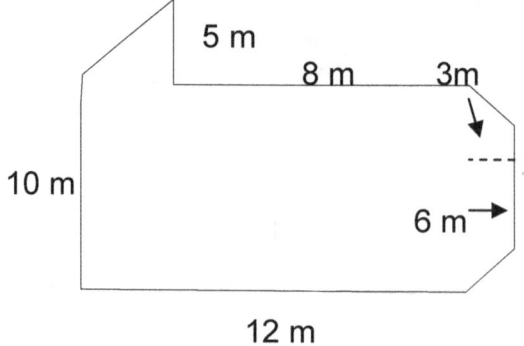

99. Compute the area of the polygon shown above. (SMR 2.2)(Rigorous)

    A. 178 m²

    B. 154 m²

    C. 43 m²

    D. 188 m²

100. Given $l_1 \parallel l_2$, which of the following is true? (SMR 2.2) (Average Rigor)

    A. ∠1 and ∠8 are congruent and alternate interior angles

    B. ∠2 and ∠3 are congruent and corresponding angles

    C. ∠3 and ∠4 are adjacent and supplementary angles

    D. ∠3 and ∠5 are adjacent and supplementary angles

101. A car is driving north at 74 miles per hour from point A. Another car is driving due east at 65 miles per hour from the same point at the same time. How far are the cars away from each other after 2 hours? (Rigorous)(SMR 2.2)

   A. 175.87

   B. 232.66

   C. 196.99

   D. 202.43

102. Which term most accurately describes two coplanar lines without any common points? (SMR 2.2)(Average Rigor)

   A. Perpendicular

   B. Parallel

   C. Intersecting

   D. skew

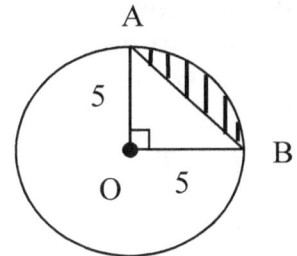

103. Compute the area of the shaded region, given a radius of 5 meters. O is the center. (SMR 2.2)(Rigorous)

   A. 7.13cm²

   B. 7.13m²
       6.13
   C. 78.5 m²

   D. 19.63 m²

104. If you have a triangle with these dimensions, solve for x if ∠B is 27°. ((Rigorous)(SMR 2.2)

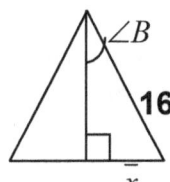

   A. 8.45

   B. 7.26

   C. 7.78

   D. 6.89

109. Find the area of the figure pictured below. (SMR 2.2)(Rigorous)

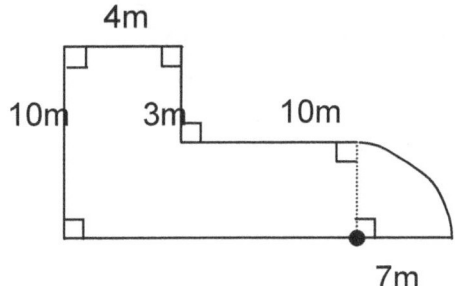

A. 136.47 m²

B. 148.48 m²

C. 293.86 m²

D. 178.47 m²

110. Solve the system of equations for x, y and z. SMR 2.2)(Rigorous)

$3x + 2y - z = 0$
$2x + 5y = 8z$
$x + 3y + 2z = 7$

A. $(-1, 2, 1)$

B. $(1, 2, -1)$

C. $(-3, 4, -1)$

D. $(0, 1, 2)$

111. Solve for x: $18 = 4 + |2x|$ (SMR 2.2)(Average Rigor)

A. $\{-11, 7\}$

B. $\{-7, 0, 7\}$

C. $\{-7, 7\}$

D. $\{-11, 11\}$

112. What is the arc length of a fourth of a circle with a diameter of 24 cm? (Average Rigor)(SMR 2.2)

A. 18.85

B. 75.4

C. 32.45

D. 20.75

113. Which theorem can be used to prove $\triangle BAK \cong \triangle MKA$? (SMR 2.2)(Rigorous)

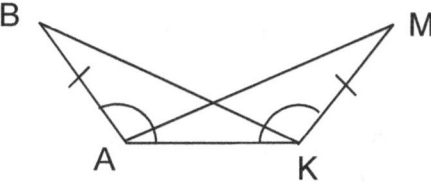

A. SSS

B. ASA

C. SAS

D. AAS

105. What is the degree measure of an interior angle of a regular 10-sided polygon?
(SMR 2.2)(Average Rigor)

   A. 18°

   B. 36°

   C. 144°

   D. 54°

106. If a ship sails due south 6 miles, then due west 8 miles, how far was it from the starting point?
(SMR 2.2)(Average Rigor)

   A. 100 miles

   B. 10 miles

   C. 14 miles

   D. 48 miles

107. What is the measure of minor arc AD, given measure of arc PS is 40° and $m<K=10°$?
(SMR 2.2)(Rigorous)

   A. 50°

   B. 20°

   D. 30°

   D. 25°

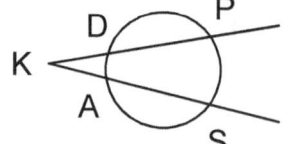

108. Choose the diagram that illustrates the construction of a perpendicular to the line at a given point on the line.
(SMR 2.2)(Average Rigor)

   A.

   B.

   C.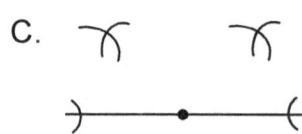

   D.

114. Given that QO⊥NP and QO=NP, quadrilateral NOPQ can most accurately be described as a (SMR 2.2)(Average Rigor)

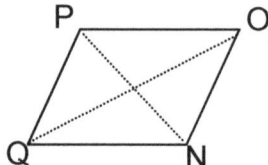

A. Parallelogram

B. Rectangle

C. Square

D. rhombus

115. Choose the correct statement concerning the median and altitude in a triangle. (SMR 2.2)(Average Rigor)

A. The median and altitude of a triangle may be the same segment.

B. The median and altitude of a triangle are always different segments.

C. The median and altitude of a right triangle are always the same segment.

D. The median and altitude of an isosceles triangle are always the same segment.

116. Given a 30 meter x 60 meter garden with a circular fountain with a 5 meter radius, calculate the area of the portion of the garden not occupied by the fountain. (SMR 2.2)(Rigorous)

A. 1721 m²

B. 1879 m²

C. 2585 m²

D. 1015 m²

117. Determine the area of the shaded region of the trapezoid in terms of x & y (the height of $\triangle ABC$). $\overline{DE}$ = 2x & $\overline{DC}$ = 3x. (SMR 2.2) (Rigorous)

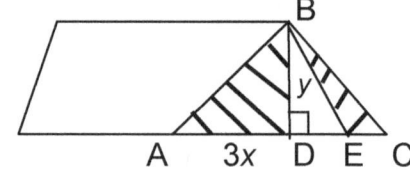

A. $4xy$

B. $2xy$

C. $3x^2y$

D. There is not enough information given.

118. Which mathematician is best known for his work in developing non-Euclidean geometry? (SMR 2.2)(Easy Rigor)

    A. Descartes

    B. Riemann

    C. Pascal

    D. Pythagoras

119. Find the surface area of a box which is 3 feet wide, 5 feet tall, and 4 feet deep. (SMR 2.3)(Rigorous)

    A. 47 sq. ft.

    B. 60 sq. ft.

    C. 94 sq. ft

    D. 188 sq. ft.

120. What happens to the volume of a square pyramid when the sides of the base are tripled? (Rigorous) (SMR 2.3)

    A. The volume is increased by a factor of 9

    B. The volume is increased by a factor of 8

    C. The volume is increased by a factor of 27

    D. The volume is increased by a factor of 16

121. The volume of water flowing through a pipe varies directly with the square is the radius of the pipe. If the water flows at a rate of 80 liters per minute through a pipe with a radius of 4 cm, at what rate would water flow through a pipe with a radius of 3 cm?
(SMR 2.3)(Rigorous)

    A. 45 liters per minute

    B. 6.67 liters per minute

    C. 60 liters per minute

    D. 4.5 liters per minute

122. What is the volume of a cylinder of a height 8 cm and a diameter of 4 cm? (Average Rigor)(SMR 2.3)

   A. 95.45

   B. 100.5

   C. 110.3

   D. 105.4

123. If the area of the base of a cone is tripled, the volume will be (SMR 2.3)(Rigorous)

   A. the same as the original

   B. 9 times the original

   C. 3 times the original

   D. 3π times the original

124. If the radius of a right cylinder is doubled, how does its volume change? (SMR 2.3)(Rigorous)

   A. no change

   B. also is doubled

   C. four times the original

   D. pi times the original

125. Which is a postulate? (SMR 2.2)(Easy Rigor)

   A. The sum of the angles in any triangle is 180°.

   B. A line intersects a plane in one point.

   C. Two intersecting lines from congruent vertical angles.

   D. Any segment is congruent to itself.

126. Determine the volume of a sphere to the nearest cm if the surface area is 113 cm^2. (SMR 2.3)(Rigorous)

   A. 113 cm^3

   B. 339 cm^3

   C. 37.7 cm^3

   D. 226 cm3

127. Find the zeroes of
   $f(x) = x^3 + x^2 - 14x - 24$
   (SMR 2.3)(Rigorous)

   A. 4, 3, 2

   B. 3, −8

   C. 7, −2, −1

   D. 4, −3, −2

128. Compute the surface area of the prism. (SMR 2.3)(Average Rigor)

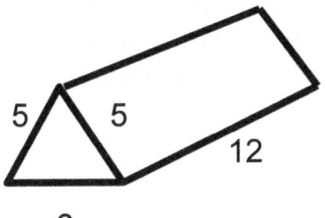

A. 204

B. 216

C. 360

D. 180

129. If the area of the base of a regular square pyramid is tripled, how does its volume change? (SMR 2.3)(Rigorous)

A. double the original

B. triple the original

C. nine times the original

D. no change

130. What is the surface area of a sphere with a circumference of 46 cm? (Rigorous)(SMR 2.3)

A. 475.6

B. 546.7

C. 673.4

D. 643.5

131. How does lateral area differ from total surface area in prisms, pyramids, and cones? (SMR 2.3) (Average Rigor)

A. For the lateral area, only use surfaces perpendicular to the base.

B. They are both the same.

C. The lateral area does not include the base.

D. The lateral area is always a factor of pi.

132. Given a drawer with 5 black socks, 3 blue socks, and 2 red socks, what is the probability that you will draw two black socks in two draws in a dark room? (SMR 4.1)(Rigorous)

A. 2/9

B. 1/4

C. 17/18

D. 1/18

133. A sack of candy has 3 peppermints, 2 butterscotch drops and 3 cinnamon drops. One candy is drawn and replaced, then another candy is drawn; what is the probability that both will be butterscotch?
(SMR 4.1) (Rigorous)

   A. 1/2

   B. 1/28

   C. 1/4

   D. 1/16

134. How many ways are there to choose a potato and two green vegetables from a choice of three potatoes and seven green vegetables?
(SMR 4.1) (Rigorous)

   A. 126

   B. 63

   C. 21

   D. 252

135. Given a spinner with the numbers one through eight, what is the probability that you will spin an even number or a number greater than four?
(SMR 4.2)(Average Rigor)

   A. 1/4

   B. 1/2

   C. 3/4

   D. 1

136. A measure of association between two variables is called:
(SMR 4.2) (Easy Rigor)

   A. Associate

   B. Correlation

   C. Confidence interval

   D. Variation

137. Compute the median for the following data set: {12, 19, 13, 16, 17, 14}
(SMR 4.2) (Average Rigor)

   A. 14.5

   B. 15.17

   C. 15

   D. 16

138. Half the students in a class scored 80% on an exam, most of the rest scored 85% except for one student who scored 10%. Which would be the best measure of central tendency for the test scores?
(SMR 4.2) (Average Rigor)

    A. Mean

    B. Median

    C. Mode

    D. either the median or the mode because they are equal

139. What is the first, second and third quartile for the following?
(SMR 4.2) (Average Rigor)

    5, 5, 5, 6, 7, 9, 9, 10, 11, 12, 13, 13, 14, 15, 16, 17, 17

    A. 5, 10, 15

    B. 6, 11, 16

    C. 7, 11, 14

    D. 6.5, 11, 14.5

140. A student scored in the 87th percentile on a standardized test. Which would be the best interpretation of his score? (SMR 4.2)(Average Rigor)

    A. Only 13% of the students who took the test scored higher.

    B. This student should be getting mostly B's on his report card.

    C. This student performed below average on the test.

    D. This is the equivalent of missing 13 questions on a question exam.

141. If a horse will probably win three races out of ten, what are the odds that he will win?
(SMR 4.1)(Average Rigor)

    A. 3:10

    B. 7:10

    C. 3:7

    D. 7:3

142. Determine the number of subsets of set K.
K = {4, 5, 6, 7}
(SMR 4.2)(Rigorous)

A. 15

B. 16

C. 17

D. 18

143. What is the range of the following numbers?
34, 14, 43, 35, 45, 18, 33, 42
(SMR 4.2)(Average Rigor)

A. 31

B. 32

C. 26

D. 19

144. Find the median of the following set of data:
14 3 7 6 11 20
(SMR 4.2)(Easy Rigor)

A. 9

B. 8.5

C. 7

D. 11

145. Corporate salaries are listed for several employees. Which would be the best measure of central tendency?
(SMR 4.2)(Average Rigor)

$24,000 $24,000
$26,000 $28,000
$30,000 $120,000

A. mean

B. median

C. mode

D. no difference

146. The tenth percentile is in what stanine?
(SMR 4.2)(Easy Rigor)

A. First

B. Second

C. Third

D. Fourth

FOUNDATION LEV. MATH.

Answer Key

1. A	38. A	75. B	112. A
2. C	39. D	76. C	113. C
3. D	40. D	77. D	114. C
4. D	41. B	78. B	115. A
5. A	42. C	79. B	116. A
6. B	43. B	80. D	117. B
7. B	44. D	81 A	118. B
8. C	45. A	82. B	119. C
9. B	46. D	83. B	120. C
10. B	47. D	84. B	121. A
11. D	48. B	85. D	122. B
12. C	49. A	86. A	123. C
13. A	50. C	87. D	124. C
14. B	51. A	88. B	125. D
15. D	52. B	89. B	126. A
16. D	53. D	90. C	127. D
17. B	54. C	91. C	128. B
18. C	55. B	92. D	129. B
19. A	56. D	93. C	130. C
20. D	57. C	94. B	131. C
21. C	58. C	95. A	132. A
22. C	59. D	96. D	133. D
23. C	60. B	97. A	134. A
24. A	61. A	98. C	135. C
25. A	62. B	99. B	136. B
26. D	63. A	100. C	137. C
27. C	64. C	101. C	138. B
28. A	65. A	102. B	139. D
29. A	66. D	103. B	140. A
30. D	67. B	104. B	141. C
31. D	68. C	105. C	142. B
32. B	69. B	106. B	143. A
33. C	70. D	107. B	144. A
34. A	71. A	108. D	145. B
35. D	72. C	109. B	146. B
36. B	73. B	110. A	
37. D	74. C	111. C	

Rigor Table

Easy Rigor 20%	Average Rigor 40%	Rigorous 40%
1, 2, 3, 4, 5, 6, 7, 8, 10, 11, 12, 13, 15, 16, 17, 19 20,21,22,26,27,55,71,83 118, 125, 136, 144, 146	9, 14, 23, 24,28,33,35,42 44,46,48,51,56,58,60,61, 63,64,65,67,68,70,72,73 74,75,79,80,84,86,87,88 89,90,91,92,93,94,100, 102,105,106,108,111,112 114,115,122,128,131,135 137,138,139,140,141,143 145	18,25,29,30,31,32,34,36 37,38,39,40,41,43,4,47, 49,50,52,53,54,57,59,62 66,69,76,77,78,81,82,85, 95,96,97,98,99,101,104, 107,109,110,113,116,117 119,120,121,123,124,126 127,129,130,132,133,134 142

Rationales for Sample Questions

The following represent one way to solve the problems and obtain a correct answer.
There are many other mathematically correct ways of determining the correct answer.

1. Given W = whole numbers
   N = natural numbers
   Z = integers
   R = rational numbers
   I = irrational numbers

   Which of the following is not true? (SMR 1.1)(Easy Rigor.)

   A. $R \subset I$
   B. $W \subset Z$
   C. $Z \subset R$
   D. $N \subset W$

Answer is A. The rational numbers are not a subset of the irrational numbers. All of the other statements are true.

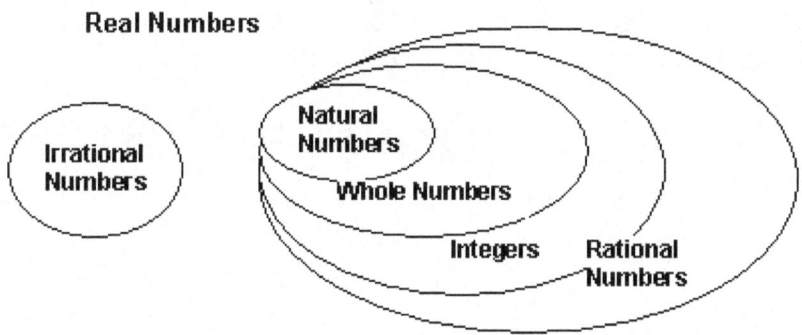

2. Which of the following is an irrational number? (SMR 1.1) (Easy Rigor)

    A. .362626262...
    B. $4^{\frac{1}{3}}$
    C. $\sqrt{5}$
    D. $-\sqrt{16}$

Answer is C. $\sqrt{5}$ is an irrational number A is a repeating decimal (decimals that do not repeat but go on are also irrational. A and B can both be expressed as fractions. D can be simplified to –4, an integer and rational number.

3. Express .0000456 in scientific notation. (SMR 1.1)(Easy Rigor)

    A. 4.56×10^{-4}
    B. 45.6×10^{-6}
    C. 4.56×10^{-6}
    D. 4.56×10^{-5}

Answer is D. In scientific notation, the decimal point belongs to the right of the 4, the first significant digit. To get from 4.56×10^{-5} back to 0.0000456, we would move the decimal point 5 places to the left.

4. Which denotes a imaginary number? (SMR 1.1)(Easy Rigor)

    A. 4.1212121212...
    B. $-\sqrt{16}$
    C. $\sqrt{127}$
    D. $\sqrt{-100}$

Answer is D. An imaginary number is the square root of a negative number. The imaginary number is defined as the square root of –1. A is rational, B is rational and C is irrational (not a perfect square under the radical sign).

TEACHER CERTIFICATION STUDY GUIDE

5. **Choose the correct statement: (SMR 1.1) (Easy Rigor)**

    A. Rational and irrational numbers are both proper subsets of the real numbers.
    B. The set of whole numbers is a proper subset of the set of natural numbers.
    C. The set of integers is a proper subset of the set of irrational numbers.
    D. The set of real numbers is a proper subset of the natural, whole, integers, rational, and irrational numbers.

Answer is A. A proper subset is completely contained in but not equal to the original set.

6. **Which statement is an example of the identity axiom of addition?(SMR 1.1) (Easy Rigor)**

    A. $3 + -3 = 0$
    B. $3x = 3x + 0$
    C. $3 \cdot \frac{1}{3} = 1$
    D. $3 + 2x = 2x + 3$

Answer is B. B illustrates the identity axiom of addition. A illustrates additive inverse, C illustrates the multiplicative inverse, and D illustrates the commutative axiom of addition.

7. **Change $.\overline{63}$ into a fraction in simplest form. (SMR 1.1) (Easy Rigor)**

    A. $63/100$
    B. $7/11$
    C. $6\ 3/10$
    D. $2/3$

Answer is B. Let N = .636363.... Then multiplying both sides of the equation by 100 or 10^2 (because there are 2 repeated numbers), we get 100N = 63.636363... Then subtracting the two equations (N = .636363... and 100N = 63.636363...), gives 99N = 63 or N = $\frac{63}{99} = \frac{7}{11}$. Answer is B

FOUNDATION LEV. MATH.

8. Which is not true? (Easy Rigor) (SMR 1.1)

   A. All irrational numbers are real numbers
   B. All integers are rational
   C. zero is a natural number
   D. All whole numbers are integers

Answer is C. Zero is not a natural number or "counting number".

9. Which axiom is incorrectly applied? (SMR 1.1) (Average Rigor)

   $3x + 4 = 7$

   Step a $3x + 4 - 4 = 7 - 4$
   additive equality

   step b $3x + 4 - 4 = 3$
   commutative axiom of addition

   Step c. $3x + 0 = 3$
   additive inverse

   Step d. $3x = 3$
   additive identity

   A. step a
   B. step b
   C. step c
   D. step d

Answer is B. In simplifying from step a to step b, 3 replaced $7 - 4$, therefore the correct justification would be subtraction or substitution.

10. Which of the following sets is closed under division? (SMR 1.1) (Easy Rigor)

   A. integers
   B. rational numbers
   C. natural numbers
   D. whole numbers

Answer is B. In order to be closed under division, when any two members of the set are divided the answer must be contained in the set. This is not true for integers, natural, or whole numbers as illustrated by the counter example 11/2 = 5.5.

11. How many real numbers lie between –1 and +1? (SMR 1.1)(Easy Rigor)

   A. 0
   B. 1
   C. 17
   D. an infinite number

Answer is D. There are an infinite number of real numbers between any two real numbers.

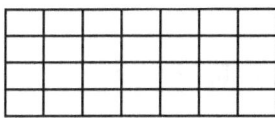

12. The above diagram would be most appropriate for illustrating which of the following? (SMR 1.1) (Easy Rigor)

   A. $7 \times 4 + 3$
   B. $31 \div 8$
   C. 28×3
   D. $31 - 3$

Answer is C. C is inappropriate. A shows a 7x4 rectangle with 3 additional units. B is the division based on 8, which makes no sense. D shows how mental subtraction might be visualized leaving a composite difference.

TEACHER CERTIFICATION STUDY GUIDE

13. 24 – 3 × 7 + 2 = (SMR 1.1) (Easy Rigor)

   A. 5
   B. 149
   C. -3
   D. 189

Answer is A. According to the order of operations PEMDAS, in this equation (which has no parentheses nor exponents) multiplication or division are performed first, then addition and subtraction from left to right (whichever comes first).

14. Which of the following does not correctly relate an inverse operation? (SMR 1.1) (Average Rigor)

   A. $a - b = a + -b$
   B. $a \times b = b \div a$
   C. $\sqrt{a^2} = a$
   D. $a \times \frac{1}{a} = 1$

Answer is B. B is always false. A, C, and D illustrate various properties of inverse relations.

15. Given that x, y, and z are prime numbers, which of the following is true? (SMR 1.1) (Easy Rigor)

   A. x + y is always prime
   B. xyz is always prime
   C. xy is sometimes prime
   D. x + y is sometimes prime

Answer is D. x + y is sometimes prime. B and C show the products of two numbers that are always composite. x + y may be true, but not always (e.g. 3 + 2 = 5 is prime but 3 + 3 = 6 is not), A.

FOUNDATION LEV. MATH.

16. Given that n is a positive even integer, 5n + 4 will always be divisible by: (SMR 1.1) (Easy Rigor)

   A. 4
   B. 5
   C. 5n
   D. 2

Answer is D. 5n is always even and even number added to an even number is always an even number, thus divisible by 2.

17. $(3.8 \times 10^{17}) \times (.5 \times 10^{-12})$ (SMR 1.1) (Easy Rigor)

   A. 19×10^5
   B. 1.9×10^5
   C. 1.9×10^6
   D. 1.9×10^7

Answer is B. Multiply the decimals and add the exponents.

18. Evaluate $16\left(4^{\frac{1}{2}}\right)$ (SMR 1.1) (Rigorous)

   A. $\left(\sqrt{4}\right)^5$
   B. $4^{\frac{5}{2}}$
   C. 32
   D. $64^{\frac{3}{4}}$

Answer is C. Getting the bases the same gives us $4^2\left(4^{\frac{1}{2}}\right)$. Adding exponents gives us $4^{\frac{5}{2}}$. But we can simplify further: $4^{\frac{5}{2}} = \left(\sqrt{4}\right)^5 = 2^5 = 32$. Answer is C.

19. Simplify: $\sqrt{27}+\sqrt{75}$ (SMR 1.1)(Easy Rigor)

   A. $8\sqrt{3}$

   B. 34

   C. $34\sqrt{3}$

   D. $15\sqrt{3}$

Answer is A. Simplifying radicals gives $\sqrt{27}+\sqrt{75}=3\sqrt{3}+5\sqrt{3}=8\sqrt{3}$. Answer is A.

20. 2^{-3} is equivalent to (SMR 1.1)(Easy Rigor)

   A. 0.8
   B. −0.8
   C. 125
   D. .125

Answer is D. Express as the fraction 1/8, then convert to a decimal.

21. Simplify: $\dfrac{3.5(10^{-10})}{.7(10^{4})}$ (SMR 1.1)(Easy Rigor)

   A. 0.5×10^{6}
   B. 5.0×10^{-6}
   C. 5.0×10^{-14}
   D. 0.5×10^{-14}

Answer is C. Divide the decimals and subtract the exponents.

22. Choose the set in which the members are <u>not</u> equivalent. (SMR 1.1)(Easy Rigor)

   A. 1/2, 0.5, 50%
   B. 10/5, 2.0, 200%
   C. 3/8, 0.385, 38.5%
   D. 7/10, 0.7, 70%

Answer is C. 3/8 is equivalent to .375 and 37.5%

23. Find the GCF of $2^2 \cdot 3^2 \cdot 5$ and $2^2 \cdot 3$. (SMR 1.2)(Average Rigor)

   A. $2^5 \cdot 3^3 \cdot 5 \cdot 7$
   B. $2 \cdot 3 \cdot 5 \cdot 7$
   C. $2^2 \cdot 3$
   D. $2^3 \cdot 3^2 \cdot 5 \cdot 7$

Answer is C. Choose the number of each prime factor that is in common.

24. Given even numbers x and y, which could be the LCM of x and y? (SMR 1.2) (Average Rigor)

   A. $\frac{xy}{2}$
   B. 2xy
   C. 4xy
   D. xy

Answer is A. Although choices B, C and D are common multiples, when both numbers are even, the product can be divided by two to obtain the least common multiple.

25. A sofa sells for $520. If the retailer makes a 30% profit, what was the wholesale price? (SMR 1.2)(Rigorous)

   A. $400
   B. $676
   C. $490
   D. $364

Answer is A. Let x be the wholesale price, then x + .30x = 520, 1.30x = 520. divide both sides by 1.30.

26. Solve for x: $\frac{4}{x} = \frac{8}{3}$ (SMR 1.2) (Easy Rigor)

   A. 0.66666...

   B. 0.6

   C. 15

   D. 1.5

Answer is D. Cross multiply to obtain 12 = 8x, then divide both sides by 8.

FOUNDATION LEV. MATH.

27) Simplify $\dfrac{a}{(\sqrt[3]{ax})^2}$ (SMR1.2)(Easy Rigor)

    A. $\dfrac{a}{(ax)^3}\,^4$

    B. $\dfrac{\sqrt{ax}}{x^2}$

    C. $\dfrac{\sqrt[3]{ax}}{x}$

    D. $\dfrac{a\sqrt{ax}}{x}$

Answer is C. multiply the numerator and denominator by $\sqrt[3]{ax}$ to get:

$$\dfrac{a\sqrt[3]{ax}}{(\sqrt[3]{ax})^2\sqrt[3]{ax}} = \dfrac{a\sqrt[3]{ax}}{(\sqrt[3]{ax})^3} = \dfrac{a\sqrt[3]{ax}}{ax} = \dfrac{\sqrt[3]{ax}}{x}$$

28. 7t − 4 •2t + 3t • 4 ÷ 2 = (SMR 1.2) (Average Rigor)

    A. 5t
    B. 0
    C. 31t
    D. 18t

Answer is A. First perform multiplication and division from left to right; 7t −8t + 6t, then add and subtract from left to right.

29. Solve for x: $3x + 5 \geq 8 + 7x$ (SMR 1.2) (Rigorous)

   A. $x \leq -\dfrac{3}{4}$

   B. $x \geq \dfrac{3}{4}$

   C. $x \leq \dfrac{3}{4}$

   D. $x \geq -\dfrac{3}{4}$

Answer is A. Using additive equality, $-4x \geq 3$. Divide both sides by -4 to obtain $x \leq -3/4$. Don't forget that when you divide or multiply an inequality by a negative number, you must reverse the inequality sign.

30. Solve for x: $|2x + 3| > 4$ (SMR 1.2)(Rigorous)

   A. $-\dfrac{7}{2} > x > \dfrac{1}{2}$

   B. $-\dfrac{1}{2} > x > \dfrac{7}{2}$

   C. $x < \dfrac{7}{2}$ or $x < -\dfrac{1}{2}$

   D. $x < -\dfrac{7}{2}$ or $x > \dfrac{1}{2}$

Answer is D. The quantity within the absolute value symbols must be either > 4 or < –4. Solve the two inequalities $2x + 3 > 4$ or $2x + 3 < -4$.

31. Solve the system of equations: $3x + 2y = 12$ $12x + 8y = 15$ (SMR 1.2) (Rigorous)

   A. all real numbers
   B. x = 4, y = 4
   C. x = 2, y = –1
   D. ∅

Answer is D. Multiplying the top equation by –4 and adding results in the equation 0 = - Since this is a false statement, the correct choice is the null set.

FOUNDATION LEV. MATH.

32. Solve the system of equations: x = 3y + 7   7x + 5y = 23 (SMR 1.2)
(Rigorous)

   A. (−1, 4)
   B. (4, −1)
   C. ($\frac{-29}{7}$, $\frac{-26}{7}$)
   D. (10, 1)

Answer is B. Substituting x in the second equation results in 7(3y + 7) + 5y = 23. Solve by distributing and grouping like terms: 26y + 49 = 23, 26y = −26, y = −1 Substitute y into the first equation to obtain x.

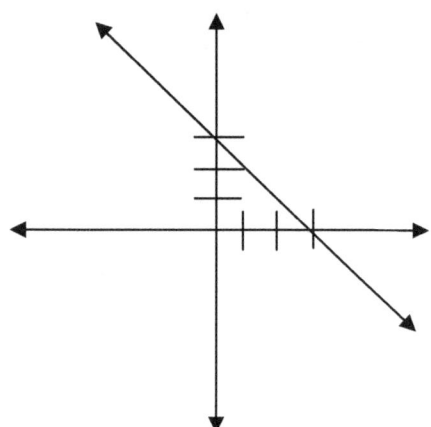

33. Which equation is represented by the above graph? (SMR 1.2)
(Average Rigor)

   A. x − y = 3
   B. x − y = −3
   C. x + y = 3
   D. x + y = −3

Answer is C. By looking at the graph, we can determine the slope to be −1 and the y-intercept to be 3. Write the slope-intercept form of the line as y = −1x + 3. Add x to both sides to obtain x + y = 3, the equation in standard form.

34. Graph the solution: $|x| + 7 < 13$ (SMR 1.2)(Rigorous)

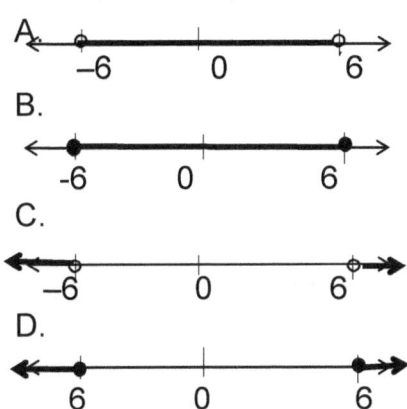

Answer is A. Solve by adding –7 to each side of the inequality. Since the absolute value of x is less than 6, x must be between –6 and 6. The end points are not included so the circles on the graph are hollow.

35. Three less than four times a number is five times the sum of that number and 6. Which equation could be used to solve this problem? (SMR 1.2)(Average rigor)

   A. $3 - 4n = 5(n + 6)$
   B. $3 - 4n + 5n = 6$
   C. $4n - 3 = 5n + 6$
   D. $4n - 3 = 5(n + 6)$

Answer is D. Be sure to enclose the sum of the number and 6 in parentheses and pay attention to the "three *less than*."

36. A boat travels 30 miles upstream in three hours. It makes the return trip in one and a half hours. What is the speed of the boat in still water? (SMR 1.2) (Rigorous)

   A. 10 mph
   B. 15 mph
   C. 20 mph
   D. 30 mph

Answer is B. Let x = the speed of the boat in still water and c = the speed of the current.

	rate	time	distance
upstream	x − c	3	30
downstream	x + c	1.5	30

Solve the system:
$3x - 3c = 30$
$1.5x + 1.5c = 30$

Multiply the 2nd equation by 2 to solve for x, then substitute in the value of x to solve for c. Always double check.

37. Which of the following is a factor of $k^3 - m^3$? (SMR 1.2)(Rigorous)

   A. $k^2 + m^2$
   B. $k + m$
   C. $k^2 - m^2$
   D. $k - m$

Answer is D. The complete factorization for a difference of cubes is $(k - m)(k^2 + mk + m^2)$.

38. Solve for x. (SMR 1.2)(Rigorous)

   $3x^2 - 2 + 4(x^2 - 3) = 0$

   A. $\{-\sqrt{2}, \sqrt{2}\}$
   B. $\{2, -2\}$
   C. $\{0, \sqrt{3}, -\sqrt{3}\}$
   D. $\{7, -7\}$

Answer is A. Distribute and combine like terms to obtain $7x^2 - 14 = 0$. Add 14 to both sides, then divide by 7. Since $x^2 = 2$, $x = \pm\sqrt{2}$

FOUNDATION LEV. MATH.

39. The discriminant of a quadratic equation is evaluated and determined to be –3. The equation has: (SMR 1.2)(Rigorous)

  A. one real root
  B. one complex root
  C. two roots, both real
  D. two roots, both complex

Answer is D. The discriminant is the number under the radical sign of the quadratic equation. Since it is negative or less than zero, the two roots of the equation are complex.

40. If y varies inversely as x and x is 4 when y is 6, what is the constant of variation? (SMR 1.2) (Rigorous)

  A. 2
  B. 12
  C. 3/2
  D. 24

Answer is D. The constant of variation for an inverse proportion is k = xy = 24.

41. If y varies directly as x and x is 2 when y is 6, what is x when y is 18? (SMR 1.2) (Rigorous)

  A. 3
  B. 6
  C. 26
  D. 36

Answer is B. The equation for direct variation is y = kx or k = $\frac{y}{x}$ or $\frac{6}{2} = 3$.
Substitute 18 for y and 3 for k and solve: 18 = 3x, x = 6.

42. The denominator of a fraction is 4 more than twice the numerator. If the numerator is doubled, and the denominator is increased by 4, the new fraction is equal to 3/4. Find the original number. (SMR 1.2)(Average Rigor)

   A. 12
   B. 8
   C. $\dfrac{3}{7}$
   D. 4

Answer is C: $\dfrac{x}{2x+4}$ and $\dfrac{2x}{2x+8} = \dfrac{3}{4}$.

Cross multiply the 2nd equation: 8x = 6x + 24. Solving for x gives x = 12 in the second equation, however, the question asks for the original value of x.

Substitute 12 into the 1st equation and solve: $\dfrac{12}{2(12)+4} = \dfrac{12}{28} = \dfrac{3}{7}$

43. Solve: (SMR 1.2)(Rigorous)

   3x + 2y = 18
   3x + 3y = 24

   A. (6,3)
   B. (2,6)
   C. (3, 4)
   D. (3,6)

Answer is B. Solving by elimination, multiply the 2nd equation by -1 and add to the first to solve for y: -y = -6 or y = 6. Then substitute 6 in for y in either equation to solve for x. x=2 or (2,6). Double check.

44. Which of the following is incorrect? (SMR 1.2)(Average Rigor)

A. $(x^2y^3)^2 = x^4y^6$

B. $m^2(2n)^3 = 8m^2n^3$

C. $\dfrac{m^3n^4}{m^2n^2} = mn^2$

D. $(x+y^2)^2 = x^2 + y^4$

Answer is D: $(x + y^2)^2 = (x + y^2)(x + y^2) = x^2 + 2xy^2 + y^4$.

45. *Solve the system of equations for* x, y *and* z. *(Rigorous)(SMR 1.2)*

$3x + 2y - z = 0$
$2x + 5y = 8z$
$x + 3y + 2z = 7$

A) $(-1, 2, 1)$

B) $(1, 2, -1)$

C) $(-3, 4, -1)$

D) $(0, 1, 2)$

Answer: A Multiplying equation 1 by 2, and equation 2 by –3, and then adding together the two resulting equations gives –11y + 22z = 0. Solving for y gives y = 2z. In the meantime, multiplying equation 3 by –2 and adding it to equation 2 gives –y – 12z = –14. Then substituting 2z for y, yields the result z = 1. Subsequently, one can easily find that y = 2, and x = –1.

46. Simplify: $\dfrac{10}{1+3i}$ (SMR 1.2)(Average Rigor)

   A. $-1.25(1-3i)$
   B. $1.25(1+3i)$
   C. $1+3i$
   D. $1-3i$

Answer is D. Multiplying numerator and denominator by the conjugate gives
$\dfrac{10}{1+3i} \times \dfrac{1-3i}{1-3i} = \dfrac{10(1-3i)}{1-9i^2} = \dfrac{10(1-3i)}{1-9(-1)} = \dfrac{10(1-3i)}{10} = 1-3i$. Answer is D.

47. Which graph represents the solution set for $x^2 - 5x > -6$?
    (SMR 1.2)(Rigorous)

   A. number line with open circles at −2 and 2, shaded outside
      −2 0 2

   B. number line with open circles at −3 and 0, shaded outside
      −3 0

   C. number line with open circles at −2 and 2, shaded between
      −2 0 2

   D. number line with open circles at 2 and 3, shaded outside
      −3 0 2 3

Answer is D. Rewriting the inequality gives $x^2 - 5x + 6 > 0$. Factoring gives $(x - 2)(x - 3) > 0$. The two cut-off points on the number line are now at $x = 2$ and $x = 3$. Choosing a random number in each of the three parts of the number line, we test them to see if they produce a true statement. If $x = 0$ or $x = 4$, $(x-2)(x-3)>0$ is true. If $x = 2.5$, $(x-2)(x-3)>0$ is false. Therefore the solution set is all numbers smaller than 2 or greater than 3. Answer is D.

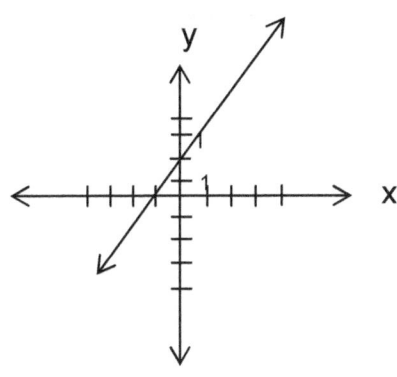

48. What is the equation of the above graph? (SMR 1.2)(Average Rigor)

A. $2x + y = 2$
B. $2x - y = -2$
C. $2x - y = 2$
D. $2x + y = -2$

Answer is B. By observation, we see that the graph has a y-intercept of 2 and a slope of 2/1 = 2. Therefore its equation is y = mx + b = 2x + 2. Rearranging the terms gives 2x – y = –2. Answer is B.

49. Which of the following is a factor of $6 + 48m^3$ (SMR 1.2)(Rigorous)

A. (1 + 2m)
B. (1 – 8m)
C. (1 + m – 2m)
D. (1 – m + 2m)

Answer is A. Removing the common factor of 6 and then factoring the sum of two cubes gives 6 + 48m³ = 6(1 + 8m³) = 6(1 + 2m)(1² – 2m + (2m)²). Answer is A.

50. Which graph represents the equation of $y = x^2 + 3x$? (SMR 1.2)(Rigorous)

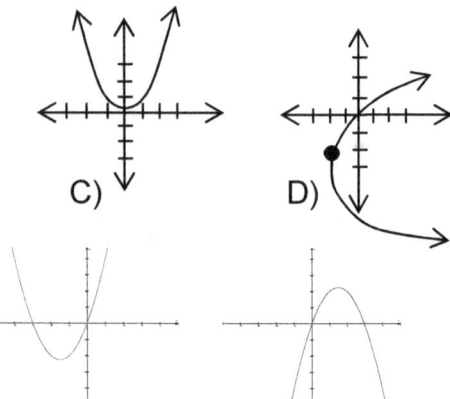

Answer is C. B is not the graph of a function. D is the graph of a parabola where the coefficient of x^2 is negative. A appears to be the graph of $y = x^2$. To find the x-intercepts of $y = x^2 + 3x$, set $y = 0$ and solve for x: $0 = x^2 + 3x = x(x + 3)$ to get $x = 0$ or $x = -3$. Therefore, the graph of the function intersects the x-axis at $x=0$ and $x=-3$. Answer is C.

51. What is the slope of the equation 2y = 4x + 3? (SMR 1.2) (Average Rigor)

    A. 2
    B. 3
    C. 1/2
    D. 4

Answer is A. y = 2x + 3/2 so slope = 2

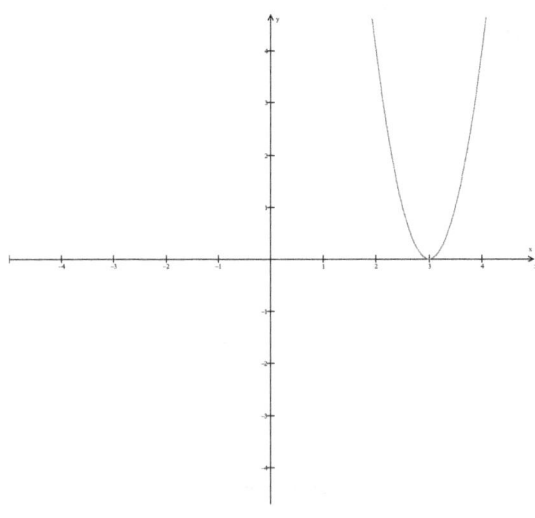

52. Which equation is graphed above? (SMR 1.3) (Rigorous)

A. y = 4 (x + 3)²
B. y = 4 (x − 3)²
C. y = 3 (x − 4)²
D. y = 3 (x + 4)²

Answer is B. Since the vertex of the parabola is three units to the right of the origin, we choose the solution where 3 is subtracted from x, then the quantity is squared.

53. $f(x) = 3x - 2;\ f^{-1}(x) =$ **(SMR 1.3)(Rigorous)**

A. $3x + 2$
B. $x/6$
C. $2x - 3$
D. $(x+2)/3$

Answer is D. To find the inverse, $f^{-1}(x)$, of the given function, reverse the variables in the given equation, y = 3x − 2, to get x = 3y − 2. Then solve for y as follows: x+2 = 3y, and y = $\frac{x+2}{3}$. Answer is D.

54. Simplify: $\sqrt{75} + \sqrt{147} - \sqrt{48}$ (SMR 1.3)(Rigorous)

   A. 174
   B. $12\sqrt{3}$
   C. $8\sqrt{3}$
   D. 74

Answer is C. Simplify each radical by factoring out the perfect squares: $5\sqrt{3} + 7\sqrt{3} - 4\sqrt{3} = 8\sqrt{3}$

55. Which set illustrates a function?(SMR 1.3)(Easy Rigor)

   A. { (0,1) (0,2) (0,3) (0,4) }
   B. (3,9) (–3,9) (4,16) (–4,16)}
   C. { (1,2) (2,3) (3,4) (1,4) }
   D. { (2,4) (3,6) (4,8) (4,16) }

Answer is B. Each number in the domain can only be matched with one number in the range. A is not a function because 0 is mapped to 4 different numbers in the range. In C, 1 is mapped to two different numbers. In D, 4 is also mapped to two different numbers.

56. Give the domain for the function over the set of real numbers:(SMR 1.3) (Average Rigor)

   $$y = \frac{3x+2}{2x^2-3}$$

   A. all real numbers
   B. all real numbers, $x \neq 0$
   C. all real numbers, $x \neq -2$ or 3
   D. all real numbers, $x \neq \frac{\pm\sqrt{6}}{2}$

Answer is D. Solve the denominator for 0. These values will be excluded from the domain.
$2x^2 - 3 = 0$
$2x^2 = 3$
$x^2 = 3/2$
$x = \sqrt{\frac{3}{2}} = \sqrt{\frac{3}{2}} \cdot \sqrt{\frac{2}{2}} = \frac{\pm\sqrt{6}}{2}$

TEACHER CERTIFICATION STUDY GUIDE

57. Factor completely: $8(x - y) + a(y - x)$ **(SMR 1.3) (Rigorous)**

    A. $(8 + a)(y - x)$
    B. $(8 - a)(y - x)$
    C. $(a - 8)(y - x)$
    D. $(a - 8)(y + x)$

Answer is C. Glancing first at the solution choices, factor $(y - x)$ from each term. This leaves -8 from the first term and a from the second term: $(a - 8)(y - x)$

58. Find the value of the determinant of this matrix: (SMR 1.3) (Average Rigor)

$$\begin{bmatrix} 4 & 5 \\ 6 & 2 \end{bmatrix}$$

    A. 22
    B. -10
    C. -22
    D. -16

Answer is C. The determinant is $(2 \times 4) - (5 \times 6) = 8 - 30 = -22$

59. Solve for x. (SMR 1.3)(Rigorous)
$$\log_6(x - 5) + \log_6 x = 2$$

    A. $x = -3, 8$
    B. $x = -1, 10$
    C. $x = 3, -9$
    D. $x = -4, 9$

Answer is D. $\log_6 x(x-5)=2$; $\log_6 x^2-5x=2$; $x^2-5x = 6^2$; $x^2-5x-36=0$ Then $(x+4)(x-9)=0$. Solving for x give you $x =-4$ and $x=9$ or Answer D.

60. Solve $\log_x 125=3$ (SMR 1.3)(Average Rigor)

    A. 4
    B. 5
    C. 6
    D. 3

Answer is B. $\log_x 125=3$ means $x^3=125$ or $x = 5$

FOUNDATION LEV. MATH.

61. What would be the total cost of a suit for $295.99 and a pair of shoes for $69.95 including 6.5% sales tax? (SMR 1.3) (Average Rigor)

   A. $389.73
   B. $398.37
   C. $237.86
   D. $315.23

Answer is A. Before the tax, the total comes to $365.94. Then .065(365.94) = 23.79. With the tax added on, the total bill is 365.94 + 23.79 = $389.73. (Quicker way: 1.065(365.94) = 389.73.) Answer is A

62. State the domain of the function $f(x) = \dfrac{3x-6}{x^2-25}$

   (SMR1.3)(Rigorous)

   A. $x \neq 2$
   B. $x \neq 5, -5$
   C. $x \neq 2, -2$
   D. $x \neq 5$

Answer is B. The values of 5 and –5 must be omitted from the domain of all real numbers because if x took on either of those values, the denominator of the fraction would have a value of 0, and therefore the fraction would be undefined. Answer is B.

63. Change $y = \log_4 32$ into exponential form. (SMR 1.3)(Average Rigor)

   A. $32 = 4^y$
   B. $y = b^x$
   C. $32 = y^4$
   D. $32y^4 = 0$

Answer is A. $y = \log_b x$ if and only if $x = b^y$

TEACHER CERTIFICATION STUDY GUIDE

64. If three cups of concentrate are needed to make 2 gallons of fruit punch, how many cups are needed to make 5 gallons?(SMR 1.3)(Average Rigor)

   A. 6 cups
   B. 7 cups
   C. 7.5 cups
   D. 10 cups

Answer is C. Set up the proportion 3/2 = x/5, cross multiply to obtain 15=2x, then divide both sides by 2.

65. Mr. Brown feeds his cat premium cat food, which costs $40 per month. Approximately how much will it cost to feed her for one year?(SMR 1.3) (Average Rigor)

   A. $500
   B. $400
   C. $80
   D. $4800

Answer is A. 12(40) = 480 which is closest to $500.

66. Find the value of the determinant of this matrix: $\begin{bmatrix} 4 & 3 & 2 \\ 5 & 7 & 8 \\ 9 & 1 & 6 \end{bmatrix}$
(SMR 1.3)(Rigorous)

   A. 309
   B. 123
   C. 213
   D. 146

Answer is D. $\begin{bmatrix} 4 & 3 & 2 \\ 5 & 7 & 8 \\ 9 & 1 & 6 \end{bmatrix} \begin{matrix} 4 & 3 \\ 5 & 7 \\ 9 & 1 \end{matrix}$ Add first two columns after the matrix and multiply the diagonal $= (a_1 b_2 c_3 + b_1 c_2 a_3 + c_1 a_2 b_3) - (a_3 b_2 c_1 + b_3 c_2 a_1 + c_3 a_2 b_1) = 168 + 216 + 10 - 126 - 32 - 90 = 146$.

FOUNDATION LEV. MATH.

TEACHER CERTIFICATION STUDY GUIDE

67. Find the center of a circle with a diameter whose endpoints are (4,5) and (-4, -6). (Average Rigor) (SMR 2.1)

   A. (-2, ½)
   B. (0, -1/2)
   C. (-1, 0)
   D. (0, 1)

Answer: B. (4+-4, 5+-6) = (0,-1/2)

68. Two non-coplanar lines that do not intersect are labeled (SMR 2.1)(Average Rigor)

   A. parallel lines
   B. perpendicular lines
   C. skew lines
   D. alternate exterior lines

Answer is C. Parallel lines do not intersect but are in the same plane.

69. Find the angles of a parallelogram if one angle is 44 degrees. (SMR 2.1) (Rigorous)

   A. 130, 130, 90
   B. 44, 136, 136
   C. 42, 140, 140
   D. 40, 132, 138

Answer is B. As the opposite angle is the same, it is 44 degrees and the other two equal angles add up to 360 – 88 = 272 degrees or 136 degrees

70. Given $\overleftrightarrow{1} \parallel \overleftrightarrow{2}$ **prove** $\angle b \cong \angle e$ **(SMR 2.1)(Average Rigor)**

1) $\angle b \cong \angle d$ 1) vertical angle theorem
2) $\angle d \cong \angle e$ 2) alternate interior angle theorem
3) $\angle b \cong \angle e$ 3) corresponding angles postulate

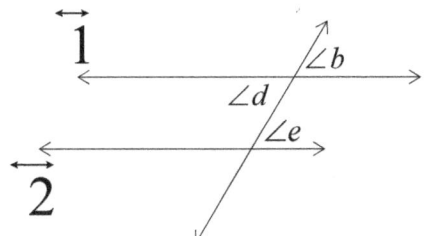

Which step is incorrectly justified?

A. step 1
B. step 2
C. step 3
D. no error

Answer is D. There is no error.

71. Given $\overline{XY} \cong \overline{ZY}$ and $\angle AYX \cong \angle AYZ$. Prove $\triangle AYZ \cong \triangle AYX$.

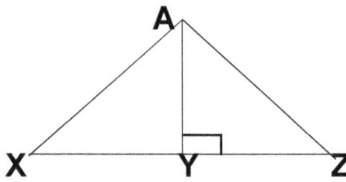

1) $\overline{XY} \cong \overline{ZY}$

2) $\angle AYX \cong \angle AYZ$

3) $\overline{AY} \cong \overline{AY}$

4) $\triangle AYZ \cong \triangle AYX$

Which property justifies step 3? SMR 2.1)(Easy Rigor)

A. reflexive
B. symmetric
C. transitive
D. identity

Answer is A. The reflexive property states that every number or variable is equal to itself and every segment is congruent to itself.

72. Define $\angle A$ (SMR 2.1) (Average Rigor)

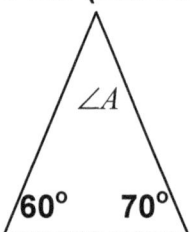

A. 30 degrees
B. 40 degrees
C. 50 degrees
D. 45 degrees

Answer is C. The sum of the angles of a triangle is 180 degrees so the answer is 50 degrees.

73. What is the supplementary angle to 75 degrees? (SMR 2.1) (Average Rigor)

   A. 15 degrees
   B. 105 degrees
   C. 95 degrees
   D. 290 degrees

Answer is B. Two supplementary angles add to 180 degrees.

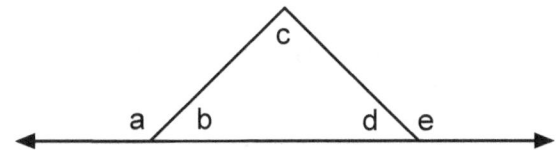

74. Which of the following statements is true about the number of degrees in each angle? (SMR 2.1) (Average Rigor)

   A. $a + b + c = 180°$
   B. $a = e$
   C. $b + c = e$
   D. $c + d = e$

Answer is C. In any triangle, an exterior angle is equal to the sum of the remote interior angles.

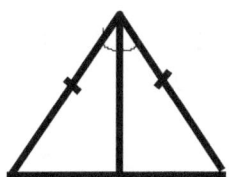

75. What method could be used to prove the above triangles congruent? (SMR 2.1)(Average Rigor)

   A. SSS
   B. SAS
   C. AAS
   D. SSA

Answer is B. Use SAS with the last side being the vertical line common to both triangles.

TEACHER CERTIFICATION STUDY GUIDE

76. Find the distance between (3, 7) and (–3, 4). (SMR 2.1) (Rigorous)

   A. 9

   B. 45

   C. $3\sqrt{5}$

   D. $5\sqrt{3}$

Answer is C. Using the distance formula $\sqrt{[3-(-3)]^2 + (7-4)^2} = \sqrt{36+9}$ = $3\sqrt{5}$

77. Find the midpoint of (2,5) and (7,–4). (SMR 2.1)(Rigorous)

   A. (9,–1)
   B. a(5, 9)
   C. 9/2, –1/2)
   D. (9/2, 1/2)

Answer is D. Using the midpoint formula

x = (2 + 7)/2   y = (5 + –4)/2

78. Given segment AC with B as its midpoint find the coordinates of C if A = (5,7) and B = (3, 6.5)> (SMR 2.1)(Rigorous)

   A. (4, 6.5)
   B. (1, 6)
   C. (2, 0.5)
   D. (16, 1)

Answer is B.
   Here is the rationale:
   Let (x,y) be the coordinates of C. Using the midpoint formula, the coordinates of B can be expressed as follows:

   3 = (5+x)/2 ; 6.5 = (7 + y)/2

   Solving for x and y we get, x = 1 and y = 6.

79.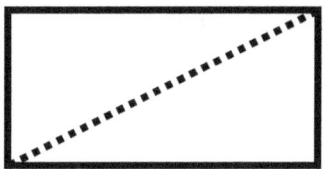

The above diagram is most likely used in deriving a formula for which of the following. (SMR 2.1)(Average Rigor)

A. the area of a rectangle
B. the area of a triangle
C. the perimeter of a triangle
D. the surface area of a prism

Answer is B.

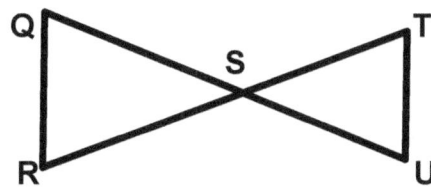

80. Given $\overline{QS} \cong \overline{TS}$ and $\overline{RS} \cong \overline{US}$, prove $\triangle QRS \cong \triangle TUS$. (SMR 2.1) (Average Rigor)

I) $\overline{QS} \cong \overline{TS}$ 1) Given
2) $\overline{RS} \cong \overline{US}$ 2) Given
3) ∠TSU ≅ ∠QSR   3) ?
4) △TSU ≅ △QSR   4) SAS

Give the reason that justifies step 3.

A. Congruent parts of congruent triangles are congruent
B. Reflexive axiom of equality
C. Alternate interior angle Theorem
D. Vertical angle theorem

Answer is D. Angles formed by intersecting lines are called vertical angles and are congruent.

81. In similar polygons, if the perimeters are in a ratio of x:y, the sides are in a ratio of (SMR 2.1)(Rigorous)

A. x : y

B. x2: y2

C. 2x : y

D. 1/2 x : y

Answer is A. The sides are in the same ratio.

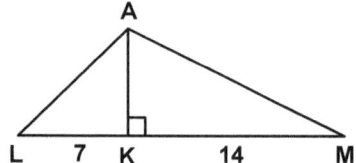

82. Given altitude AK in the right triangle ALM with measurements as indicated, determine the length of AK. (SMR 2.1)(Rigorous)

A. 98
B. $7\sqrt{2}$
C. $\sqrt{21}$
D. $7\sqrt{3}$

Answer is B. The attitude from the right angle to the hypotenuse of any right triangle is the geometric mean of the two segments that are formed. Multiply 7 x 14 and take the square root.

83. Which of the following can be defined? (SMR 2.1)(Easy rigor)

A. point
B. ray
C. line
D. plane

Answer is B. The point, line, and plane are the three undefined concepts on which plane geometry is based.

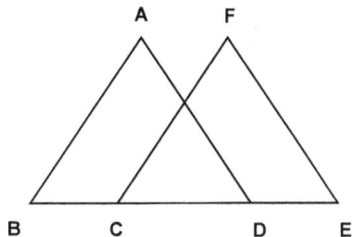

84. Which theorem could be used to prove △ABD ≅ △FEC, given $\overline{BC} \cong \overline{DE}$, ∠C ≅ ∠D, and $\overline{AD} \cong \overline{CF}$? (SMR 2.2)(Average Rigor)

   A. ASA
   B. SAS
   C. SAA
   D. SSS

Answer is B. To obtain the final side, add CD to both BC and DE.

85. Prove △HYM ≅ △KZL, given $\overline{XZ} \cong \overline{XY}$, ∠L ≅ ∠M and $\overline{YL} \cong \overline{MZ}$

1) $\overline{XZ} \cong \overline{XY}$ 1) Given
2) ∠Y ≅ ∠Z   2) ?
3) ∠L ≅ ∠M   3) Given
4) $\overline{YL} \cong \overline{MZ}$ 4) Given
5) $\overline{LM} \cong \overline{LM}$ 5) ?
6) $\overline{YM} \cong \overline{LZ}$ 6) Add
7) △HYM ≅ △KZL   7) ASA

Which could be used to justify steps 2 and 5? (SMR 2.2) (Rigorous)

A. CPCTC, Identity
B. Isosceles Triangle Theorem, Identity
C. SAS, Reflexive
D. Isosceles Triangle Theorem, Reflexive

Answer is D. The isosceles triangle theorem states that the base angles are congruent, and the reflexive property states that every segment is congruent to itself.

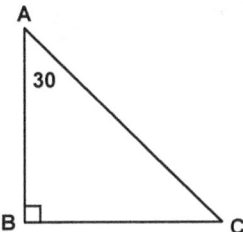

86. If $\overline{AC}$ = 12, determine $\overline{BC}$. (SMR 2.2)(Average Rigor)

   A. 6
   B. 4
   C. $6\sqrt{3}$
   D. $3\sqrt{6}$

Answer is A. In a 30-60-90 right triangle, the leg opposite the 30° angle is half the length of the hypotenuse.

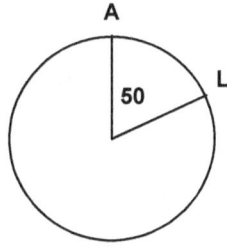

87. What is the measure of major arc AL ? (SMR 2.2)(Average Rigor)

   A. 50°
   B. 25°
   C. 100°
   D. 310°

Answer is D. Minor arc $\overparen{AC}$ measures 50°, the same as the central angle. To determine the measure of the major arc, subtract from 360.

88. Given similar polygons with corresponding sides 6 and 8, what is the area of the smaller if the area of the larger is 64? (SMR 2.2)(Average Rigor)

   A. 48
   B. 36
   C. 144
   D. 78

Answer is B. In similar polygons, the areas are proportional to the squares of the sides. 36/64 = x/64

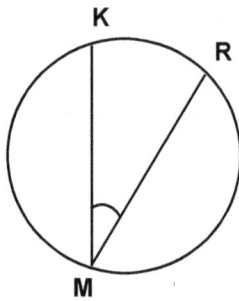

89. If arc KR = 70° what is the measure of ∠M? (SMR 2.2)(Average Rigor)

   A. 290°
   B. 35°
   C. 140°
   D. 110°

Answer is B. An inscribed angle is equal to one half the measure of the intercepted arc.

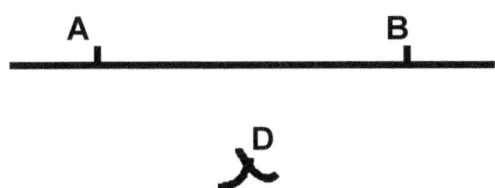

90. The above construction can be completed to make (SMR 2.2)(Average Rigor)

   A. an angle bisector
   B. parallel lines
   C. a perpendicular bisector
   D. skew lines

Answer is C. The points marked C and D are the intersection of the circles with centers A and B.

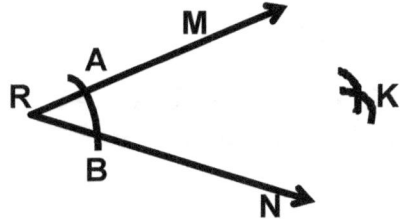

91. A line from R to K will form (SMR 2.2)(Average Rigor)

   A. an altitude of ∠ RMN

   B. a perpendicular bisector of $\overline{MN}$

   C. a bisector of ∠ MRN

   D. a vertical angle

Answer is C. Using a compass, point K is found to be equidistant from A and B.

92. Find the missing side: (Average Rigor)(SMR 2.2)

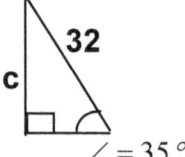
$\angle = 35°$

A. 11.65
B. 19.5
C. 23
D. 27.13

Answer is D. Cos 35 = adjacent /hypotenuse or 0.8480=c/32 or c=18

93. 4 square yards is equivalent to (SMR 2.2)(Average Rigor)

A. 12 square feet
B. 48 square feet
C. 36 square feet
D. 108 square feet

Answer is C. There are 9 square feet in a square yard.

94. If a circle has an area of 25 cm^2, what is its circumference to the nearest tenth of a centimeter? (SMR 2.2)(Average Rigor)

A. 78.5 cm
B. 17.7 cm
C. 8.9 cm
D. 15.7 cm

Answer is B. Find the radius by solving $\Pi r^2 = 25$. Then substitute r=2.82 into C = 2Πr to obtain the circumference.

95. Find the area of the figure low. (SMR 2.2)Rigorous)

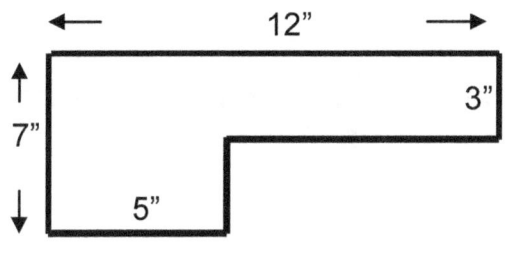

A. 56 in²
B. 27 in²
C. 71 in²
D. 170 in²

Answer is A. Divide the figure into two rectangles with a horizontal line. The area of the top rectangle is 36 in, and the bottom is 20 in.

96. Find the area of the shaded region given square ABCD with side $\overline{AB}$ =10m and circle E. (SMR 2.2)(Rigorous)

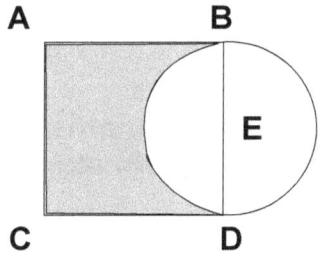

A. 178.5 m²
B. 139.25 m²
C. 71 m²
D. 60.75 m²

Answer is D. Find the area of the square 10^2 = 100, then subtract 1/2 the area of the circle. The area of the circle is Πr^2 = (3.14)(5)(5)=78.5. Therefore the area of the shaded region is 100 – 39.25 = 60.75.

97. Given the regular hexagon in the circle above, determine the degree of the hexagon's central angle. (SMR 2.2) (Rigorous)

   A. 60°

   B. 30°

   C. 120°

   D. 90°

Answer is A. A regular hexagon is composed of 6 isosceles triangles because the legs of the triangle are the radius of the circle ▢ the central angle must be $\frac{360°}{6°} = 60°$.

98. Given similar polygons with corresponding sides of lengths 9 and 15, find the perimeter of the smaller polygon if the perimeter of the larger polygon is 150 units. (SMR 2.2)(Rigorous)

   A. 54
   B. 135
   C. 90
   D. 126

Answer is C. The perimeters of similar polygons are directly proportional to the lengths of their sides, therefore 9/15 = x/150. Cross multiply to obtain 1350 = 15x, then divide by 15 to obtain the perimeter of the smaller polygon.

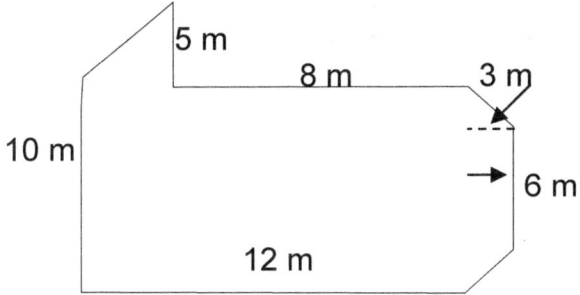

99. Compute the area of the polygon shown above. (SMR 2.2)(Rigorous)

  A. 178 m²
  B. 154 m²
  C. 43 m²
  D. 188 m²

Answer is B. Divide the figure into a triangle, a rectangle and a trapezoid. The area of the triangle is 1/2 bh = 1/2 (4)(5) = 10. The area of the rectangle is bh = 12(10) = 120. The area of the trapezoid is 1/2(b + B)h = 1/2(6 + 10)(3) = 1/2 (16)(3) = 24. Thus, the area of the figure is 10 + 120 + 24 = 154.

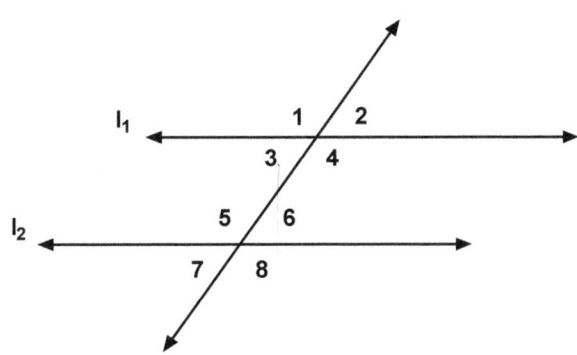

100. Given $l_1 \parallel l_2$, which of the following is true? (SMR 2.2) (Average Rigor)

  A. ∠1 and ∠8 are congruent and alternate interior angles
  B. ∠2 and ∠3 are congruent and corresponding angles
  C. ∠3 and ∠4 are adjacent and supplementary angles
  D. ∠3 and ∠5 are adjacent and supplementary angles

Answer is C. The angles in A are exterior. In B, the angles are vertical. The angles in D are consecutive, not adjacent.

101. A car is driving north at 74 miles per hour from point A. Another car is driving due east at 65 miles per hour starting from the same point at the same time. How far are the cars away from each other after 2 hours? (Rigorous)(SMR 2.2)

   A. 175.87
   B. 232.66
   C. 196.99
   D. 202.43

Answer is C. The route the cars take form a right triangle with edges 74 x 2 and 65 x 2. This gives two sides of a right triangle of 148 and 130. Using the Pythagorean Theorem, we get 148^2 and 130^2 = distance^2. Distance = $\sqrt{21904+16900}$ = 196.99

102. Which term most accurately describes two coplanar lines without any common points? (SMR 2.2)(Average Rigor)

   A. Perpendicular
   B. Parallel
   C. Intersecting
   D. skew

Answer is B. By definition, parallel lines are coplanar lines without any common points.

103. Compute the area of the shaded region, given a radius of 5 meters. O is the center. (SMR 2.2)(Rigorous)

   A. 7.13cm²
   B. 7.13m²
   C. 78.5 m²
   D. 19.63 m²

Answer is B. Area of triangle AOB is .5(5)(5) = 12.5 square meters. Since $\frac{90}{360} = .25$, the area of sector AOB (pie-shaped piece) is approximately $.25(\pi)5^2$ = 19.63. Subtracting the triangle area from the sector area to get the area of segment AB, we get approximately 19.63–12.5 = 7.13 square meters.

104. If you have a triangle with these dimensions, solve for x if ∠B is 27°. ((Rigorous)(SMR 2.2)

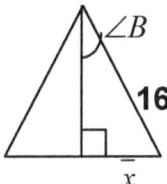

A. 8.45
B. 7.26
C. 7.78
D. 6.89

Answer is B. sin(B) = opposite/hypotenuse or sin(27) = 0.454 = x/16 or x=7.26

105. What is the degree measure of an interior angle of a regular 10-sided polygon? (SMR 2.2)(Average Rigor)

A. 18°
B. 36°
C. 144°
D. 54°

Answer is C. Formula for finding the measure of each interior angle of a regular polygon with n sides is $\frac{(n-2)180}{n}$. For n=10, we get $\frac{8(180)}{10} = 144$.

106. If a ship sails due south 6 miles, then due west 8 miles, how far was it from the starting point? (SMR 2.2)(Average Rigor)

A. 100 miles
B. 10 miles
C. 14 miles
D. 48 miles

Answer is B. Draw a right triangle with legs of 6 and 8. Find the hypotenuse using the Pythagorean Theorem. $6^2 + 8^2 = c^2$. Therefore, c = 10 miles.

107. What is the measure of minor arc AD, given measure of $\overarc{PS}$ is 40° and $m < K = 10°$? (SMR 2.2)(Rigorous)

A. 50°
B. 20°
C. 30°
D. 25°

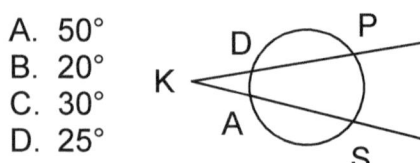

Answer is B. The formula relating the measure of angle K and the two arcs it intercepts is $m\angle K = \frac{1}{2}(mPS - mAD)$. Substituting the known values, we get $10 = \frac{1}{2}(40 - mAD)$. Solving for mAD gives an answer of 20 degrees.

108. Choose the diagram that illustrates the construction of a perpendicular to the line at a given point on the line. (SMR 2.2)(Average Rigor)

A.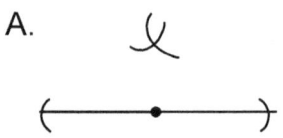

B.

C.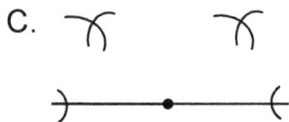

D.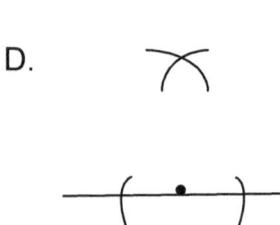

Answer is D. Given a point on a line, place the compass point there and draw two arcs intersecting the line in two points, one on either side of the given point. Then using any radius larger than half the new segment produced, and with the pointer at each end of the new segment, draw arcs that intersect above the line. Connect this new point with the given point.

109. Find the area of the figure pictured below. (SMR 2.2)(Rigorous)

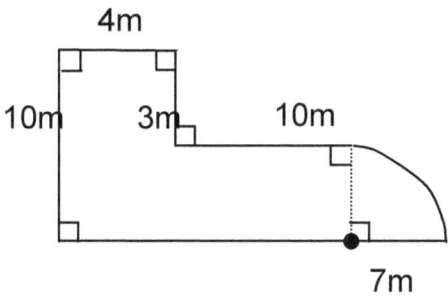

A. 136.47 m²
B. 148.48 m²
C. 293.86 m²
D. 178.47 m²

Answer is B. Divide the figure into 2 rectangles and one quarter circle. The tall rectangle on the left will have dimensions 10 by 4 and area 40. The rectangle in the center will have dimensions 7 by 10 and area 70. The quarter circle will have area $.25(\pi)7^2$ = 38.48. The total area is therefore approximately 148.48.

110. Solve the system of equations for x, y and z. SMR 2.2)(Rigorous)

$$3x + 2y - z = 0$$
$$2x + 5y = 8z$$
$$x + 3y + 2z = 7$$

A. $(-1, 2, 1)$

B. $(1, 2, -1)$

C. $(-3, 4, -1)$

D. $(0, 1, 2)$

Answer is A. Multiplying equation 1 by 2, and equation 2 by –3, and then adding together the two resulting equations gives –11y + 22z = 0. Solving for y gives y = 2z. In the meantime, multiplying equation 3 by –2 and adding it to equation 2 gives –y – 12z = –14. Then substituting 2z for y, yields the result z = 1. Subsequently, one can easily find that y = 2, and x = –1.

111. Solve for x: $18 = 4 + |2x|$ (SMR 2.2)(Average Rigor)

   A. $\{-11, 7\}$
   B. $\{-7, 0, 7\}$
   C. $\{-7, 7\}$
   D. $\{-11, 11\}$

Answer is C. Using the definition of absolute value, two equations are possible: 18 = 4 + 2x or 18 = 4 – 2x. Solving for x gives x = 7 or x = –7.

112. What is the arc length of a fourth of a circle with a diameter of 24 cm? (Average Rigor)(SMR 2.2)

   A. 18.85
   B. 75.4
   C. 32.45
   D. 20.75

Answer is A. The circumference of the circle is πd where d is 24. Π(24)= 75.4. One fourth of that is 18.85.

113. Which theorem can be used to prove $\triangle BAK \cong \triangle MKA$? (SMR 2.2)(Rigorous)

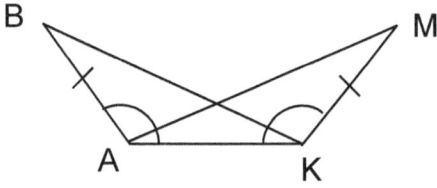

   A. SSS
   B. ASA
   C. SAS
   D. AAS

Answer is C. Since side AK is common to both triangles, the triangles can be proved congruent by using the Side-Angle-Side Postulate.

114. Given that QO⊥NP and QO=NP, quadrilateral NOPQ can most accurately be described as a (SMR 2.2)(Average Rigor)

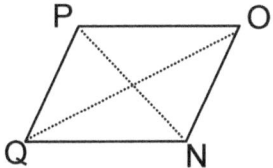

A. Parallelogram
B. Rectangle
C. Square
D. rhombus

Answer is C. In an ordinary parallelogram, the diagonals are not perpendicular or equal in length. In a rectangle, the diagonals are not necessarily perpendicular. In a rhombus, the diagonals are not equal in length. In a square, the diagonals are both perpendicular and congruent.

115. Choose the correct statement concerning the median and altitude in a triangle. (SMR 2.2)(Average Rigor)

A. The median and altitude of a triangle may be the same segment.
B. The median and altitude of a triangle are always different segments.
C. The median and altitude of a right triangle are always the same segment.
D. The median and altitude of an isosceles triangle are always the same segment.

Answer is A. The most one can say with certainty is that the median (segment drawn to the midpoint of the opposite side) and the altitude (segment drawn perpendicular to the opposite side) of a triangle may coincide, but they more often do not. In an isosceles triangle, the median and the altitude to the base are the same segment.

116. Given a 30 meter x 60 meter garden with a circular fountain with a 5 meter radius, calculate the area of the portion of the garden not occupied by the fountain. (SMR 2.2)(Rigorous)

   A. 1721 m²
   B. 1879 m²
   C. 2585 m²
   D. 1015 m²

Answer is A. Find the area of the garden and then subtract the area of the fountain: $30(60) - \pi(5)^2$ or approximately 1721 square meters.

117) Determine the area of the shaded region of the trapezoid in terms of *x* & *y* (the height of $\triangle ABC$). $\overline{DE}$ = 2x & $\overline{DC}$ = 3x.
(SMR 2.2) (Rigorous)

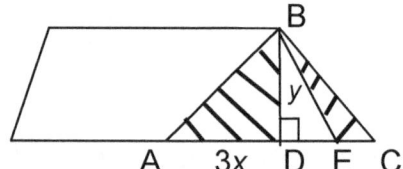

   A. $4xy$
   B. $2xy$
   C. $3x^2 y$
   D. There is not enough information given.

Answer is B. To find the area of the shaded regions, 1st find the area of triangle ABC and then subtract the area of triangle DBE. The area of triangle ABC is .5(6x)(y) = 3xy. The area of triangle DBE is .5(2x)(y) = xy. The difference is 2xy, which is the area of shaded area.

118. Which mathematician is best known for his work in developing non-Euclidean geometry? (SMR 2.2)(Easy Rigor)

   A. Descartes
   B. Riemann
   C. Pascal
   D. Pythagoras

Answer is B. In the mid-nineteenth century, Reimann and other mathematicians developed elliptic geometry.

119. Find the surface area of a box which is 3 feet wide, 5 feet tall, and 4 feet deep. (SMR 2.3)(Rigorous)

   A. 47 sq. ft.
   B. 60 sq. ft.
   C. 94 sq. ft
   D. 188 sq. ft.

Answer is C. Let's assume the base of the rectangular solid (box) is 3 by 4, and the height is 5. Surface area = 2(lw) + 2(wh) + 2(lh). Then the surface area of the top and bottom together is 2(12) = 24. The sum of the areas of the front and back are 2(15) = 30, while the sum of the areas of the sides are 2(20)=40. The total surface area is therefore 94 square feet.

120. What happens to the volume of a square pyramid when the sides of the base are tripled? (Rigorous)(SMR 2.3)

   A. The volume is increased by a factor of 9
   B. The volume is increased by a factor of 8
   C. The volume is increased by a factor of 27
   D. The volume is increased by a factor of 16

Answer is C. The formula for the volume of a square pyramid is $V = \dfrac{h(L^2)}{3}$. Assuming h, the height, remains constant, then if the side (L) of the base is tripled, the overall volume would increase by a factor of 9: $V = \dfrac{h(3L)^2}{3}$ and $3^2 = 9$.

121. The volume of water flowing through a pipe varies directly with the square is the radius of the pipe. If the water flows at a rate of 80 liters per minute through a pipe with a radius of 4 cm, at what rate would water flow through a pipe with a radius of 3 cm? (SMR 2.3)(Rigorous)

   A. 45 liters per minute
   B. 6.67 liters per minute
   C. 60 liters per minute
   D. 4.5 liters per minute

Answer is A. Set up the direct variation: $\dfrac{V}{r^2} = \dfrac{V}{r^2}$. Substituting gives $\dfrac{80}{16} = \dfrac{V}{9}$. Solving for V gives 45 liters per minute.

122. What is the volume of a cylinder of a height 8 cm and a diameter of 4 cm? (Average Rigor)(SMR 2.3)

   A. 95.45
   B. 100.5
   C. 110.3
   D. 105.4

Answer is B. The volume = $\pi r^2 h$ or $8\pi 2^2$ = 100.5 cm^3

123. If the area of the base of a cone is tripled, the volume will be (SMR 2.3)(Rigorous)

   A. the same as the original
   B. 9 times the original
   C. 3 times the original
   D. 3 π times the original

Answer is C. The formula for the volume of a cone is $V = \frac{1}{3}Bh$, where B is the area of the circular base and h is the height. If the area of the base is tripled, the volume becomes $V = \frac{1}{3}(3B)h = Bh$, or three times the original area.

124. If the radius of a right cylinder is doubled, how does its volume change? (SMR 2.3)(Rigorous)

   A. no change
   B. also is doubled
   C. four times the original
   D. pi times the original

Answer is C. If the radius of a right circular cylinder is doubled, the volume is multiplied by four because in the formula, the radius is squared, therefore the new volume is 2 x 2 or four times the original.

125. Which is a postulate? (SMR 2.2)(Easy Rigor)

    A. The sum of the angles in any triangle is 180o.
    B. A line intersects a plane in one point.
    C. Two intersecting lines from congruent vertical angles.
    D. Any segment is congruent to itself.

Answer is D. A postulate is an accepted property of real numbers or geometric figures that cannot be proven, A, B and C are theorems that can be proven.

126. Determine the volume of a sphere to the nearest cm if the surface area is 113 cm^2. (SMR 2.3)(Rigorous)

    A. 113 cm3
    B. 339 cm3
    C. 37.7 cm3
    D. 226 cm3

Answer is A. Solve for the radius of the sphere using A = 4πr^2. The radius is 3. Then, find the volume using 4/3 πr^3. Only when the radius is 3 are the volume and surface area equivalent.

127. Find the zeroes of $f(x) = x^3 + x^2 - 14x - 24$ (SMR 2.3)(Rigorous)

    A. 4, 3, 2
    B. 3, –8
    C. 7, –2, –1
    D. 4, –3, –2

Answer is D. Possible rational roots of the equation 0 = x^3 + x^2 – 14x –24 are all the positive and negative factors of 24. By substituting into the equation, we find that –2 is a root, and therefore that x+2 is a factor. By performing the long division (x^3 + x^2 – 14x – 24)/(x+2), we can find that another factor of the original equation is x^2 – x – 12 or (x–4)(x+3). Therefore the zeros of the original function are –2, –3, and 4.

128. Compute the surface area of the prism. (SMR 2.3)(Average Rigor)

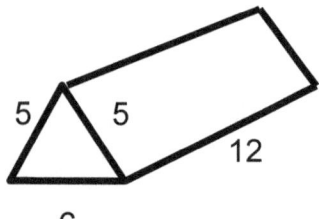

A. 204
B. 216
C. 360
D. 180

Answer is B. There are five surfaces that make up the prism. The bottom rectangle has area 6 x 12 = 72. The sloping sides are two rectangles each with an area of 5 x 12 = 60. The height of the and triangles is determined to be 4 using the Pythagorean theorem. Therefore each triangle has area 1/2bh = 1/2(6)(4) –12. Thus, the surface area is 72 + 60 + 60 + 12 + 12 = 216.

129. If the area of the base of a regular square pyramid is tripled, how does its volume change? (SMR 2.3)(Rigorous)

   A. double the original
   B. triple the original
   C. nine times the original
   D. no change

Answer is B. Using the general formula for a pyramid $V = \dfrac{h(L^2)}{3}$, since the base is tripled and is not squared or cubed in the formula, the volume is also tripled.

130. What is the surface area of a sphere with a circumference of 46 cm? (Rigorous)(SMR 2.3)

   A. 475.6
   B. 546.7
   C. 673.4
   D. 643.5

Answer is C. If the circumference is 46, the radius is 7.32. The surface area is $4\pi r^2 = 673.4$ cm^2

131. How does lateral area differ from total surface area in prisms, pyramids, and cones? (SMR 2.3) (Average Rigor)

   A. For the lateral area, only use surfaces perpendicular to the base.
   B. They are both the same.
   C. The lateral area does not include the base.
   D. The lateral area is always a factor of pi.

Answer is C. The lateral area does not include the base.

132. Given a drawer with 5 black socks, 3 blue socks, and 2 red socks, what is the probability that you will draw two black socks in two draws in a dark room? (SMR 4.1)(Rigorous)

   A. 2/9
   B. 1/4
   C. 17/18
   D. 1/18

Answer is A. In this example of conditional probability, the probability of drawing a black sock on the first draw is 5/10. It is implied in the problem that there is no replacement, therefore the probability of obtaining a black sock in the second draw is 4/9. Multiply the two probabilities and reduce to lowest terms.

133. A sack of candy has 3 peppermints, 2 butterscotch drops and 3 cinnamon drops. One candy is drawn and replaced, then another candy is drawn; what is the probability that both will be butterscotch? (SMR 4.1)(Rigorous)

   A. 1/2
   B. 1/28
   C. 1/4
   D. 1/16

Answer is D. With replacement, the probability of obtaining a butterscotch on the first draw is 2/8 and the probability of drawing a butterscotch on the second draw is also 2/8. Multiply and reduce to lowest terms.

TEACHER CERTIFICATION STUDY GUIDE

134. How many ways are there to choose a potato and two green vegetables from a choice of three potatoes and seven green vegetables? (SMR 4.1)(Rigorous)

   A. 126
   B. 63
   C. 21
   D. 252

Answer is A. There are 3 slots to fill. There are 3 choices for the first, 7 for the second, and 6 for the third. Therefore, the total number of choices is 3(7)(6) = 126.

135. Given a spinner with the numbers one through eight, what is the probability that you will spin an even number or a number greater than four? (SMR 4.2)(Average Rigor)

   A. 1/4
   B. 1/2
   C. 3/4
   D. 1

Answer is C. There are 6 favorable outcomes: 2,4,5,6,7,8 and 8 possibilities. Reduce 6/8 to 3/4.

136. A measure of association between two variables is called: (SMR 4.2) (Easy Rigor)

   A. Associate
   B. Correlation
   C. Confidence interval
   D. Variation

Answer is B. Correlation is the measure of association between two variables.

137. Compute the median for the following data set: (SMR 4.2)(Average Rigor)

{12, 19, 13, 16, 17, 14}

A. 14.5
B. 15.17
C. 15
D. 16

Answer is C. Arrange the data in ascending order: 12,13,14,16,17,19. The median is the middle value in a list with an odd number of entries. When there is an even number of entries, the median is the mean of the two center entries. Here the average of 14 and 16 is 15.

138. Half the students in a class scored 80% on an exam, most of the rest scored 85% except for one student who scored 10%. Which would be the best measure of central tendency for the test scores? (SMR 4.2) (Average Rigor)

A. Mean
B. Median
C. Mode
D. either the median or the mode because they are equal

Answer is B. In this set of data, the median (see #14) would be the most representative measure of central tendency since the median is independent of extreme values. Because of the 10% outlier, the mean (average) would be disproportionately skewed. In this data set, it is true that the median and the mode (number that occurs most often) are the same, but the median remains the best choice because of its special properties.

TEACHER CERTIFICATION STUDY GUIDE

139. What is the first, second and third quartile for the following? (SMR 4.2)(Average Rigor)

5, 5, 5, 6, 7, 9, 9, 10, 11, 12, 13, 13, 14, 15, 16, 17, 17

A. 5, 10, 15
B. 6, 11, 16
C. 7, 11, 14
D. 6.5, 11, 14.5

Answer is D. The second quartile is the median of the whole while the first and third quartiles are the median of the first half and the second half respectively; since the median was part of the first calculation in an odd number of data, it isn't included in determining the quartiles. There is no consensus on how the mean should be calculated for an odd number of data. If using a TI86 calculator, the answer will be D. However, the correct answer could also be 7, 11, 14 (C).

140. A student scored in the 87th percentile on a standardized test. Which would be the best interpretation of his score? (SMR 4.2)(Average Rigor)

A. Only 13% of the students who took the test scored higher.
B. This student should be getting mostly B's on his report card.
C. This student performed below average on the test.
D. This is the equivalent of missing 13 questions on a question exam.

Answer is A. Percentile ranking tells how the student compared to the norm or the other students taking the test. It does not correspond to the percentage answered correctly, but can indicate how the student compared to the average student tested.

141. If a horse will probably win three races out of ten, what are the odds that he will win? (SMR 4.1)(Average Rigor)

A. 3:10
B. 7:10
C. 3:7
D. 7:3

Answer is C. The odds are that he will win 3 and lose 7.

FOUNDATION LEV. MATH.

142. Determine the number of subsets of set K.
    K = {4, 5, 6, 7}
    (SMR 4.2)(Rigorous)

    A. 15
    B. 16
    C. 17
    D. 18

Answer is B. A set of n objects has 2^n subsets. Therefore, here we have $2^4 =$ 16 subsets. These subsets include four that each have 1 element only, six that each have 2 elements, four that each have 3 elements, plus the original set, and the empty set.

143. What is the range of the following numbers? (SMR 4.2)(Average Rigor)
    34, 14, 43, 35, 45, 18, 33, 42

    A. 31
    B. 32
    C. 26
    D. 19

Answer is A. The range is the difference between the highest and lowest number or is 45-14=31.

144. Find the median of the following set of data:
    14 3 7 6 11 20
    (SMR 4.2)(Easy Rigor)

    A. 9
    B. 8.5
    C. 7
    D. 11

Answer is A. Place the numbers is ascending order: 3 6 7 11 14 20. Find the average of the middle two numbers (7+11)/2 =9

145. Corporate salaries are listed for several employees. Which would be the best measure of central tendency? (SMR 4.2)(Average Rigor)

   $24,000 $24,000 $26,000 $28,000 $30,000 $120,000

   A. mean
   B. median
   C. mode
   D. no difference

Answer is B. The median provides the best measure of central tendency in this case where the mode is the lowest number and the mean would be disproportionately skewed by the outlier $120,000.

146. The tenth percentile is in what stanine? (SMR 4.2)(Easy Rigor)

   A. First
   B. Second
   C. Third
   D. Fourth

Answer is B. The tenth percentile is in the second stanine. Stanines represent a 9-point scale with 9 being the highest. **Stanine scores are** derived from standard deviations and have a mean of 5 and standard deviation of 2. To relate stanine scores to other scores by use the "Rule of Four." Start with either end of the stanine scale, 1 or 9, 4% of the cases in a normal distribution fall into the end of the stanines. Stanine 5 falls in the middle and has 20%, 6 has 16%, 7 has 12%, 8 has 8%, and 9 has 4%. To find the stanine corresponding to any percentile, start from stanine 1 and add up the percents included in consecutive stanines until you find the stanine that includes the percentile you are interested in. So 10 percentile = (4% stanine 1 +8% stanine 2 = 12% which is in stanine 2). 10% is between 5% and 12%, the 2nd stanine.

XAMonline, INC. 21 Orient Ave. Melrose, MA 02176

Toll Free number 800-509-4128

TO ORDER Fax 781-662-9268 OR www.XAMonline.com

CALIFORNIA SUBJECT EXAMINATIONS - CSET - 2008

PO#　　　　　　Store/School:

Address 1:

Address 2 (Ship to other):

City, State Zip

Credit card number_____-_____-_____-_____   expiration_____

EMAIL _____

PHONE　　　　　　　　　　　　**FAX**

ISBN	TITLE	Qty	Retail	Total
978-1-58197-595-6	RICA Reading Instruction Competence Assessment			
978-1-58197-596-3	CBEST CA Basic Educational Skills			
978-1-58197-398-3	CSET French Sample Test 149, 150			
978-1-58197-622-9	CSET Spanish 145, 146, 147			
978-1-58197-803-2	CSET MSAT Multiple Subject 101, 102, 103			
978-1-58197-261-0	CSET English 105, 106, 107			
978-1-58197-049-4	CSET Foundational-Level Mathematics 110, 111			
978-1-58197-285-6	CSET Mathematics 110, 111, 112			
978-1-58197-340-2	CSET Social Science 114, 115			
978-1-58197-342-6	CSET General Science 118, 119			
978-1-58197-585-7	CSET Biology-Life Science 120, 124			
978-1-58197-395-2	CSET Chemistry 121, 125			
978-1-58197-399-0	CSET Earth and Planetary Science 122, 126			
978-1-58197-224-5	CSET Physics 123, 127			
978-1-58197-299-3	CSET Physical Education, 129, 130, 131			
978-1-58197-397-6	CSET Art Sample Subtest 140			
			SUBTOTAL	
			Ship	$8.70
			TOTAL	

www.ingramcontent.com/pod-product-compliance
Lightning Source LLC
Chambersburg PA
CBHW080534300426
44111CB00017B/2725